# Lecture Notes of the Institute for Computer Sciences, Social Informatics and Telecommunications Engineering    376

Paolo Perego · Nima TaheriNejad ·
Maurizio Caon (Eds.)

# Wearables
# in Healthcare

Second EAI International Conference, HealthWear 2020
Virtual Event, December 10–11, 2020
Proceedings

 Springer

*Editors*
Paolo Perego (iD)
Department of Design
Politecnico di Milano
Milan, Italy

Nima TaheriNejad (iD)
Institute for Computer Technology
TU Wien
Vienna, Austria

Maurizio Caon (iD)
Haute école de gestion
University of Applied Sciences and Arts
Fribourg, Fribourg, Switzerland

ISSN 1867-8211 ISSN 1867-822X (electronic)
Lecture Notes of the Institute for Computer Sciences, Social Informatics
and Telecommunications Engineering
ISBN 978-3-030-76065-6 ISBN 978-3-030-76066-3 (eBook)
https://doi.org/10.1007/978-3-030-76066-3

This Springer imprint is published by the registered company Springer Nature Switzerland AG
The registered company address is: Gewerbestrasse 11, 6330 Cham, Switzerland

# Preface

I am delighted to introduce the proceedings of the 2nd EAI International Conference on Wearables in Healthcare (HealthWear 2020) an event that brought together experts who focus their research on wearable devices and systems for healthcare and wellbeing.

HealthWear 2020 assumed a different configuration than the first edition of the conference due to the COVID-19 pandemic situation, which has affected all of us, we have been forced to live through difficult months of isolation, social distancing and trying to continue our work despite all the difficulties. This situation led to the second edition of the conference being held completely online, without the possibility of networking with other researchers: an indispensable tool for boosting technology. The virtual HealthWear 2020, took place on December 10, focused both on design and technological aspects. Professor David Atienza from EPFL, Switzerland, gave a keynote on how to mimic brain functions to reduce energy consumption in wearable systems. The conference included four sessions, with tens of authors from all over the world presenting new methods, approaches and applications in the field of wearables in healthcare.

HealthWear started in 2016 in Budapest, Hungary, bringing together researchers, developers, and industry professionals from both healthcare and academic communities to discuss key issues, opportunities, and obstacles for personal health data research. With the second edition, the conference evolved towards an interdisciplinary approach, including authors and research from more humanistic research fields and taking into consideration aspects of acceptability and usability, which too often are left unexamined. This volume includes the papers presented during the online conference. HealthWear 2020 received around 40 papers which were subject to a double-blind review process, involving tens of reviewers: members of the Technical Program Committee and experts from different countries. This highly selective review process resulted in a full paper rejection rate of 50%, thereby guaranteeing that high-quality scientific papers were accepted for both presentation and publication. The technical program of HealthWear 2020 consisted of 16 papers divided into four different tracks: PPG and Algorithms, IoT and Smart Sensors, Innovation by Design, and Wearable Applications.

The first track, PPG and Algorithms, consisted of three papers focused on photoplethysmography. The first paper by TaheriNejad et al. showed a new algorithm for estimating systolic blood pressure using a simple smartwatch PPG sensor. Shibam et al. presented a paper on the use of a multi-level singular value decomposition technique for the reduction of motion artifact during PPG monitoring. The last paper of the first track concerned the use of an intraoral PPG sensor for cardiorespiratory measurement.

The second track IoT and Smart Sensors, included five papers on the use of wearable devices and systems for Internet of Medical Things applications. The first paper by Vargiu et al. presented the approach followed in the CarpeDiem project, which uses an IoT-based self-management system to encourage citizens to improve their quality of life. The second work, presented by Colman et al. introduced the use and potentiality of blockchain for wearable health data. This second paper was also awarded best paper of the conference. Khokhlova et al. presented a new wearable textile-based muscle activity and motion sensing device for lower limbs. Mosna et al. presented a practical and feasible approach based on low-cost IMU-based wearable devices and mobile applications to rapidly collect 3D motion information coming from different body segments. The last paper of the track, by Perego et al. presented a new integrated design method for wearable development, and its application for a MoCap wearable system.

The third track, Innovation by Design, was a new session introduced for the second edition of the conference. This track focused on the intrinsic multidisciplinary nature of wearable devices, and includes works on methodology and design aspects of wearable research. The first paper by Kolasa et al. presented a quality-by-design approach to the development of an e-monitoring solution, underlining the experiments and assessments implemented during the study. The second paper by Bianchini et al. introduced a design and open source wearables project for healthcare solutions. Pontilo et al. illustrated research based on the development of orthopedic devices, characterized by the integration of parametric design and data visualization, for product customization on specific morphologies and needs of users. Sironi et al. in the fourth paper, introduced the development of a parametric upper limb prosthesis with integrated sensors and its development method. The last paper of the track by Kritikos et al. examined whether the presence of a virtual guided master using participant modeling in a virtual environment was as effective as standard exposure therapy in the treatment of anxiety disorders.

The last track comprised three different works on Wearable Applications. The first paper, by Fusca et al. concerned the application of wearable actigraphy for Parkinson monitoring. The second paper, by Marzaroli et al. discussed the use of a wearable system for foot-transmitted vibration monitoring; while the last paper, by Poli et al. discussed the use of a simple wearable device for Human Activity Recognition.

The papers in this book are the result of an extensive and selective review process, and are astonishing works. We hope they can be a starting point for new research and discovery for wearable devices and technology. We would like to thank the Program Committee members for the effort dedicated in the reviewing process, and all the authors of these beautiful papers for all the work and the preparation of the conference presentations. We would like also to thank the European Alliance for Innovation for sponsoring this event and supporting us in the organization.

We hope that the experiences contained in this book can be a starting point for new research and, perhaps, can accompany you through 2021, which still promises to be as strange as 2020!

January 2021                                                         Paolo Perego

# Organization

## Steering Committee

Imrich Chlamtac        University of Trento, Italy

## Organizing Committee

### General Chair

Paolo Perego        Politecnico di Milano, Italy

### General Co-chair

Nima Taherinejad        TU Wien, Austria

### Technical Program Committee Chair and Co-chair

Amir Rahamani        TU Wien, Austria/University of California, USA
Sharmistha Bhadra        McGill University, Canada

### Sponsorship and Exhibit Chairs

Marta Sesana        Politecnico di Milano, Italy
Valentina Brunetti        Politecnico di Milano, Italy

### Local Chair

Giuseppe Andreoni        Politecnico di Milano, Italy

### Workshops Chair

Mario Covarubbias        Politecnico di Milano, Italy

### Publicity and Social Media Chair

Roberto Sironi        Politecnico di Milano, Italy

### Publications Chair

Maurizio Caon        HES-SO, Switzerland

### Web Chair

Maria Terraroli        Politecnico di Milano, Italy

## Technical Program Committee

| | |
|---|---|
| Sharmistha Bhadra | McGill University, Canada |
| Maurizio Caon | HES-SO, Switzerland |
| Mira El Kamali | HES-SO, Switzerland |
| Venere Ferraro | Politecnico di Milano, Italy |
| Nicola Francesco Lopomo | Università degli Studi di Brescia, Italy |
| Paolo Perego | Politecnico di Milano, Italy |
| Amir Rahmani | University of California, USA |
| Martina Scagnoli | Politecnico di Milano, Italy |
| Mauro Serpelloni | Università degli Studi di Brescia, Italy |
| Roberto Sironi | Politecnico di Milano, Italy |
| Carlo Emilio | Politecnico di Milano, Italy |
| Alessandro Tognetti | University of Pisa, Italy |

# Contents

## Innovation by Design

## Wearable Applications

# PPG and Algorithms

# Blood Pressure Estimation Using a Single PPG Signal

Nima TaheriNejad[(✉)] [ⓘ] and Yasaman Rahmati

Institute of Computer Technology, TU Wien, Vienna, Austria
nima.taherinejad@tuwien.ac.at

**Abstract.** Early Warning Score (EWS) is a measure commonly used in hospitals since 90's to quantitatively assess the health of patients and predict its deterioration. Currently, nurses perform this assessment periodically by measuring respiration rate, oxygen saturation, systolic blood pressure, heart rate, core body temperature, and level of consciousness. Automation of this process using wearable devices allows for continuous monitoring inside and outside hospitals while reducing nurses' workload and monitoring costs. Current systems designed for this purpose use a separate device for measuring each of those bio-metric signals. This presents a challenge for the comfort and practicality of use in a real-life setup and increases its associated costs. In this work, we present a new method for estimation of systolic blood pressure, which allows reduction of the number of sensors. In our proposed method we use a smartwatch Photoplethysmogram (PPG) signal, which is mainly used for heart rate estimation, to estimate the (systolic) blood pressure too. An important feature of this system, in contrast to State-of-the-Art (SoA), is continuous, easy, and comfortable monitoring of blood pressure.

**Keywords:** Blood pressure · Smartwatch · Single PPG sensor · EWS

## 1 Introduction

Wearable devices have claimed many areas of our life; sports [12,22], physical [3,6] and mental [12,13,19,20] health being only a few of them. Despite several challenges such as constrained resources [7,17], changes in the environmental conditions [4,5,17], and excessive noise and artefact introduced by users' activities [14–16], they have been thriving and proved themselves helpful. A key factor in their current and future growth is their design and ease of use [17,18]. In this work, we follow this direction by proposing a method that allows a further extended health monitoring using smart watches.

A patient's health status can be assessed based on their vital signs. Research on cardiac arrests shows that certain symptoms can be observed long before the situation turns into a case of emergency; symptoms may appear even 24 h before

© ICST Institute for Computer Sciences, Social Informatics and Telecommunications Engineering 2021
Published by Springer Nature Switzerland AG 2021. All Rights Reserved
P. Perego et al. (Eds.): ICWH 2020, LNICST 376, pp. 3–11, 2021.
https://doi.org/10.1007/978-3-030-76066-3_1

actual health deterioration [10]. Early Warning Score (EWS) is a standard manual tool for assessing patients' health status and predicting health deterioration. Healthcare professionals periodically monitor patients' vital signs (heart rate, respiratory rate, body temperature, blood pressure, and blood's oxygen saturation) and assess their health status by a criticality level defined as EWS [11]. Each vital value is assessed and assigned a score based on Table 1. A score of 0 indicates an ideal health condition of a vital sign, while score 3 corresponds to the worst. The EWS is the aggregate value of all the individual vital sign scores. The higher the score, the higher the criticality.

**Table 1.** A conventional Early Warning Score (EWS) chart [21].

| Vital sign score | 3 | 2 | 1 | 0 | 1 | 2 | 3 |
|---|---|---|---|---|---|---|---|
| Heart rate (beats per minute) | 0–39 | 40–50 | 51–59 | 60–100 | 101–110 | 111–129 | ≥130 |
| Systolic blood pressure (mmHg) | 0–69 | 70–80 | 81–100 | 101–149 | 150–169 | 170–179 | ≥180 |
| Respiratory rate (breaths per minute) | | 0–8 | | 9–14 | 15–20 | 21–29 | ≥30 |
| Body temperature ($^\circ$C) | | ≤35 | | 35.1–38 | | 38.1–39.5 | ≥39.6 |
| Blood oxygen saturation (%) | 0–84 | 85–89 | 90–94 | 95–100 | | | |

This manual procedure has been applied to hospitalized patients, which takes a considerable amount of time from the nurses. A portable device that automates the procedure would save time for the nurses and allow patients to pursue their daily lives with a much higher chance of survival. However, currently, each of these measurements require a separate sensor and separate wearable device which makes the system bulky and impractical. This is the issue that we try to address by extracting Blood Pressure (BP) from the Photoplethysmogram (PPG) signal of a smartwatch, which is easy to wear and measures heart rate as well. In other works [16] authors have proposed a novel method, which can extract Respiratory Rate (RR) from the same PPG signal, accurate enough for EWS and in a fashion much more reliable than other existing works [14]. The reliability of measuring EWS using portable devices (even with dedicated sensors) is an important issue, which has been discussed in many previous works and many methods were proposed for improvement of different issues [3–6].

Regarding the extraction of BP from PPG, however, we are not the first ones. Johnson et al. [9] proposed using Pulse transit time (PTT) and linear regression. In this method, two PPG sensors are required, and the time that a peak requires to travel between the two points is used to estimate the BP. They achieve a high accuracy but their approach has shown to be sensitive to hand movements. A more similar study has been performed in [8]. They use the change of blood volume (BV) and blood vessel resistance (VR), considering of the influence of two external factors, namely the pressure between index finger and sensor and the temperature of the interest region. Even though this approach has a good accuracy, it is more complex and it needs to be worn on the finger, which is less convenient than a smartwatch, which is the approach we propose here.

The rest of this work is organized as follow; In Sect. 2, we propose our novel method for extracting the BP information from PPG signals. Next, we present the setup and result of our experiments in Sect. 3, and finally draw the conclusions in Sect. 4.

## 2 Proposed Method

Since the amount of light that returns to the photo-detector of the smartwatch PPG sensor is proportional to the volume of blood in the tissue, the PPG signal represents an average of all blood volume in the arteries and any other tissue, through which the light has passed. Therefore, changes in the Blood Volume Pulse (BVP) signal can indicate increase or decrease in blood perfusion as well as changes in the elasticity of the vascular walls, reflecting changes in BP. We plan to use this phenomenon to extract systolic and diastolic BP from the BVP signal captured by PPG optical sensor. Figure 1 shows a typical PPG signal and various Points of Interest (PINs) on that signal, particularly systolic and diastolic points.

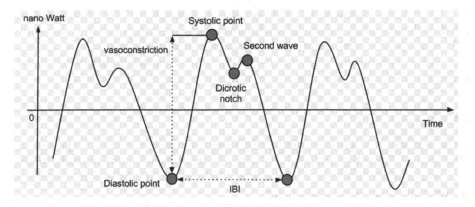

**Fig. 1.** PINs related to BP on a BVP signal.

### 2.1 Pre-processing

The pre-processing step includes Inter beat interval (IBI) extraction and band-pass filtering. In the IBI extraction, "good" heart beats (cycles) are separated from "bad" heart beat cycles. That is, the extremely noisy portion of the signal, which do not assimilate normal heart beats in a typical BVP, are tagged for removal. This process is symbolically shown in Fig. 2.

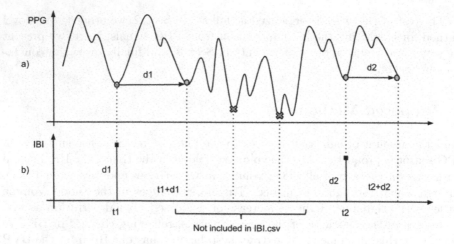

**Fig. 2.** Corrupted portions of the signals removed by IBI pre-processing.

## 2.2   Band-Pass Filtering

The BVP signal captured by PPG sensor of a smartwatch is often contaminated with noise, and especially with movement artifacts. Therefore, we apply a $4^{th}$ order Butterworth band-pass filter in the range of $[\frac{0.8}{f_s}0.8/f_s, \; 4.4/f_s]$ with $f_s = 64$ Hz. This proved to be very helpful in improving the quality of the signal, hence, the PINs, and consequently overall performance of the system.

## 2.3   Extracting PINs

In the next step, five critical points or PINs were extracted from each cycle of the PPG signal. These five PINs, shown Fig. 1, are: systolic point, diastolic point, dicrotic notch, second wave peak, and the fifth point. The fifth point is defined as $\frac{1}{2}$(systolic point + diastolic point).

It is important to bear in mind that the shape of the PPG signal changes depending on age of the subject. As shown in Fig. 3, for older people, second wave peak points are somehow smoothed out and dicrotic notches are placed at higher positions in comparison with people at younger ages.

## 2.4   Linear Estimation

We studied the correlation between the systolic and diastolic BPs and sundry of variables such as the mean, median and Standard Deviation (STD) of the PINs, as well as the ratio of the medians of four PINs over the median of the diastolic points. In addition, we studied their correlation with the difference and sum of the systolic and diastolic points. We found out that there are moderate to strong correlations between some of these parameters. This means that we

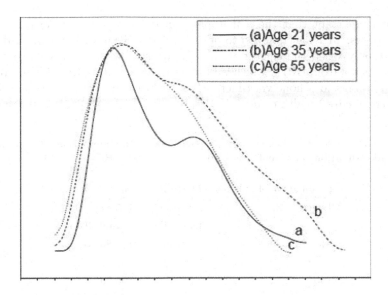

**Fig. 3.** Shape of PPG signal, particularly regarding second wave peak and dicrotic notch, changes based on the age.

can calculate such parameters, specifically BPs, one from another using a simple linear regression, i.e.;

$$y = \beta_1 x + \beta_0, \tag{1}$$

where $y$ is the desired parameter, $x$ the measured value, and $\beta_i$ respective coefficients. In Sect. 3.2, we present the $\beta_i$ values obtained through our experiments.

## 3 Experiments

### 3.1 Setup

We conducted our experiments on 36 subjects aged 6–80 years old, the distribution of which is shown in Table 2. Three subjects were removed from the data since due to excessive noise contamination (no clean part was detected in the pre-processing step.). In addition, due to reasons which we will describe in the next subsection, we collected another data set consisting of 11 subjects 20–40 years old. The subjects were asked not to drink alcohol or coffee and not to smoke for at least 2 h before the experiment.

During the experiments, the subjects were asked to sit relaxed and wear Empatica smartwatch [1], which measures the BVP using a PPG sensors, on their right wrist. The watch was connected via Bluetooth to an iPhone to record and monitor the output signals from all sensors in real time. One minute after starting to record a session, blood pressure was measured via the Smart Blood Pressure Wrist Monitor (BP7S) [2], which was worn on the subjects' left wrist. The BP7S took approximately 40 s to measure systolic and diastolic BP. Since it is very important that the cuff is positioned at our heart level during BP measurements, BP7S is equipped to detect wrist position and the measurement will start only when the correct position is detected. This helps us to obtain accurate results from BP7S, which we use as ground truth. BP7S is also able to sync its readings to iPhone via Bluetooth using iHealth MyVitals App and save data to the secure iHealth cloud.

**Table 2.** The division of collected data into age ranges, the number of subjects in each group, and estimation coefficients for systolic and diastolic BPs.

| Age range | # of subjects | Estimation | $\beta_0$ | $\beta_1$ |
|---|---|---|---|---|
| All ages | 32 | Systolic | 115.61 | −0.41 |
| | | Diastolic | 74.66 | 0.75 |
| Under 20 | 6 | Systolic | 119.86 | −0.41 |
| | | Diastolic | 87.83 | 0.29 |
| 20–40 | 12 | Systolic | 105.79 | 0.80 |
| | | Diastolic | 76.60 | 0.17 |
| 40–60 | 10 | Systolic | 78.87 | 0.77 |
| | | Diastolic | 53.99 | 0.41 |
| Over 60 | 4 | Systolic | 123.12 | 4.96 |
| | | Diastolic | 73.63 | 0.01 |

## 3.2   Results

We first studied the correlations between different parameters across the entire age range. The strongest correlation —with a large margin— was 0.483, between diastolic BP and the median of the sum of the systolic and diastolic points. However, this correlation is not very strong. Therefore, we divided the collected data to the age ranges shown in Table 2 and extracted the estimation coefficients, $\beta_i$, of Eq. (1) for each group. This grouping based on age increased the highest correlation to 0.77. However, once we used our linear estimation model, Eq. (1), the uniform model (extracted for all ages) provided better results in most cases and on average too. These results are inserted in Table 3, where we observe that except for the age range of 20–40, the uniform model has a smaller error.

To further verify this observation, we collected an extra set consisting of 11 subjects aged between 20–40 years old, which was not included in our previous analysis and extraction of the coefficients. We then ran both unified and the model adjust to 20–40 years data on this new test data set and obtained the following results, shown in Table 4. This is consistent with the previous results, reported in Table 3.

**Table 3.** Error percentage in systolic and diastolic BPs estimation using different methods.

| Age range | Uniform model | | | Age-based | | |
|-----------|---------|-----------|---------|----------|-----------|---------|
|           | Systolic | Diastolic | Average | Systolic | Diastolic | Average |
| Under 20  | 14.10   | 12.64     | 13.37   | 15.20    | 27.94     | 21.57   |
| 20–40     | 15.08   | 11.51     | 13.30   | 7.85     | 10.31     | 9.08    |
| 40–60     | 9.70    | 7.50      | 8.60    | 41.12    | 21.17     | 31.15   |
| Over 60   | 7.70    | 6.12      | 6.91    | 23.42    | 4.60      | 14.00   |
| Average   | 12.29   | 09.80     | 11.04   | 21.57    | 16.30     | 18.93   |

Even though the average of these two estimations is not considerably different, given that in EWS, systolic BP is the main used metric and the difference of estimation for this metric is higher between the two methods, we propose a combination of two as the final solution. In other words, to use the coefficients fitted to the 20–40 years old data for subjects in that age range, and the unified model for everyone else. That is;

$$SysBP = \begin{cases} 0.8x + 105.79 & 20 \leq \text{age} \leq 40 \\ -0.41x + 115.61 & \text{otherwise} \end{cases} \tag{2}$$

where

$$x = Med(\text{SP} + \text{DP}), \tag{3}$$

that is, the median of the Systolic Point (SP) and the Diastolic Point (DP), extracted from the PPG signal, as explained in Sect. 2.

**Table 4.** Error percentage in systolic and diastolic BPs estimation using different methods.

| Age range | Uniform model | | | Age-based | | |
|-----------|---------|-----------|---------|----------|-----------|---------|
|           | Systolic | Diastolic | Average | Systolic | Diastolic | Average |
| 20–40     | 14.43   | 11.61     | 13.02   | 9.36     | 10.80     | 10.08   |

This gives us an average error of 9.52% for the systolic BP estimation over all 43 data sets. Even though, this error is not ideal, it is acceptable for the purpose of EWS, since in most cases it not very likely lead to any error. Particularly for the normal range (healthy subject or score 0), which has a 43% width with respect to its middle point. In other blood pressure ranges this width is lower, however, 9.52% error in such cases, the worst case scenario, will lead to maximum 1 score error.

# 4    Conclusions

In this paper, we presented a new method for estimating BP based on the SP and the DP of the PPG signal. This method requires only a single PPG signal, which is available -virtually- in all smartwatches. Therefore, it is cheap (no additional costs if integrated in a smartwatch) and comfortable to use. The average accuracy of this method is 90.48%, which is acceptable for many applications such as EWS[1]. Moreover, by reusing PPG signal that is used for heart rate estimation, it reduces the number of sensors required for monitoring patients. Thus taking one step towards a practical, comfortable, and continous monitoring of EWS.

# References

1. Empatica smart watch. https://support.empatica.com/hc/en-us/categories/200023126-E4-wristband. Accessed 15 May 2019
2. ihealth wireless wrist blood pressure monitor. https://ihealthlabs.com/blood-pressure-monitors/wireless-blood-pressure-wrist-monitor-view-bp7s/. Accessed 15 Feb 2020
3. Anzanpour, A., et al.: Self-awareness in remote health monitoring systems using wearable electronics. In: Proceedings of Design and Test Europe Conference (DATE). Lausanne, Switzerland, March 2017
4. Götzinger, M., et al.: Confidence-enhanced early warning score based on fuzzy logic. ACM/Springer Mob. Netw. Appl. 1–18 (2019). https://doi.org/10.1007/s11036-019-01324-5
5. Götzinger, M., Anzanpour, A., Azimi, I., TaheriNejad, N., Rahmani, A.M.: Enhancing the self-aware early warning score system through fuzzified data reliability assessment. In: Perego, P., Rahmani, A.M., TaheriNejad, N. (eds.) MobiHealth 2017. LNICST, vol. 247, pp. 3–11. Springer, Cham (2018). https://doi.org/10.1007/978-3-319-98551-0_1
6. Götzinger, M., Taherinejad, N., Rahmani, A.M., Liljeberg, P., Jantsch, A., Tenhunen, H.: Enhancing the early warning score system using data confidence. In: Perego, P., Andreoni, G., Rizzo, G. (eds.) MobiHealth 2016. LNICST, vol. 192, pp. 91–99. Springer, Cham (2017). https://doi.org/10.1007/978-3-319-58877-3_12
7. Hadizadeh, E., Elmi, M., TaheriNejad, N., Fotowat, A., Mirabbasi, S.: A low-power signal-dependent sampling technique: analysis, implementation, and application. IEEE Trans. Circ. Syst. I: Regular Papers, 1–14 (2020)
8. Jeong, I.C., Ko, J.I., Hwang, S.O., Yoon, H.R.: A new method to estimate arterial blood pressure using photoplethysmographic signal. In: 2006 International Conference of the IEEE Engineering in Medicine and Biology Society, pp. 4667–4670, August 2006. https://doi.org/10.1109/IEMBS.2006.260663

---

[1] We note that as shown in Table 1, the values of various vital signal used in EWS assessment are abstracted to a score and in this abstraction often a range of numbers lead to the same score. At the border of various scores smaller errors may lead to a change of score, however, a single point error in the overall score is often negligible. For a patient to be considered in a critical condition, the aggregate score of many vital signs is important.

9. Johnson, A.M., Jegan, R., Mary, X.A.: Performance measures on blood pressure and heart rate measurement from PPG signal for biomedical applications. In: 2017 International Conference on Innovations in Electrical, Electronics, Instrumentation and Media Technology (ICEEIMT), pp. 311–315, February 2017. https://doi.org/10.1109/ICIEEIMT.2017.8116856

10. McGaughey, J., et al.: Outreach and early warning systems (EWS) for the prevention of intensive care admission and death of critically ill adult patients on general hospital wards. The Cochrane Library (2007)

11. Morgan, R.J.M., et al.: An early warning scoring system for detecting developing critical illness. Clin. Intensive Care **8**(2), 100 (1997)

12. Perego, P., Rahmani, A., Taherinejad, N. (eds.): Proceedings of the 7th International Conference on Wireless Mobile Communication and Healthcare, MobiHealth 2017, Vienna, Austria, 14–15 November 2017 (2017). https://doi.org/10.1007/978-3-319-98551-0

13. Pollreisz, D., TaheriNejad, N.: A simple algorithm for emotion recognition, using physiological signals of a smart watch. In: 2017 39th Annual International Conference of the IEEE Engineering in Medicine and Biology Society (EMBC), pp. 2353–2356, July 2017. https://doi.org/10.1109/EMBC.2017.8037328

14. Pollreisz, D., TaheriNejad, N.: Detection and removal of motion artifacts in PPG signals. ACM/Springer Mob. Netw. Appl. 1–10 (2019)

15. Pollreisz, D., TaheriNejad, N.: Efficient respiratory rate extraction on smartwatch. In: 42nd Annual International Conferences of the IEEE Engineering in Medicine and Biology Society in conjunction with the 43rd Annual Conference of the Canadian Medical and Biological Engineering Society EMBC. Montreal, Canada, pp. 1–4, July 2020

16. Pollreisz, D., TaheriNejad, N.: Reliable respiratory rate extraction using PPG. In: 11th IEEE Latin American Symposium on Circuits and Systems - LASCAS, San José, Costa Rica, pp. 1–4, February 2020

17. TaheriNejad, N.: Wearable medical devices: challenges and self-aware solutions. IEEE Life Sci. Newslett. **2**, 5–6 (2019)

18. TaheriNejad, N.: Functional or fictional. IEEE Life Sci. Special Issue on: Consumer Technology meets Health Care, 13–15, February 2020

19. TaheriNejad, N., Jantsch, A., Pollreisz, D.: Comprehensive observation and its role in self-awareness: an emotion recognition system example. In: the Federated Conference on Computer Science and Information Systems (FedCSIS), September 2016

20. TaheriNejad, N., Pollreisz, D.: Assessment of physiological signals during happiness, sadness, pain or anger. In: 6th MobiHealth (2016)

21. Urban, R.W., et al.: Modified early warning system as a predictor for hospital admissions and previous visits in emergency departments. Adv. Emerg. Nursing J. **37**(4), 281–289 (2015)

22. Yin, H., Akmandor, A.O., Mosenia, A., Jha, N.K.: Smart healthcare. Found. Trends® Electron. Des. Autom. **2**(14), 401–466 (2018)

# Multi-level Motion Artifacts Reduction in Photoplethysmography Signal Using Singular Value Decomposition

Shibam Debbarma[✉] [iD], Seyed F. Nabavi [iD], and Sharmistha Bhadra [iD]

Department of Electrical and Computer Engineering, McGill University, Montreal,
QC H3A 0E8, Canada
shibam.debbarma@mail.mcgill.ca, {seyed.nabavi,
sharmistha.bhadra}@mcgill.ca

**Abstract.** Photoplethysmography (PPG) is used for measuring vital cardiopulmonary indices such as heart rate and blood oxygen saturation ($SpO_2$). But PPG signals get inevitably corrupted by movements of the patient and results in inaccurate calculation of heart rate and $SpO_2$. In this paper, we report a method that uses a multi-level singular value decomposition (SVD) technique for effective reduction of motion artifacts while preserving the PPG morphology along with baseline. Results show impressive improvement on the signal quality and suppression of motion artifacts of the PPG signal. The PPG signals without motion artifacts obtained using out proposed method shows an average error of 0.69% in heart rate measurement with respect to the reference signal and an average max difference of 1.73% in the $SpO_2$ estimation (in comparison to the average max difference of 1.69% for the reference signal). The proposed method has potential for accurate estimation of heart rate and $SpO_2$ from PPG signal.

**Keywords:** Photoplethysmography · Heart rate · Blood oxygen saturation · Motion artifacts · Singular value decomposition · Singular values

## 1 Introduction

In recent decades, Photoplethysmoghraphy (PPG) has become a standard, low-cost, and non-invasive technique in clinical and in-house healthcare setups for monitoring cardiopulmonary parameters such as heart rate (HR) and blood-oxygen saturation ($SpO_2$) [1, 2]. A PPG sensor, shown in Fig. 1, uses a source light on a skin periphery like finger, earlobe. The transmitted/reflected light from/through the skin is detected by a photodetector [2]. It measures the blood volumetric changes due to cardiopulmonary activity. The measurement is known as PPG signal. However, PPG signal is extremely sensitive to motion and gets affected easily even by a slight movement at the point of contact between sensor and skin surface [3]. Such artifacts due to motion lead to erroneous estimation of HR and $SpO_2$ [1], and difficult to remove from the PPG signal when it appears in the desired signal band. Therefore, an effective method is needed to remove these motion artifacts from the signal while preserving its basic morphology.

© ICST Institute for Computer Sciences, Social Informatics and Telecommunications Engineering 2021
Published by Springer Nature Switzerland AG 2021. All Rights Reserved
P. Perego et al. (Eds.): ICWH 2020, LNICST 376, pp. 12–22, 2021.
https://doi.org/10.1007/978-3-030-76066-3_2

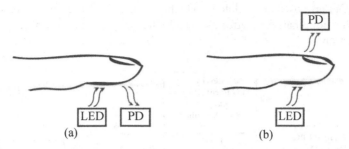

**Fig. 1.** PPG sensor configurations with light source (LED) and photodetector (PD): (a) reflection mode PPG and (b) transmission mode PPG.

Several techniques have already been proposed to reduce motion artifacts in the PPG signal. One among the easiest method is the use of moving average filter, proposed by Rusch et al. [4]. However, it is only effective for a limited range of motion artifact. Another approach of employing independent component analysis (ICA) for motion artifact removal was proposed by Kim and Yoo [5]. It is based on the assumption that the PPG and motion artifacts components are statistically independent of each other, which doesn't hold true in practical scenario [6].

Adaptive filtering is also considered as another attractive technique for reducing motion artifact from the PPG signal [7–9]. However, this technique always requires a reference motion artifact signal which can be processed directly from the corrupted PPG signal [7] or using accelerometer sensor [8, 9]. The performance of the adaptive filter is dependent on a highly correlated reference motion artifact signal, which is difficult to generate. This limits the reliability of this method.

Singular value decomposition (SVD) is a powerful statistical method. It can be used to decompose data matrix of a signal into orthonormal data matrices. The singular values of the data matrices contain information of noise levels present in that signal [10]. Reddy and Kumar reported an SVD based technique for strongest component extraction from a PPG signal [11]. This method selects a segment of a PPG signal (say first six cycles) and converts it into a data matrix depending on its strongest periodic component. In the data matrix each row represents a single PPG signal cycle. To remove motion artifacts the PPG data rows are averaged column-wise to output a PPG signal cycle (represented by a single row data, in this case the first cycle). After that, the first cycle is removed from the selected segment and a new cycle is inserted at the end of the segment. The process described above is repeated to compute the second artifact free PPG cycle and so on. However, this technique fails if all the cycles in the data-matrix are corrupted with motion artifact.

In order to overcome the issue with the SVD based technique discussed above, we propose a new SVD based algorithm as shown in Fig. 2. The method employs SVD at the first stage to select the data matrix with strongest component. Then the singular values of that data matrix are exploited to estimate noise in multiple levels and an averaging technique is employed to reconstruct a motion artifacts reduced PPG signal. Next, the signal is passed through a smoothening filter and used for HR and SpO$_2$

calculation. Our proposed methodology, which does not need a certain reference signal, can reduce the motion artifacts effectively and efficiently and provide accurate HR and SpO$_2$ calculation.

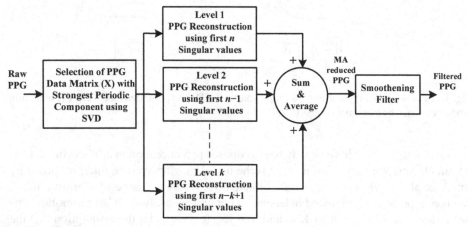

**Fig. 2.** The proposed algorithm based on singular value decomposition (SVD), multi-level PPG signal reconstruction, averaging, and smoothening filter.

## 2   Singular Value Decomposition and the Proposed Algorithm for Motion Artifacts Reduction

Singular value decomposition (SVD) method plays a key role in this new algorithm. It not only converts the PPG signal into a data matrix based on the strongest periodic component, but also reduces noise by exploiting the singular values of the data matrix. Therefore, a basic concept of SVD is needed to explain the working principle and effectiveness of the proposed algorithm.

### 2.1   Singular Value Decomposition (SVD)

SVD is a competent tool in linear algebra. The SVD of a real-valued data matrix $X$ of dimension $p \times q$ is given as follows [10],

$$X = USV^T \tag{1}$$

where $U$ and $V$ are $p \times p$ and $q \times q$ unitary matrices such that $U^T U = I$ and $V^T V = I$, where $I$ is an identity matrix. The column values of $U$ and $V$ are called left and right singular vector of $X$, respectively. $S$ is a diagonal matrix of dimension $p \times q$ and its elements are called singular values, which are in fact positive square-roots of the Eigen values of $X^T X$. The diagonal values of $S$ can be presented as $S = diag(\sigma_1, \sigma_2, \sigma_3 \ldots)$ and they are always in the descending order i.e. $(\sigma_1 > \sigma_2 > \sigma_3 \ldots)$. The singular values of $X$ can actually be analyzed to determine its true rank, noise level, energy [12], and period detection [10].

## 2.2 The Proposed Algorithm

Let's say $X$ is a data matrix of a periodic signal with each row containing one period, as shown in (2). When SVD is applied on the $X$, its $S$ matrix contains only one non-zero singular value i.e. $\sigma_1 \neq 0$ representing its one and only dominant component, while other singular values are zero.

$$X = \begin{bmatrix} x(1) & x(2) & \cdots x(j) \\ x(j+1) & x(j+2) & \cdots x(2j) \\ \vdots & \vdots & \vdots & \vdots \\ x((i-1)j+1) & x((i-1)j+2) & \cdots x(ij) \end{bmatrix} \tag{2}$$

However, for a quasi-periodic signal like PPG, once $X$ is decomposed, $S$ matrix will have several non-zero singular values with $\sigma_1 > \sigma_2 > \sigma_3 \ldots$, interpreting its several components in descending order. This information can be used to determine the dominant frequency in a PPG signal and convert it into a data matrix $X$, with each row containing one PPG signal cycle [11]. The singular values of data matrix $X$ get affected by the presence of noise or artifacts in the PPG signal. Generally, the lower singular values ($\sigma_1 - \sigma_6$, or less) in the $S$ matrix represent almost all the signal components, whereas the higher singular values represent the noise or artifacts [13]. Therefore, by reducing the rank of the $S$ matrix, in other words by making the higher singular values zero, a noise free signal can be reconstructed.

Our method incorporates both applications of SVD discussed above. In the first block (see Fig. 2), the raw PPG data is converted into data matrix $X$ using the same technique proposed in [11]. A segment of PPG data, sampled in 100 Hz, is converted into multiple matrices with different periodicities represented by the row length. The row lengths of the matrices are varied from 125 to 33 elements, representing periodicities from 0.8 Hz to 3.03 Hz (48 to 182 heart beats per minute). Then SVD is employed to all of the matrices and the ratio of their first two singular values i.e. $\sigma_1/\sigma_2$ are computed. The data matrix with highest value of $\sigma_1/\sigma_2$ is chosen as $X$.

Once $X$ is determined, the corresponding $S$ matrix is analyzed for noise reduction. The data matrix is reconstructed by reducing the rank of $S$ to $n$, (where $n <$ total number of singular values), in other words by selecting first $n$ singular values, using formula (1). The reconstructed data matrix then converted into a 1-dimensional PPG signal, marked as level 1 in Fig. 2. The value of $n$ is selected carefully to retain the PPG morphology, which still may contain some noise, referred as in-band noise [13]. The PPG signal can be reconstructed using lesser singular values to remove in-band noise but the signal pattern is compromised, which is a trade-off [13]. To overcome this trade-off, the PPG signal is reconstructed in multiple levels. In level 1 the signal morphology is retained with in-band noise components. In the subsequent levels, $n$ is reduced by 1 up to $n - k + 1$ until $k$ levels (where $k < n$ and $k > 0$), making sure the in-band noise components (along with some signal components) are eliminated from the PPG signal. Next, the reconstructed PPG signals from $k$ levels are averaged to remove the in-band noise while recovering the most of lost signal components. At last, a smoothening filter is applied on the averaged signal to remove any glitches present at the reconstructed signal. Then, the entire algorithm is repeated for the next segment of the data.

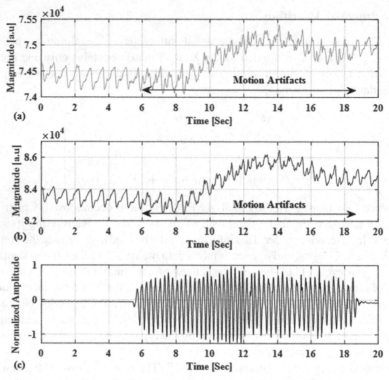

**Fig. 3.** Recorded PPG signal with motion artifacts: (a) red signal, (b) infra-red signal, and (c) accelerometer data.

## 3   Experimental Results

The experimental procedure in this study is in accordance with the Deceleration of Helsinki and was approved by Institutional Review Board of McGill University (study number: A04-M21-19B, approval date: 04/17/2019). This study was carried out using a commercial PPG sensor kit (MAX30101ACCEVKIT, by Maxim Integrated). This PPG sensor kit also contains an accelerometer. This PPG sensor has two LEDs (Red and Infra-red) which is necessary for $SpO_2$ calculation. The sensor was placed on the left index fingertip of a healthy subject and motion artifacts are introduced during the measurement. The recorded signals were sampled at 100 Hz. A portion of the signals (duration 20 s) is shown in Fig. 3. As we can see, the motion artifacts introduced during the measurement corrupts the recorded PPG signal. The corrupted part of the signal perfectly aligns with the accelerometer events. Another PPG sensor was placed on the right index fingertip for motion artifact free reference measurement, which is discussed in the next section. The signal from the left and right index fingertip are considered as measured and reference PPG signal, respectively.

The proposed algorithm, in Fig. 2, was applied to a measured PPG signals at infra-red wavelength shown in Fig. 4(a). The algorithm identified the PPG data matrix with strong component and decomposed its singular matrix $S$. At first stage, the rank of the rank of

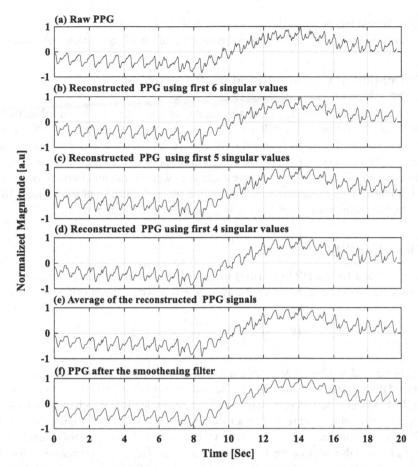

**Fig. 4.** Proposed method: (a) raw PPG signal; (b), (c), (d) PPG signal reconstructed with 6, 5, 4 singular values, respectively; (e) average of the reconstructed PPGs; and (f) smoothened PPG output at the final stage.

the singular matrix $S$ was reduced up to its first six ($n = 6$) singular values ($\sigma_1$ to $\sigma_6$) to reconstruct the PPG signal shown in Fig. 4(b). The signal in Fig. 4(b) retained the PPG signal features and removed the high frequency noise. In the subsequent stages ($k = 3$), the singular values were eliminated one at a time and the PPG signal was reconstructed using first five ($n = 5$) and then four ($n = 4$) singular values, respectively, as shown in 4(c) and Fig. 4(d). The average of these three level signals is shown in Fig. 4(e). The average signal was then smoothen out as shown 4(f). It is worth pointing out that the number of levels $k$ aren't limited to 3 and can be more or less depending on the sampling frequency and quality of the signal. However, singular values being chosen from $\sigma_4$ to $\sigma_6$ (i.e. $n = 4$ to 6) for 3 levels (i.e. $k = 3$) was found optimal for motion artifacts estimation for a signal sampled at 100 Hz. It can be the seen from the final signal (shown in Fig. 4(f)) our proposed method can remove the motion artifacts effectively while this motion reduction has minimal impact on nature of the PPG signals, i.e., amplitude and baseline, in addition to the ability of preserving the unaffected region as the original one.

## 4  Estimation of Cardiopulmonary Parameters

As mentioned earlier, a PPG data contain significant information about a subject's HR and $SpO_2$ levels. Whereas, the HR can be calculated from time domain PPG signal, $SpO_2$ can be calculating by analyzing the DC and AC levels of red and infra-red signals. To see the effectiveness of the proposed algorithm, both HR and $SpO_2$ are calculated from measured PPG signals of 5 subjects while they were sitting and introduced motion in the left index finger in random times. A motion free reference PPG signal taken from their right index finger was used to calculate the reference HR and $SpO_2$.

### 4.1  Heart Rate (HR)

We estimated beat-to-beat HR first in the time domain by calculating the distance between two consecutive PPG peaks and then the average HR was calculated using this formula:

$$HR = \frac{1}{n-1} \sum_{i=1}^{n} \frac{60}{t_{i+1} - t_i}; n \geq 2 \tag{3}$$

where $n$ is the total number of detected peaks in a given segment of PPG data and $t_i$ is the $i^{th}$ detected peak in that segment. The idea behind this is to show how the motion artifacts affects the PPG signal and thereby leads to a false peak selection, which eventually leads to erroneous HR value. Figure 5 shows PPG signal from subject 1. Figure 5(a) shows the PPG signal with motion artifacts along with its selected peaks. In this signal, some of the peaks are false peaks detected due to motion artifacts. The average HR for that duration is found out to be 88 beats per minute (bpm) from the signal with motion artifact. Figure 5(b) shows the motion artifact free signal obtained after applying our proposed method. It can be seen that the PPG peaks are selected accurately in this signal leading to an average HR of 87 bpm which perfectly matches with the average HR of the reference signal shown in Fig. 5(c). To validate this information, PPG data with motion artifacts from 5 subjects were analyzed using the proposed method. Their average HR were calculated from the PPG signal with motion artifact, reconstructed PPG signal after motion artifact removal using our method, and reference PPG signal. The results are tabulated in Table 1. It can be seen that the average HR from motion artifact free signals are closer to the values obtained from reference signal than the average HR obtained from the signal with motion artifacts. For the motion artifact free signal, it shows an average error of 0.69% with respect to the reference signal, affirming the usefulness of the proposed method.

### 4.2  Blood Oxygen Saturation ($SpO_2$)

The blood oxygen saturation ($SpO_2$) is another important metric, representing percentage amount of oxygenated blood in a healthy subject and should always remain close to

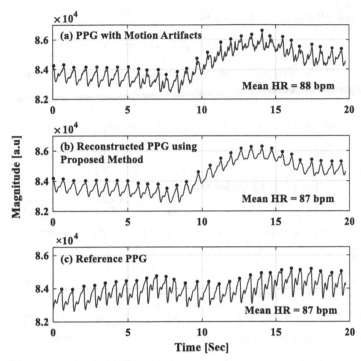

**Fig. 5.** Average Heart Rate (HR) calculation using: (a) PPG signal with motion artifacts, (b) reconstructed PPG signal using our proposed method, and (c) reference PPG signal.

**Table 1.** Average HR calculation from raw PPG signal, PPG signal using proposed method, and the reference signal.

| Subjects | Average HR from PPG signal with motion artifact | Average HR from PPG signal after motion artifact removal | Average HR from Reference PPG signal | Abs. Error for motion artifact free signal |
|---|---|---|---|---|
| 1 | 88 bpm | 87 bpm | 87 bpm | 0% |
| 2 | 81 bpm | 81 bpm | 80 bpm | 1.25% |
| 3 | 84 bpm | 86 bpm | 86 bpm | 0% |
| 4 | 90 bpm | 89 bpm | 88 bpm | 1.14% |
| 5 | 90 bpm | 92 bpm | 93 bpm | 1.08% |

100%. The %SpO$_2$ was calculated by utilizing the ratio AC and DC part of both red and infra-red signals, using the following formula;

$$Ratio = \frac{AC_{Red}/DC_{Red}}{AC_{IR}/DC_{IR}} \qquad (4)$$

And the overall %SpO$_2$ was calculated by;

$$\%SpO_2 = \alpha.(Ratio)^2 + \beta.(Ratio) + \gamma \qquad (5)$$

where $\alpha$, $\beta$, and $\gamma$ are calibration coefficients and are generally determined empirically by studying groups of people.

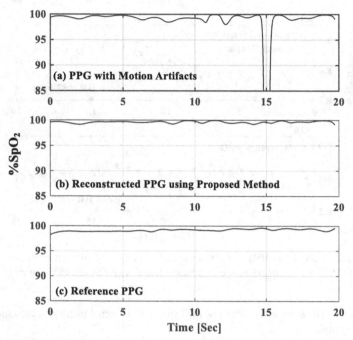

**Fig. 6.** Blood oxygen saturation (%SpO$_2$) estimation from: (a) PPG signal with motion artifacts, (b) reconstructed PPG signal using our proposed method, and (c) reference PPG signal.

Due to the presence of motion artifacts in the signal, calculated %SpO$_2$ may vary significantly and show a false value below 90%, which is considered to be fatal in terms of clinical standards. Therefore, it becomes essential to have motion free PPG signal for better estimation of %SpO$_2$. For our study, the values of $\alpha$, $\beta$, and $\gamma$ were chosen to be $-45.060$, $30.354$, and $94.84$, respectively [14]. Figure 6 shows the SpO$_2$ estimation for subject 1 using the PPG signals shown in Fig. 5. The estimation of %SpO$_2$ for a PPG signal with motion artifacts, reconstructed PPG signal after removing the motion artifacts using proposed method and reference signal are shown in Fig. 6(a), Fig. 6(b), Fig. 6(c), respectively. We can clearly see a few downward fluctuations of %SpO$_2$ in Fig. 6(a). Even one of them is reaching below 85%. These fluctuation are restored closer to 100% in Fig. 6(b) after the PPG signal is processed with the proposed method. The estimated SpO$_2$ from the motion artifact free PPG signal is close to the estimated SpO$_2$ from the reference signal. To further support this information, SpO$_2$ was estimated from acquired PPG signals from the 5 subjects. For each subject SpO$_2$ was estimated from PPG signal after removing the motion artifacts using the proposed method and the reference signal.

The results are shown in Table 2. It shows an average max difference of 1.73% and 1.69% in the $SpO_2$ estimation from the PPG signal without motion artifact and the reference signal, respectively.

**Table 2.** $\%SpO_2$ calculation from PPG signal using proposed method and the reference signal.

| Subjects | %SpO₂ range from PPG signal after motion artifact removal | %SpO₂ range from reference PPG signal |
|---|---|---|
| 1 | 99.12—99.95% | 98.25—99.61% |
| 2 | 98.89—99.92% | 97.23—99.95% |
| 3 | 96.88—99.95% | 96.8—99.76% |
| 4 | 97.99—99.95% | 98—98.84% |
| 5 | 98.21—99.95% | 98.26—98.84% |

## 5　Conclusion

In this paper, a novel SVD based multi-level motion artifact reduction method is presented to remove the motion artifacts present in PPG signals. The multi-level averaging technique efficiently removed the in-band noise and out of band noise introduced by motion artifacts while retaining the signal features. Estimated HR and $\%SpO_2$ from the motion artifact free PPG signal obtained from our proposed method shows an average error of 0.69% in HR measurement with respect to the reference signal and an average max difference of 1.73% in the $SpO_2$ estimation (in comparison to the average max difference of 1.69% for the reference signal). The close agreement of the estimated value from the motion artifact free signal and the reference signal validates the effectiveness of the proposed method.

## References

1. Allen, J.: Photoplethysmography and its application in clinical physiological measurement. Physiol. Meas. **28**(3), R1–R39 (2007)
2. Webster, J.G.: Design of Pulse Oximeters. Taylor & Francis, New York (1997)
3. Maeda, Y., Sekine, M., Tamura, T.: Relationship between measurement site and motion artifacts in wearable reflected photoplethysmography. J. Med. Syst. **35**(5), 969–976 (2011)
4. Rusch, T.L., Sankar, R., Scharf, J.E.: Signal processing methods for pulse oximetry. Comput. Biol. Med. **26**(2), 143–159 (1996)
5. Kim, B.S., Yoo, S.K.: Motion artifact reduction in photoplethysmography using independent component analysis. IEEE Trans. Biomed. Eng. **53**(3), 566–568 (2006)
6. Yao, J., Warren, S.: A short study to assess the potential of independent component analysis for motion artifact separation in wearable pulse oximeter signals. In: 27th Proceedings on Annual Conference of IEEE Engineering in Medicine and Biology (EMBC), Shanghai, pp. 3585–3588 (2005)

7. Ram, M.R., Madhav, K.V., Krishna, E.H., Komalla, N.R., Reddy, K.A.: A novel approach for motion artifact reduction in PPG signals based on AS-LMS adaptive filter. IEEE Trans. Instrum. Meas. **61**(5), 1445–1457 (2011)
8. Ye, Y., Cheng, Y., He, W., Hou, M., Zhang, Z.: Combining nonlinear adaptive filtering and signal decomposition for motion artifact removal in wearable photoplethysmography. IEEE Sens. J. **16**(19), 7133–7141 (2016)
9. Wu, C.C., Chen, I.W., Fang, W.C.: An implementation of motion artifacts elimination for PPG signal processing based on recursive least squares adaptive filter. In: 13th IEEE Biomedical Circuits and Systems Conference (BioCAS), Turin, pp. 1–4 (2017)
10. Klema, V.C., Laub, A.J.: The singular value decomposition: Its computation and some applications. IEEE Trans. Autom. Control **25**(2), 164–176 (1980)
11. Reddy, K.A., Kumar, V.J.: Motion Artifact reduction in Photoplethysmography Signals using Singular Value Decomposition. In: Proceedings on IEEE Instrumentation and Measurement Technology Conference (IMTC), Warsaw, pp. 1–4 (2007)
12. Kanjilal, P.P., Palit, S.: On multiple pattern extraction using singular value decomposition. IEEE Trans. Signal Process. **43**(6), 1536–1540 (1995)
13. Rojano, J.F., Isaza, C.V.: Singular Value decomposition of the time frequency distribution of PPG signals for motion artifact reduction. Int. J. Sig. Process. Syst. **4**(6), 475–482 (2016)
14. Maxim Integrated, MAXREFDES117#: Heart-rate and pulse-oximetry monitor. https://media.digikey.com/pdf/Data%20Sheets/Maxim%20PDFs/MAXREFDES117_Web.pdf. Accessed 19 June 2019

# Intraoral Monitoring of Photoplethysmogram Signal to Estimate Cardiorespiratory Parameters

Shibam Debbarma$^{(\boxtimes)}$ ⓘ and Sharmistha Bhadra ⓘ

Department of Electrical and Computer Engineering, McGill University, Montreal,
QC H3A 0E8, Canada
`shibam.debbarma@mail.mcgill.ca, sharmistha.bhadra@mcgill.ca`

**Abstract.** Photoplethysmograpghy (PPG) is a simple, non-invasive, optical method already known in clinical and home monitoring setups for its wide applications in cardiorespiratory measurements such as heart rate, breathing, and blood oxygen saturation ($SpO_2$). Here, we present an intraoral measurement of such cardiorespiratory parameters using a photoplethysmogram (PPG) sensor. A reflective PPG sensor is placed inside the oral cavity, facing the buccal mucosa opposite to upper jaw, and PPG signal is obtained. The average heart rate, breathing signal and average $SpO_2$ variation are calculated from the intraoral PPG signal. Accuracy of the measured parameters are validated against standard monitoring methods: a commercial PPG sensor mounted on the left index fingertip to monitor heart rate and $SpO_2$ levels and a respiration monitoring belt worn around the diaphragm for breathing. Results obtained from subject's tests show an average absolute error of 0.75% in heart rate measurement and 5.83% in breathing detection compared to standard references. Whereas, the average variation in $SpO_2$ levels are 2.41% and 1.35% from the intra-oral measurement and the reference measurement, respectively. Intraoral measurement of such cardiorespiratory parameters can have useful applications such as smart mandibular advancement devices to monitor sleep while treating patients with sleep apnea.

**Keywords:** Photoplethysmography · Photoplethysmogram sensor · Intraoral monitoring · Heart Rate · Blood oxygen saturation · Breathing · Sleep Apnea

## 1 Introduction

Obstructive Sleep Apnea (OSA) is a health condition where patients suffer from multiple episodes of decreased or cessation of breathing events while sleeping [1]. If not treated, OSA may contribute to several medical conditions like Alzheimer's disease [2], cognitive issues, day-time sleepiness, hypertension, high blood pressure, cardiovascular diseases and may have an impact on the quality of our day-to-day life [3]. To diagnose OSA, a sleep study is required. Sleep studies include overnight monitoring of physiological parameters such as heart rate, $SpO_2$ saturation, breathing, EEG and EMG to detect restless leg syndrome. Intraoral mandibular advancement devices (MADs) provide safe and effective treatments of OSA [4]. Due to limited number of sleep labs across the world, sleep studies are not typically performed after the initiation of MAD treatment [5]. While sleep studies are typically done as a preliminary diagnostic step, data collected from an intraoral MAD could provide long-term monitoring of patients and their condition.

Developing a smart MAD, with an integrated sensing platform to monitor physiological parameters intraorally, would monitor both the state of the patient and the effectiveness of the treatment. To date, compliance monitoring during MAD treatment has been limited to rudimentary thermal recording [6]. There is a lack of research in intraoral monitoring of physiological parameters. One research group designed a pacifier with a reflective photoplethysmogram (PPG) sensor for acquiring oxygen saturation ($SpO_2$) intraorally, mainly for infants and critically burned subjects [7]. A possible study of acquiring some of those above mentioned health parameters intraorally will definitely provide a boon to the smart MAD technologies.

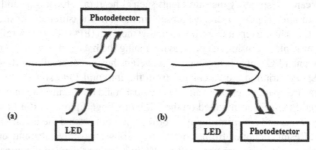

**Fig. 1.** Sensor placement configurations in photoplethysmography (PPG) with light source (LED) and photodetector: (a) transmissive PPG and (b) reflective PPG.

Photoplethysmography (PPG), a non-invasive method, is well known for its simplicity and widely used for monitoring cardiac parameters such as heart rate and blood oxygen saturation (SpO2) levels [8, 9]. It has also been employed as an indirect method for reliable monitoring of respiratory activity [10, 11]. In this method, a PPG sensor is placed on a skin surface such as fingertip, earlobe etc. to monitor the changes during blood flow [8]. This optical method uses a light source, see Fig. 1, to illuminate the sensor-skin contact area and the transmitted or reflected light is acquired using a photodetector from the opposite or same side of the light source. The former and the latter configurations are known as transmissive and reflective photoplethymsography, respectively.

In this study, we have investigated few intraoral locations for acquiring the PPG signal using a reflective PPG sensor. A good PPG signal is observed when the PPG sensor is placed inside the oral cavity in such a way so that it faces the buccal mucosa opposite to upper jaw. The acquired PPG signal is then processed to extract cardiorespiratory parameters like heart rate (HR), $SpO_2$, and breathing signal. The extracted heart rate and SpO2 from the intraoral PPG signal are validated against another reference PPG signal taken from the subject's left index finger. The breathing signal extracted from the intraoral PPG signal is compared with the breathing events recorded using a respiration monitoring belt worn around the subject's diaphragm. Results show potential for monitoring cardiorespiratory parameters intraorally and suggest that longitudinal sleep studies could be conducted for patients with sleep apnea by integrating a reflective PPG sensor into a MAD.

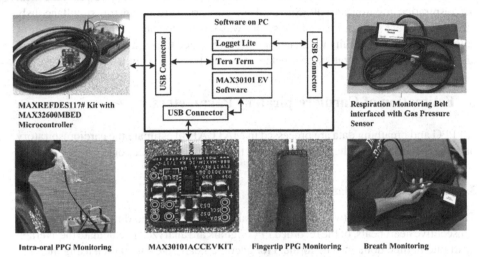

**Fig. 2.** Complete experimental setup of the sensors: MAXREFDES117# sensor kit for intra-oral PPG signal monitoring (left), MAX30101ACCEVKIT sensor kit for fingertip PPG signal monitoring (middle), and respiration monitoring belt with gas pressure sensor for breath monitoring (right); all are connected to a PC

## 2    Sensors and Experimental Setup

The complete experimental setup is shown in Fig. 2. To monitoring PPG signals intraorally, we used the sensor kit MAXREFDES117# containing MAX30102 reflective PPG sensor by Maxim integrated [12, 13]. This dual wavelength (Red and Infra-red) PPG sensor, designed for wearables, is compact in size and can be easily configured and programmed in any microcontroller with $I^2C$ ports. To validate our calculated heart rate and $SpO_2$, another reference signal is recorded using a PPG sensor kit MAX30101ACCEVKIT [14], mounted on the fingertip of the index finger of the test subject's left hand. To validate breathing signal extracted from the intraoral PPG, another reference breathing signal is obtained using a respiration monitoring belt interfaced with a gas pressure sensor, by Vernier [15, 16]. The belt is generally worn around the diaphragm to monitor breathing. It is worth pointing out that the subjects were in complete resting position when the intraoral PPG and other reference signals are recorded and no artifacts (being motion, coughing etc.) were introduced during PPG and breathing monitoring. The objecting of this study is to acquire a good PPG signal intraorally and see if parameters heart rate, $SpO_2$, and breathing can be extracted from that location.

The intraoral PPG data are compared to fingertip PPG data, both recorded in 100 samples per second. A serial communication freeware 'Tera Term' was used to record the digitized intraoral PPG data on a personal computer (PC). The sensor kit MAX30101ACCEVKIT comes with a specific controller board, and a software. The software was used to log the data from the fingertip PPG signal to a PC. The breathing data was also sampled at 100 Hz and recorded on a PC with software provided with the respiration monitoring belt. Since all the sensors were being run simultaneously through different software, an 'autoit script' was written to start all the software almost at the same time for simultaneous data monitoring. Once the data are recorded, they are analyzed for cardiorespiratory parameters, given in the next section.

## 3  Estimation of Cardiorespiratory Parameters

All PPG and breathing data are processed in MATLAB to estimate the cardiorespiratory parameters and each of them are detailed in the following subsections:

### 3.1  Heart-Rate Calculation

The difference between two consecutive peaks, representing the duration between two consecutive heart beats, of the recorded PPG signals are analyzed to calculate the average heart rate in time domain. The formula for average heart-rate calculation using the PPG peaks is given as follows:

$$HR = \frac{1}{n-1} \sum_{i=1}^{n} \frac{60}{t_{i+1} - t_i}; n \geq 2 \qquad (1)$$

where $n$ is the total number of detected peaks and $t_i$ is the $i^{th}$ detected peak, in a given segment of PPG signal.

### 3.2  Estimation of SpO2

The estimation of $SpO_2$ require both the red and infra-red wavelength PPG signals and can be given using the following formulas:

$$Ratio = \frac{AC_{Red}/DC_{Red}}{AC_{IR}/DC_{IR}} \qquad (2)$$

and

$$\%SpO_2 = \alpha.(Ratio)^2 + \beta.(Ratio) + \gamma \qquad (3)$$

Here $\alpha$, $\beta$, and $\gamma$ are called calibration coefficients and are determined empirically by acquiring data from a large set of people. The values of $\alpha$, $\beta$, and $\gamma$ are used as $-45.060$, $30.354$, and $94.84$, respectively, for $\%SpO_2$ calculation [12]. The estimated $\%SpO_2$ in a healthy subject should always be closer to 100%.

### 3.3  Breathing Monitoring and Estimation

The PPG signal has also been reported to have breathing information in them and can be used as an indirect method for respiration detection [10, 11]. A way of extracting respiration signal from the PPG signal is by observing respiration sinus arrhythmia (RSA), an event where the beat-to-beat heart rate interval decreases during inhalation and increases during exhalation [10]. Therefore, the peak-to-peak time interval of the heart rate variation (HRV) curve should correspond to the breathing events [11].

Only because of this reason the average heart rate is also calculated in time domain by selecting PPG peak-to-peak distances and thereby determining beat-to-beat heart rates for a given segment of PPG data. The beat-to-beat heart rate data is also known as the heart rate variation i.e. HRV. In the next step, the HRV data extracted from intraoral PPG is then smoothened out and a curve is obtained which can be interpreted as a breathing signal.

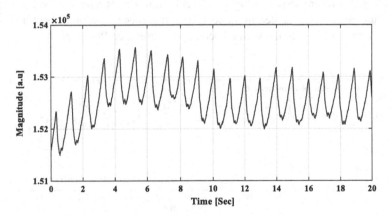

**Fig. 3.** Example PPG signal recorded intraorally.

## 4  Results and Analysis

The experimental procedure in this study is in accordance with the Deceleration of Helsinki and was approved by Institutional Review Board of McGill University (study number: A04-M21-19B, approval date: 04/17/2019). In this experiment, the intraoral PPG sensor was wrapped in a transparent plastic material for isolation. The transparent plastic material was safe to use inside the mouth. Several locations inside the oral cavity, like the tongue surface, mouth roof, interior and exterior gum of the upper and lower jaw, and buccal mucosa are tested to obtain a good optimal PPG signal. The locations in the interior part of the oral cavity such as mouth roof are not suitable for the measurement since PPG sensors are sensitive to motion and a slight movement of the tongue disturbs the recording. The exterior gum of the upper jaw could not be tested properly because of the relatively small headroom to place the PPG sensor. The buccal mucosa area facing opposite to both the upper and lower jaw is found to be the best location for PPG sensor placement and the area gets isolated from the tongue when the jaws are closed. Since the PPG sensor did not get affected by any ambient light source inside the oral cavity, very clear PPG signals were recorded. Figure 3 shows an example PPG signal recorded intraorally for 20 s. To further investigate the study, five subjects are tested and PPG signals are recorded for a duration of 1 to 2 min intraorally as well as from their left index fingertip as reference measurement. At the same time as this intraoral PPG signal measurement, breathing signals from a respiration monitoring belt are recorded, simultaneously.

### 4.1  Validation of Heart Rate

The average heart rates for all five subjects are calculated from the intraoral PPG and the reference PPG signal after selecting the peaks (in MATLAB) and using the formula given in (1). One example of the intraoral and reference PPG signals with their selected peaks (in MATLAB) are shown in Fig. 4. The calculated heart rates for 5 subjects along with absolute error are presented in Table 1, which shows an average absolute error of 0.75% for intraoral PPG signal, with respect to the reference PPG signal.

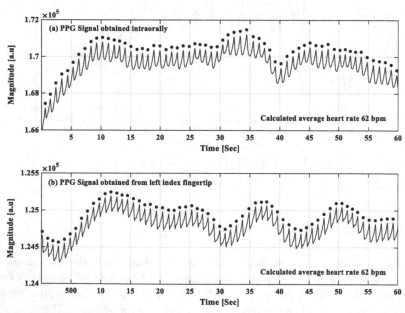

**Fig. 4.** Average heart rate calculations from: (a) intraoral PPG signal and (b) reference PPG signal taken from the left index fingertip.

**Table 1.** Average heart rate calculation from intraoral signals and reference PPG signals taken from left index fingertip in beats per minute (bpm).

| Subjects | Average heart rate from intraoral PPG (in bpm) | Average heart rate from reference PPG (in bpm) | % Absolute error |
|---|---|---|---|
| 1 | 62 | 62 | 0% |
| 2 | 66 | 65 | 1.54% |
| 3 | 68 | 68 | 0% |
| 4 | 87 | 88 | 1.14% |
| 5 | 92 | 93 | 1.08% |

**Table 2.** Estimated %SpO$_2$ range from intraoral signals and reference PPG signals taken from left index fingertip.

| Subjects | Average %SpO$_2$ range from intraoral PPG | Variation | Average %SpO$_2$ range from reference PPG | Variation |
|---|---|---|---|---|
| 1 | 98.75–99.95% | 1.2% | 97.71–99.95% | 2.24% |
| 2 | 97.65–99.95% | 2.3% | 99.79–99.95% | 0.16% |
| 3 | 95.76–99.95% | 4.19% | 97.15–99.95% | 2.8% |
| 4 | 95.97–99.95% | 3.98% | 99.06–99.95% | 0.89% |
| 5 | 99.55–99.95% | 0.4% | 99.28–99.95% | 0.67% |

## 4.2  Validation of Percentage SpO$_2$ (%SpO$_2$)

To estimate the %SpO$_2$ for all the five subjects, Eqs. (2) and (3) are used. The calculated range of %SpO$_2$ levels is presented in Table 2 and one reading is presented in Fig. 5. The average variation in %SpO$_2$ for intraoral PPG signal is calculated to be 2.41%, whereas for the reference PPG signal taken from the left index fingertip is 1.35%.

## 4.3  Validation of Breathing Patterns

To study the effect of breathing on PPG signals, different breathing patterns like normal breathing, slow breathing, fast breathing, shallow breathing, and breath holds are performed with the subjects. Figure 6 and 7 show the HRV curve obtained from intraoral measurement along with breathing signal obtained from the respiration monitoring belt (standard breathing measurement) during two new tests, separate from the test cases used for heart rate and %SpO2 estimation. This is done to see how the PPG signals respond to different kinds of breathing pattern and if the intended HRV data can capture those patterns. For the test shown in Fig. 6, the subject performed slow breathing (SLB) at first followed by normal (NB), again slow (SLB) and then fast breathing (FB). If we compare the intraoral HRV curve with the standard breathing measurement it can be seen that the HRV curve can properly detect all the peaks for normal and slow breathing. The five

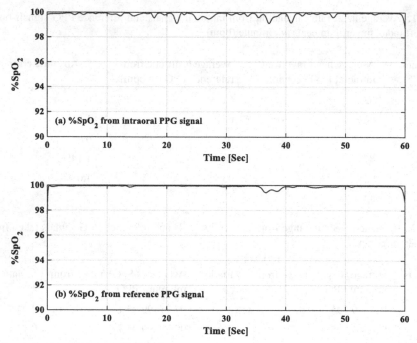

**Fig. 5.** Estimation of %SpO$_2$ levels from: (a) intraoral PPG signal and (b) reference PPG signal taken from the left index fingertip.

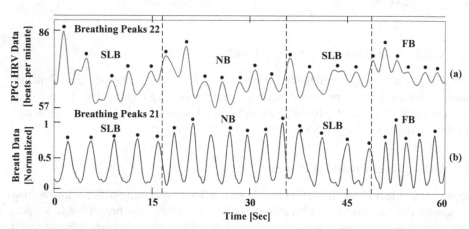

**Fig. 6.** Respiratory waveforms of a subject: (a) PPG HRV data in beats per minute from the PPG sensor and (b) Normalized Breath data from the respiration monitoring belt, with the following breathing patterns: slow breathing (SLB), normal breathing (NB), and fast breathing (FB).

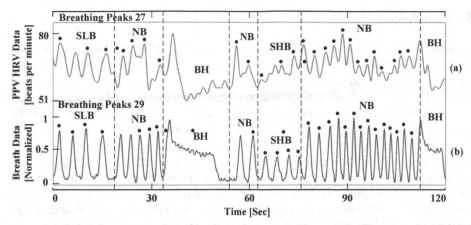

**Fig. 7.** Respiratory waveforms of a subject: (a) PPG HRV data in beats per minute from the PPG sensor and (b) Normalized Breath data from the respiration monitoring tube, with the following breathing patterns: slow breathing (SLB), normal breathing (NB), shallow breathing (FB), and breath holds (BH).

peaks for the fast breathing pattern are also visible in the HRV curve. However, the peak to valley differences are small for fast breathing in HRV curve in comparison to the other breathing patterns. This behavior is expected since the heart activity does not get much affected during a simulated fast breathing and the gaseous exchange happen in small amount. In some cases, we see dual peaks in the HRV curve for a corresponding single peak in the respiration curve. This is an artifact generated by the MATLAB interpolation function when it sees same heart rate value in the two consecutive points in the discrete HRV data.

For the test shown in Fig. 7, the subject performed breathing patterns as followed: slow breathing (SLB), normal breathing (NB), a breath hold (BH), normal breathing (NB), shallow breathing (SHB), normal breathing (NB), and at the end another breath hold (BH) event. If we compare the intraoral HRV curve with the standard breathing measurement it can be seen that the HRV curve can detect all the peaks for normal, slow, and shallow breathing properly. The amplitude of HRV curve goes down significantly during the breathing hold event and fluctuates very little during the entire breath hold event. This pattern can easily detect a breath hold event (an indicator of sleep apnea patients).

Now, for the test given in Fig. 6, the breathing peaks are counted as 22 and 21 from HRV curve extracted from intraoral PPG signal and the reference breathing signal from the respiration monitoring belt, respectively. Whereas, for Fig. 7, the counted breathing peaks (excluding the breath hold event) are 27 and 29 from HRV curve extracted from intraoral PPG signal and the reference breathing signal from the respiration monitoring belt, respectively. The overall absolute error of this two readings is found out to be 5.83%, thus showing the potential of intraoral PPG measurements in smart MAD technologies.

# 5  Conclusion

To assess cardiorespiratory parameters during sleep, the intraoral monitoring of PPG signals can be utilized. In this regard, the PPG sensor can be integrated with a mandibular advancement device (MAD) to monitor patients who suffer from obstructive sleep apnea (OSA). This is a non-invasive technique and doesn't require any kind of incision while placing the PPG sensor in the oral cavity. We provide a detailed study of monitoring PPG signals intraorally for extracting cardiorespiratory parameters like average heart rate, $\%SpO_2$, and respiratory (or breathing) events. The estimated heart rate, $\%SpO_2$, and breathing events from the intraoral PPG signal are validated with a fingertip PPG sensor and a respiration belt, respectively. The intraoral heart rate measurement for five subjects provided an average error of 0.75% with respect to the reference PPG measurement. The same readings yielded an average variation of 2.41% in $\%SpO_2$ from the intraoral PPG, whereas the reference PPG yielded an average variation of 1.35%. Different kinds of breathing patterns, such as normal, slow, fast, shallow, and breath-hold, recorded from the PPG signal were compared with the reference measurement. Intraoral measurement were able to capture almost all the breathing peaks intraorally showing an average error of 5.83%. This intraoral monitoring showed the reliability of capturing intraoral PPG signal to detect cardiorespiratory parameters by the MADs.

# References

1. Punjabi, N.M.: The epidemiology of adult obstructive sleep apnea. Proc. Am. Thoracic Soc. **5**(2), 136–143 (2008)
2. Somers, V.K., White, D.P., Amin, R., Abraham, W.T., Costa, F.: Sleep apnea and cardiovascular disease: an american heart association/american college of cardiology foundation scientific statement (...). Circulation **118**(10), 1080–1111 (2008)
3. Sharma, R.A., Varga, A.W., Bubu, O.M., Pirraglia, E., Kam, K., Parekh, A.: Obstructive sleep apnea severity affects amyloid burden in cognitively normal elderly: a longitudinal study. Am. J. Respir. Crit. Care Med. **197**(7), 933–943 (2017)
4. Bratton, D.J., Gaisl, T., Wons, A.M., Kohler, M.: CPAP vs mandibular advancement devices and blood pressure in patients with obstructive sleep apnea: a systematic review and meta-analysis. JAMA **314**(21), 2280–2293 (2015)
5. Flemons W. W., Douglas N. J., Kuna S. T., Rodenstein D. O., Wheatley J.: Access to diagnosis and treatment of patients with suspected sleep apnea. World J. Am. J. Respir. Crit. Care Med., **169(6)**, 668–672, (2004).
6. Sutherland, K., et al.: Oral appliance treatment for obstructive sleep apnea: an update. J. Clin. Sleep Med. **10**(2), 215–27 (2014)
7. Walker, S.C., Alexander, J.G., Shepherd, J.M.: Pacifier pulse oximeter sensor. US patent US6470200B2, 22 October 2002
8. Webster, J.G.: Design of Pulse Oximeters. Taylor & Francis, New York (1997)
9. Sahni, R.: Noninvasive monitoring by photoplethysmography. Clin. Perinatol. **39**(3), 573–583 (2012)
10. Yasuma, F., Hayano, J.: Respiratory sinus arrhythmia: why does the heartbeat synchronize with respiratory rhythm? Chest **125**(2), 683–690 (2004)
11. Shahshahami, A., Zilic, Z., Bhadra, S.: Motion artifact reduction for respiratory monitoring: a multichannel ultrasound sensor for diaphragm tracking. IEEE Sens. J. (2019). https://doi.org/10.1109/JSEN.2019.2930461

12. Maxim Integrated, MAXREFDES117#: Heart-rate and pulse-oximetry monitor. https://media.digikey.com/pdf/Data%20Sheets/Maxim%20PDFs/MAXREFDES117_Web.pdf. Accessed 19 June 2019
13. Maxim Integrated, MAX30102: High-sensitivity pulse oximeter and heart-rate sensor for wearable health, https://datasheets.maximintegrated.com/en/ds/MAX30102.pdf. Accessed 19 June 2019
14. Maxim Integrated, MAX30101 evaluation system. https://datasheets.maximintegrated.com/en/ds/MAX30101DBEVKIT.pdf. Accessed 20 June 2019
15. Vernier: Respiration monitoring belt. https://www.vernier.com/files/manuals/rmb.pdf. Accessed 21 June 2019
16. Vernier: Gas pressure sensor. https://www.vernier.com/files/manuals/gps-bta/gps-bta.pdf. Accessed 21 June 2019

# IoT and Smart Sensors

# Empowering the Citizen in the Main Pillars of Health by Using IoT

Meritxell Gómez-Martínez, Silvia Orte, Laura Ros-Freixedes, Kian Seif, and Eloisa Vargiu(✉) ⓘ

Eurecat, Centre Tecnòlogic, eHealth Unit, Barcelona, Spain
{meritxell.gomez-martinez,silvia.orte,
laura.ros-freixedes,kian.seif,eloisa.vargiu}@eurecat.org

**Abstract.** To live longer, healthier, and more active, people at any age have to follow simple and clear suggestions that cover the 3 main pillars of health: physical activity, nutrition, and sleeping. Unfortunately, due to the intrinsic (e.g., daily-life habits) and extrinsic (e.g., environmental change) factors, people are far to have a healthy life and, thus, there is an increase of chronic diseases, mental disorders, and premature death. Approaches to increase citizen empowerment vary from self-management programs to those for promoting citizen (especially patients) involvement in treatment shared decision-making, to those to facilitating also the clinician-patient cooperation, when required. This paper presents the approach followed in CarpeDiem, an IoT-based system focused on self-management as a way to engage and empower citizens in order to improve their quality of life, to allow a better follow-up by clinicians in case of patients or elderly people, and to improve training in case of sportsmen.

**Keywords:** Healthy habits · Citizen empowerment · Physical activity · Nutrition · Sleeping activity · Activity monitoring · Recommender system

## 1 Introduction

Digital tools represent a valuable potential resource for healthcare systems, especially when addressing populations with a high prevalence of risk factor clustering. However, although technological innovations may provide monitoring instruments which can improve person-centred care, they are often ineffective or underutilised due to barriers associated with implementation. These include issues such as the incompatibility of the technology to the local context, limited interoperability, poor system performance, increased cost, lack of financial incentives, inadequacy of legislation and policies, poor organisation of work, health

M. Gómez-Martínez, S. Orte, L. Ros-Freixedes, K. Seif—Contributed equally to the work.

P. Perego et al. (Eds.): ICWH 2020, LNICST 376, pp. 37–53, 2021.
https://doi.org/10.1007/978-3-030-76066-3_4

professionals' resistance, lack of leadership, negative attitudes and beliefs, lack of planning [25].

In this scenario and according to the P4 medicine paradigm [19], we claim that facilitating new forms of active participation by patients, citizens, and consumers in the self-management of personal health data will allow disease prevention for healthy citizens [10, 28].

There is not a universally accepted definition of self-management [4]. Alderson et al. refers to it as "an inter-disciplinary group education, based on the principles of adult learning, individualized treatment and case management theory" [2]. On the other hand, in [22], authors define self-management as a treatment that combines biological, psychological, and social intervention techniques, with a goal of maximal functioning of regulatory processes. In contrast, in [10], authors interpret self-management as the "day-to-day tasks an individual must undertake to control or reduce the impact of disease on physical status.". Accordingly, four kinds of self-management approaches have been identified, depending on the role of the healthy citizen or the patient [5]: subordinate, structured, collaborative, and autonomous. Subordinate tools are those that provide modest patient discretion through controlling and supervisory technology. Structured tools require more active, though still limited, patient participation. Collaborative ones involve patient drawing on their own knowledge and making decisions jointly with clinicians. Finally, autonomous tools support patients take matters in hand without much participation from clinicians.

In this paper, we present the CarpeDiem IoT-based self-management system aimed at providing intelligent and automatic support to people who want to maintain a healthy lifestyle. CarpeDiem target users are people who need to follow a strict diet, athletes who want to control their weight and stay healthy, or simply, citizens who want to follow a healthy diet (in a comprehensive way, taking into account nutrition, physical activity, and sleep).

The CarpeDiem self-management system is intelligent and autonomous, and it is aimed at monitoring physical- and sleeping-activity, nutrition, as well as environmental data and lifestyle habits, with the final goal of providing personalized recommendations and nudges to foster behaviour change towards healthier behaviours. The self-management system is composed of a micro-services-based back-end [29], in which intelligent techniques have been implemented for personalization and automatic monitoring, and a front-end in form of an app to be installed in the citizen's smartphone. The first prototype of the system is available for Android and 14 healthy users are currently testing it.

The rest of the paper is organized as follow. Section 2 illustrates the overall solution for monitoring activities, environmental data, and lifestyle habits. In Sect. 3, we present the current prototype available in the Android market place. Section 4 summarizes similar works currently available pointing out limitations and differences with CarpeDiem. Finally, Sect. 5 ends the paper with conclusions and future directions.

## 2    The IoT Self-management System

With the aim of improving healthy habits in the population, we propose an automatic and intelligent system that empowers and supports the citizens giving them personalized recommendations and nudges.

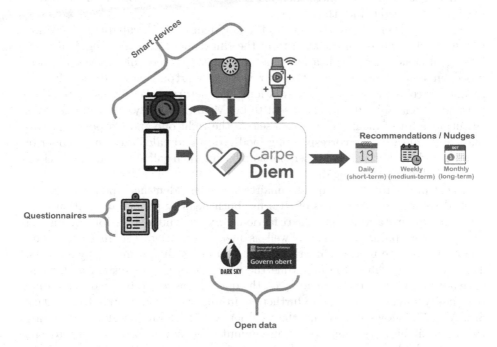

**Fig. 1.** The CarpeDiem IoT system at a glance.

Figure 1 shows the CarpeDiem IoT-based self-management system that put together data from smart devices (i.e., an activity tracker, a scale, and a smartphone), questionnaires, and open sources (i.e., Dark Sky API[1] and Dades Obertes (open data) from Generalitat de Catalunya[2]).

### 2.1    Data Collection

As depicted in Fig. 1, the IoT-based self-management system works with a set of data coming from different sources.

CarpeDiem users wear an off-the-shelf activity tracker 24/7. Physical- and sleep-activity are monitored in terms of: number of steps, total number of minutes of activity per level (i.e., low, medium, high, and sedentary), total number of sleeping hours, number of sleeping hours during the night, number of sleeping

---

[1] https://darksky.net/dev.
[2] http://governobert.gencat.cat/en/dades_obertes/.

hours during the day, number of naps, onset time, offset time, minutes awake, and sleep efficiency. Moreover, the energy expenditure in terms of calories is constantly monitored. Smart scales measure the weight and calculate the body fat scale and uploads the measurements to the cloud by using the WiFi connection [21]. CarpeDiem users are asked to monitor her/his weight once a week in order to take under control her/his Body Mass Index (BMI) and to avoid reaching overweight and, thus, obesity.

The CarpeDiem system integrates the LogMeal API [7], capable of recognizing meals through pictures taken from the smartphone camera. LogMeal is an intelligent cloud-based application which automatically recognizes several dishes, based on images acquired by the user with a smartphone to objectively and seamlessly collect food intake information. The pictures taken by using the CarpeDiem system are automatically sent to LogMeal that analyzes them and gives as output a list of meals. The citizen selects the right one and CarpeDiem automatically indicates the corresponding food group and calculates the number of calories and key nutrients of a dish portion, basing such calculation on the recipes also available through LogMeal.

In the literature, several questionnaires have been identified and are currently applied to monitor the status of citizens (both healthy people and patients) in terms of, for instance, overall satisfaction, anxiety and depression, quality of life, perceived pain, self-care, as well as mental disorder [15]. In CarpeDiem, questionnaires are used to directly ask the users regarding some lifestyle habits. They have to be filled the first time the user enters to the system and, then, once a week or everyday, depending on the questionnaire. To be aware regarding seasonality, daylight hours, and further environmental data, we rely to the Dark Sky API[3]. It allows to look up the weather anywhere on the globe, returning (where available): weather conditions, minute-by-minute forecasts out to one hour, hour-by-hour and day-by-day forecasts out to seven days, hour-by-hour and day-by-day observations going back decades, weather alerts, and humidity.

Finally, to monitor the air quality in Catalonia, the Dades Obertes by Generalitat de Catalunya is used[4].

## 2.2   The Recommender Systems

The CarpeDiem IoT-based self-management system collects and fuses the heterogeneous data coming from all the data sources and sends personalised nudges and recommendations to empower citizens in better follow-up healthy habits concerning the main pillars of health, according to their profile. Recommendations and nudges are sent on a daily (short-term), weekly (medium-term), and monthly (long-term) basis.

A specific recommender system for each of the pillars has been defined and developed.

---

[3] https://darksky.net/dev.
[4] http://governobert.gencat.cat/en/dades_obertes/.

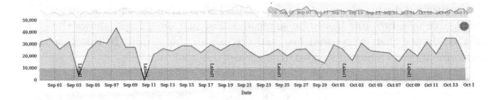

**Fig. 2.** Example of a volunteer that overpasses her goal every day.

**Physical Activity.** The Physical Activity recommender system of CarpeDiem improves and extends the one proposed in [17].

Its main functionalities are:

- Computation of the daily adherence of the patient;
- Computation of the adherence profile of the patient;
- Computation of activities during the week;
- Computation of improvements during the month.

Daily adherence is calculated as a percentage of the amount of activity fulfilled against the goal in terms of number of steps. The adherence computation takes also into consideration, for each user, her/his "best" and "worse" days of the week and also National holidays. In doing so, different messages will be sent those days, accordingly. Thanks to the integration of the Dark Sky API, we also consider the weather in order to not push the users to walk if it is snowing or during a storm.

The adherence profile considers prolonged time periods, so as to assess how adherence fluctuates during time. The recommender system relies on two counters, one for the number of consecutive days in which the patients achieved the goal (winstreak), and one for the number of consecutive days in which the patients did not achieve the goal (losestreak). Any time the patient moves from achieving to not achieving the goal, the winstreak counter is reset to 0. The same with losestreak when moving from not achieving to achieving. Early in the morning, the recommender system checks if the day before the goal has been achieved or not, and it updates the counters, accordingly. Depending on the number of days that the patient is achieving/not achieving the goal, the message will be more or less effective. The more the number of days s/he is not achieving, the stronger the message to push the patient to improve. The more the number of days s/he is achieving, the stronger the message to compliment the patient and to push her/him to doing better and better.

Activities during the week are calculated considering the adherence weekly seasonality. The weekdays with less adherence over time are stored. Depending on the day the patient is achieving/not achieving the goal, the message will be different. We do not push the users to walk during the days of the week where the adherence is usually lower, which may be due to impossibility of the user to perform physical activity at certain moments of the week.

Improving during the month are calculated to check if the current goal is still applicable or a new one has to be suggested. For instance, Fig. 2 shows the case of a volunteer that overpassed her goal during all the period. In this case, the recommender system will suggest to increase the goal.

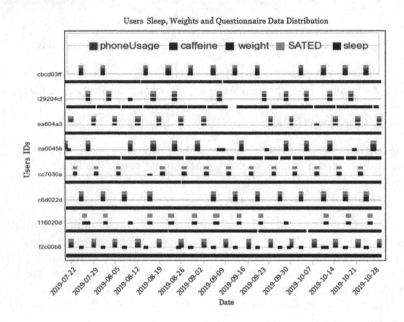

**Fig. 3.** Data distribution of the 8 selected users collected during the pilot.

**Sleeping.** In order to define the Sleeping recommender system, data from a 8-months pilot performed during 2019 have been used to create the models [30]. A total of 30 volunteers have been recruited in Barcelona and Lleida (Spain). Volunteers were asked to wear their activity tracker 24/7, to weight once a week, and to answer selected questionnaires at the end of the week. The day of the inclusion, we also took note of the comfort of the bed of each volunteer, as well as her/his address to take into consideration the environmental factors. Due to technical problems and adherence issues, 6 of the 30 volunteers dropped-out before finishing the first month of the study. Thus, the analysis of the data have been done using the data of 24 volunteers ($38.43 \pm 11.46$ years old; 15 females; and $23.09 \pm 3.66$ BMI). The pilot started on May 2019 and finished in December 2019.

A static profile is first created considering gender and age together with data coming from the questionnaires. That profile will be dynamically and continuously updated by considering the data gathered from the wristband, the changes in the BMI, if any, the questionnaire answers, and the environmental data.

Once the profile is built, the citizen is automatically clustered according to fixed groups of habits defined considering the intersections among the three

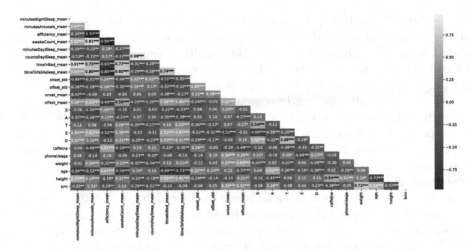

**Fig. 4.** The correlation matrix between the sleep features collected by using the activity tracker and the questionnaires. The Pearson correlation coefficient is displayed for each parameter pair. Legend of parameter names: *minutesNightSleep_mean* - weekly average of the minutes spent sleeping during the night, *minutesArousals_mean* - weekly average of the minutes spent awake during the night, *efficiency_mean* - weekly average of the sleep efficiency, *awakeCount_mean* - weekly average of the number of awakening times during the night sleep, *minutesDaySleep_mean* - weekly average of the minutes spent sleeping during the day, *countsDaySleep_mean* - weekly average of the number of the sleep periods during the day, *timeInBed_mean* - weekly average of the total time spent in bed, *timeToFallAsleep_mean* - weekly average of the time it takes to fall asleep, *onset_std* - weekly variation of the onset time, *offset_std* - weekly variation of the offset time, *onset_mean* - weekly average of the onset time, *offset_mean* - weekly average of the offset time, $S$ - weekly satisfaction answer from SATED questionnaire, $A$ - weekly alertness answer from SATED questionnaire, $T$ - weekly timing answer from SATED questionnaire, $E$ - weekly efficiency answer from the SATED questionnaire, $D$ - weekly duration answer from the SATED questionnaire, *caffeine* - weekly averaged caffeine consumption, *phoneUsage* - weekly electronic device minutes of usage before bedtime, *weight* - citizen weight, *age* - citizen age, *bmi* - citizen body mass index. The (*) symbol indicates the significance level: *** if p-value $\leq 0.01$, ** if p-value $\leq 0.05$ and * if p-value $\leq 0.1$.

categories: number of sleeping hours (less than the recommended hours, the recommended hours, more than the recommended hours), sleep efficiency (below or above 85%), and satisfaction with the sleep. The recommended hours are defined taking into account the citizen age, according to what defined in the literature [18]. Similarly, the efficiency threshold is defined according to the work in [23]. Finally, satisfaction is assessed by using the 5 levels of the SATED questionnaire [6]: 1 = Never, 2 = Rarely, 3 = Sometimes, 4 = Usually, 5 = Always.

To study the correlation among the features to start automatically profiling the users, we selected the 8 volunteers who had a higher adherence to the pilot during a time frame of 15 weeks in order to study the relationship between the features (see Fig. 3). In Fig. 4, the correlation matrix is shown. A weak but significant correlation is found between caffeine consumption and the time spent awake during the night by the users. Additionally, a negative weak correlation is found between the time spent awake and the citizen sleep satisfaction, which could indicate an indirect impact of caffeine consumption on sleep quality. Nevertheless, no correlation is found between caffeine consumption and onset time, although in the literature it has been shown that a delay should take place [8,14]. As expected [9], a correlation is found between the averaged time that a citizen goes to bed and the usage of electronic devices before bedtime. Overall, these results showed the usefulness of using questionnaire to detect bad sleep habits and finding ways of improving the sleep quality and satisfaction of the citizens, such as by recommending a reduction the caffeine consumption or the electronic devices usage before bedtime. However, the lack of strong significant relationships between the questionnaire answers and the sleep parameters lead into changes in the question wording. Stronger relationships are expected to be found during the next pilot, in accordance to what the literature states.

We also studied the impact of environmental factors (e.g., pollution concentration levels) in the sleeping activities. Unfortunately, preliminary experiments do not show any evidence.

**Nutrition.** Given the heterogeneity of nutritional habits, and the involvement of nutritional experts in the project, the Nutrition recommender system follows an expert-based approach following the specifications proposed by nutritionists from Eurecat. Its main objective is to provide recommendations based on the user profile to trigger behaviour change towards healthier nutritional behaviours, for example, increase fruit consumption or decrease salty food. It uses as input the food diary built from the pictures taken by users through their smartphone camera, and some questionnaires triggered at a convenient time throughout all the intervention. Based on the recipe coming from the LogMeal API, the recommender system computes the number of nutrients consumed by the user and the corresponding food groups contained on it, with the objective of calculating the adherence of the user to the corresponding behaviours. To do so, a nutritional database with more than 450 ingredients based on the CIQUAL[5] database was built and contains information about food groups and key nutrients. The results of these calculations are exploited with a rule-based reasoning (RBR) approach which decides what recommendations to be triggered during the intervention. The RBR bases its rules on the guidelines about food group intake specified by nutritionists. Aiming at not being very intrusive and repetitive, the Nutritional recommender system manages differently the required actions needed to be performed by the user, depending on the specific moment. The first week, the user is asked for taking pictures of all her/his meals, so that the behavioural and nutritional profile can be built. At the end of this phase, the nutritional objective of the user is set (e.g., increase fruit consumption) taking into account a) the food groups to work on, and b) distribution and types of recommendations. After

---

[5] https://ciqual.anses.fr/.

that, the user will be receiving personalised recommendations for 3 weeks with checkpoints each week to check the progression. In each checkpoint, the nutritional profile is updated with the new data coming from the past week, and the nutritional objective is adjusted accordingly. After one month, the user receives follow-up questions, so that the system can evaluate the progression and, if the system detects that the proposed behaviour has been adopted, it will propose the user to change to another objective. Figure 5 sketches the overall workflow.

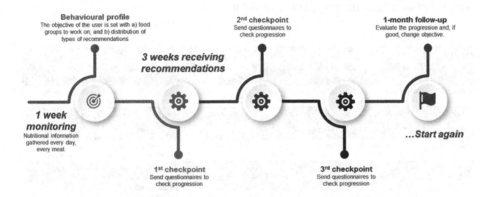

**Fig. 5.** The workflow adopted by the Nutrition recommender.

## 3   The Current Prototype

The CarpeDiem self-management system front-end is an app available in the Google Play (early access) for Android smartphones[6].

### 3.1   Data Collection

In its current version, the self-management system integrates all the devices and external sources described in Sect. 2.1:

- activity trackers from Fitbit[7] and Withings[8] for monitoring steps, sleeping habits, and energy expenditure;
- smart scales from Withings, for monitoring the weight and the BMI;
- LogMeal, for the automatic food recognition from pictures;
- Dark Sky API and Dades Obertes, for monitoring weather and air pollution, respectively.

---

[6] https://play.google.com/store/apps/details?id=com.eurecat.carpediem.
[7] https://www.fitbit.com/.
[8] https://www.withings.com/.

Users are asked to wear the wristband 24/7. Moreover, during the first week, they have also to take pictures to all the meals they eat. Finally, they have to fill, through the app, 3 questionnaires on her/his habits once a week and 1 more every day. The questionnaires are: SATED, about the satisfaction of the citizen regarding her/his sleep; Smoke, on the number of cigarettes smoked on average during the week; Use of technology, concerning the number of minutes spent on average using the smartphone or a tablet just before going to sleep; and Caffeine, to check the number of coffees, teas, and energy drinks the user drunk during the 7 h before going to sleep, the day before.

| Feature(s) | Value | Frequency | Title | Modifier | Message |
|---|---|---|---|---|---|
| Steps | More than the goal | Daily (today) | Goal achieved | Generic | Congratulations! You have already exceeded your goal for today by 200 steps! Good job! |
| Steps | More than the goal | Daily (Today) | Goal achieved | Worst days | Congratulations! You have already reached your goal although it is Tuesday! |
| Steps | Less than the goal | Daily (Today) | Goal not achieved | Generic | Right now you are 7500 steps away to complete today's goal. Let's try to improve this tomorrow! |
| Steps | Less than the goal | Daily (Today) | Goal not achieved | Almost | Right now you are only 50 steps away to complete today's goal! You almost got it! |
| Steps | More than the goal | Daily (Yesterday) | Goal achieved | Generic | Congratulations! Yesterday you reached your goal, keep going! |
| Steps | More than the goal | Daily (Yesterday) | Goal achieved | Consecutive | Congratulations! Yesterday you achieved your goal for the last 5 consecutive days! |
| Steps | Less than the goal | Daily (Yesterday) | Goal not achieved | Generic | Yesterday you did not reach your goal, that means you have more energy to achieve it today! |
| Steps | Less than the goal | Daily (Yesterday) | Goal not achieved | Adverse weather | Right now you are 3000 steps away to complete today's goal, but we know it's because it is raining. |
| Steps | More than the goal on average | Monthly | New month, new goals! | None | We have noticed your performance has been awesome the past month, would you like to increase your goal? |
| Steps | Less than the goal on average | Monthly | New month, new goals! | None | We have noticed you have been struggling to keep up with your goal the past month, would you like to decrease your goal? |

**Fig. 6.** Example of recommendations and nudges for improving the physical activity.

## 3.2 Nudges and Recommendations

**Physical Activity.** As described above, the Physical Activity recommender system sends nudges and recommendations considering the daily adherence and the adherence profile. Figure 6 shows some of the nudges and recommendations that have been defined. Some of them are totally generic and can be sent without considering the profile of the user. On the other hand, some others consider the day of the week (e.g., the "worst day"), the number of consecutive days the goal has (has not) been achieved, or the weather (e.g., a raining day). As shown in the Figure, monthly nudges are more oriented to suggest to change the goal depending on the overall trend of the last month.

**Sleeping.** For each cluster, together with the clinicians from the Biomedical Research Institute (IRB) in Lleida, we defined a suitable set of recommendations and nudges with the final goal of moving all the citizens in the healthiest cluster, corresponding to the number of hours suggested depending on the age, a sleep efficiency higher than 85%, and a satisfaction of 4 or 5 (i.e., normally or always satisfied). Recommendations and nudges on daily basis are based on the number of slept hours, the efficiency, the performed physical activity, and the questionnaire answers. Figure 7 shows an example of the nudges and recommendations that have been defined for each of the timing (daily, weekly, and monthly).

| Feature(s) | Value | Frequency | Title | Message |
|---|---|---|---|---|
| Sleeping hours | Less than the minimum recommended hours | Daily | Not enough sleep! | Today you slept less than what is recommended. Try to sleep between 7 and 9 hours! |
| Satisfaction | Satisfaction "normally" (high) but less than the previous week | Weekly | Satisfaction worsening! | Your sleep satisfaction is high, but it is worsening! Pay attention to the sleep recommendations to improve it! |
| Sleep duration, Sleep efficiency, Satisfaction | Between the recommended hours Less than the threshold "Sometimes" | Monthly | You are doing a good job but there is room for improvement! | This month you slept the recommended hours, but we can still work together to improve your sleep satisfaction. Try to follow the advices to improve your sleep quality. If this is not enough, look for professional help. |

**Fig. 7.** Example of recommendations and nudges for improving the sleeping activity.

**Nutrition.** Thanks to the expertise of Eurecat nutritionists, a database containing 130 recommendations of different types was constructed. Each of them is tagged with different labels (i.e. food group to increase/decrease, triggering time, and type of profile which it applies to). The database is used by the Nutritional recommender system to assure that the nutritional guidelines concerning food group consumption are met. The ones which frequency is daily and weekly, are automatically triggered through a scheduler at specific times manually specified. In contrast, the ones marked with "at a convenient time" frequency, are triggered through a rule-based reasoning system, which considers both the nutritional user profile and the recommendations already delivered. Figure 8 shows some of the nudges and recommendations that have been defined.

## 3.3 The Front-End

Figure 9 shows some screenshots of the app: (a) the home page where the user has an overview of her/his status and may answer to the questionnaires; (b) a list of received notification, each pillar represented by a different icon; (c) the setting page that shows, besides other information, that the app is linked to Fitbit; (d) the physical activity page with the summary of the steps a day that the goal was achieved; (e) the sleeping page with the summary of the current

| Feature(s) | Value | Frequency | Title | Message |
|---|---|---|---|---|
| Daily food groups | Information about the consumption of the daily food groups | Daily | These are the food groups detected today | An image with the food groups detected today, compared with the recommendations. |
| Weekly food groups | Information about the consumption of the weekly food groups. | Weekly | These are the food groups detected this week | An image with the food groups detected during the week, compared with the recommendations. |
| Diversity | Ideas to add diversity to the diet. | At convenient time | Increase vegetables and fruit consumption | Try to eat raw vegetables cooking recipes like tomato soup, mixed salads or vegetable snacks. |
| Hydratation | Water and other recommendations to keep the hydratation | At convenient time | Take an infusion! | Adding infusions or soups to your diet will help you to be more hydrated. |
| Reducing bad behaviours | Step by step reduction of bad behaviours | At convenient time | Add less sugar to your coffee | Try to add half of the usual quantity of sugar to your coffee! |
| Recipes | Recipes to cook specific food groups | At convenient time | Increase the vegetable consumption | Cook different vegetable recipes, for example: "https://www.directoalpaladar.com/rec etas-de-legumbres-y-verduras/receta-de-ratatouille" |
| Healthy diet | Recommendations to follow a healthy diet | At convenient time | Cook home made desserts | Choose desserts cooked at home. For example, fruit salads. |
| Expertise | Explain important nutritional features | At convenient time | | Make sure that, at lunch and dinner, there is a part of protein (legumes, fish, chicken, eggs, ...), grains (pasta, rice, quinoa, ...), and don't forget the vegetables! |

**Fig. 8.** Example of recommendations and nudges for improving the nutritional habits.

weak showing the sleeping hours and the efficiency as calculated by Fitbit; and (f) an example of recognized food (meatballs).

### 3.4 The Pilot

On July 2020, a pilot started with 14 healthy volunteers that have been recruited in Eurecat ($35.64 \pm 8.58$ years old; 5 females; and $22.96 \pm 2.67$ BMI). The pilot, which will end at the end of the year, has a threefold objective: (1) collecting feedback to improve the app and/or correct bugs; (2) testing the usability and evaluating the user experience; and (3) gathering new data to improve the 3 recommender systems and start implementing the holistic one. Results of the pilot will be calculated in terms of usability once the pilot ends.

## 4   Discussion

Self-management plays a central role in the P4 medicine paradigm, as it has a beneficial impact on both physical and psychological health status [10]. From a technological standpoint, personalisation, adaptation, and scalability are key

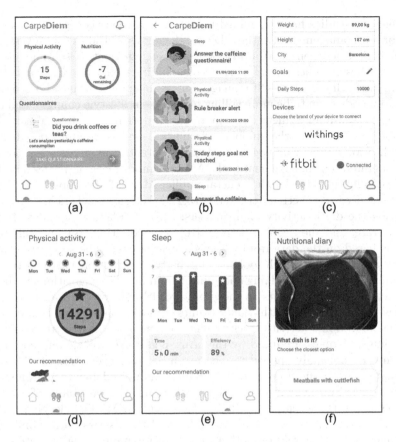

**Fig. 9.** The CarpeDiem app: (a) the main page with an overview of the activities; (b) a list of received notifications; (c) the setting page; (d) the physical activity details; (e) the sleeping activity details; (f) an example of food recognized by its picture.

properties to leverage when designing and developing software solutions promoting self-management through, for instance, patient empowerment [27]. One way of empowering patient so as to let them self-manage not only disease, in case of patients, but also day-to-day life, in case of any citizen, is to let them be aware of their healthy or unhealthy habits with the goal of, respectively, encourage them to improve or not. For instance, a common strategy regarding physical activity practicing is to provide regular reminders based on objectively measured levels of adherence [1]. This is true for both activities of healthy subjects and prescriptions to patients suffering of some chronic condition [26].

Many studies have shown that patients who engage in healthy diet, exercise, or other aspects of self-management have healthy benefits in terms of fewer symptoms, better functional capability, and fewer complications than those who do not in various diseases (e.g., HIV/AIDS [11], rheumatoid arthritis [24], asthma or chronic obstructive pulmonary disease [3], diabetes [31], and heart failure [20]).

Most relevant studies have examined the association between poor adjustment and poor self-management. On the other hand, there are studies that investigated the connection between good adjustment and engagement in self-management practices. These studies show evidence of a bidirectional association between wellbeing and adherence to self-management regimens. Citizens who can maintain good moods seem to be more willing to engage in lifestyle changes, and those who practice self-management behaviours also report improved wellbeing [12].

Mobile phones and other mobile information and communication technology applications and technologies hold great potential as a basis for powerful citizen-operated self-management tools. Apps for monitoring activities have been enthusiastically adopted by the general public. Most of the apps are linked to wearable devices (i.e., activity trackers) [13,21]. Activity trackers are capable of monitoring the daily activity of their users, in particular the number of steps, the heart rate, and the sleeping activity [16]. The counting steps module of the devices is based on the data from a 3-axis accelerometer. The steps are counted by using an algorithm which looks for intensity and motion patterns that are most indicative of people walking and running and includes algorithms to discard other acceleration movements as those produced by other transportation (e.g., cars, bus, train). The algorithm only counts a motion as a step if its duration is long enough. Some activity trackers measures also the heart rate considering blood volume changes produced by the heart beats. Automatic and continuous algorithms are normally applied to measure heart rate every minute. The algorithm that monitors the sleep activity is slightly different depending on the brand and the model. New generation activity trackers use the variability of the heart rate to estimate the sleep phases: light, deep, and REM. The sleeping activity data can be divided into summary variables and time series data. Similarly to CarpeDiem, apps that rely on activity trackers for monitoring activities focus on physical activities (e.g., steps, distance, and performed exercises), sleeping habits (number of sleeping hours and sleep phases), and, some of them, also nutrition (burned calories, food and drinks intake) and weight. Unfortunately, they are more based on monitoring activities than giving suggestions and recommendations to improve habits. Moreover, no personalisation is provided and only general nudges are given.

Apps specifically aimed at monitoring nutrition are also currently available in the market: for managing a daily food diary, track activities and lose weight successfully[9]; for registring or for scanning food care products to decipher their ingredients and evaluate their impact on your health[10,11]. Unfortunately, those solutions continuously need the manual intervention from the user that stops using them.

CarpeDiem advances current solutions because it is an IoT solution that fuses together data from different sources and, considering the profile of each user, provides personalized recommendations and nudges. Moreover, it considers not only

---

[9] https://play.google.com/store/apps/details?id=com.yazio.android.

[10] https://play.google.com/store/apps/details?id=io.yuka.android.

[11] https://myrealfood.app/.

data from an activity tracker or manually input by the user (i.e., questionnaires or food images), but also environmental data that may influence daily life activities. Thus, CarpeDiem takes into account preferences, habits, weather conditions, and further data when compiling recommendations and nudges. Currently, CarpeDiem provides support to healthy people that want to follow healthy habits. Next versions of the system will allow also to follow a plan for reducing weight, improving training, or having a plan specialized for a specific need (e.g., elderly adults or chronic patients).

## 5   Conclusions and Future Directions

This paper presented the CarpeDiem self-management system, an IoT solution aimed at providing intelligent and automatic support to people who want to follow a diet to lose weight, or to maintain a healthy lifestyle. The CarpeDiem approach integrates smart devices and open data sources, as well as input from the user. It monitors physical- and sleeping-activity, nutrition, as well as environmental data and lifestyle habits, and provides personalised recommendations and nudges. The first prototype of the system is available for Android and 14 healthy users are currently testing it.

As for the future directions, we will start first from the feedback we are receiving from the volunteers. In particular, we will improve the nutrition monitoring allowing the volunteers to select suggested recipes or to upload their owns. They will be allowed also to specify the size of the dish. The smartphone will be used also to detect the luminosity of the bedroom during the sleeping time and the citizen will be asked regarding the comfort of the bed, since especially vulnerable or at risk citizens often sleep on truly old or uncomfortable beds. Furthermore, data gathered from the pilot will be used to re-train the models of the recommender systems improving them. From those data, we will investigate and develop also an holistic recommender system that considers all the pillars together to give more personalised recommendations that take into account all the lifestyle habits together. Collaborative approaches will be also followed to consider similarities among citizens in order to send recommendations and nudges, adding also gamification. Finally, mindfulness, the fourth pillar of the health, will be also considered to give support to the citizens in managing anxiety and stress, as well as improve sleeping quality.

**Acknowledgments.** The Project has been partially funded by ACCÍÓ Pla de Recerca i Innovació 2019/2020, under the project CarpeDiem (Collaborative and Adaptive Recommender for PErsonalized DIEt Management). The authors would like to express their sincerest gratitude to all the participating volunteers. We want also to thank Juan Ruiz Zaldivar for his precious support in the development of the system, as well as the involved domain experts: Lucia Tarro from Eurecat (Spain), for nutrition, and Ferran Barbe and Adriano Targa from IRB in Lleida (Spain), for sleeping.

# References

1. den Akkera, H., Cabrita, M., den Akker, R., Jones, V.M., Hermens, H.J.: Tailored motivational message generation: a model and practical framework for real-time physical activity coaching. J. Biomed. Inform. **55**, 104–115 (2015)
2. Alderson, M., Starr, L., Gow, S., Moreland, J.: The program for rheumatic independent self-management: a pilot evaluation. Clin. Rheumatol. **18**(4), 283–292 (1999). https://doi.org/10.1007/s100670050103
3. Bailey, W.C., et al.: Asthma self-management: do patient education programs always have an impact? Arch. Intern. Med. **159**(20), 2422–2428 (1999)
4. Barlow, J., Wright, C., Sheasby, J., Turner, A., Hainsworth, J.: Self-management approaches for people with chronic conditions: a review. Patient Educ. Couns. **48**(2), 177–187 (2002)
5. Barrett, M.J.: Patient self-management tools: an overview. California HealthCare Foundation (2005)
6. Benítez, I., et al.: Validation of the satisfaction, alertness, timing, efficiency and duration (SATED) questionnaire for sleep health measurement. Ann. Am. Thorac. Soc. **17**(3), 338–343 (2020)
7. Bolaños, M., Valdivia, M., Radeva, P.: Where and what am i eating? Image-based food menu recognition. In: Leal-Taixé, L., Roth, S. (eds.) ECCV 2018. LNCS, vol. 11134, pp. 590–605. Springer, Cham (2019). https://doi.org/10.1007/978-3-030-11024-6_45
8. Burke, T.M., et al.: Effects of caffeine on the human circadian clock in vivo and in vitro. Sci. Transl. Med. **7**(305), 305ra146 (2015)
9. Calamaro, C.J., Yang, K., Ratcliffe, S., Chasens, E.R.: Wired at a young age: the effect of caffeine and technology on sleep duration and body mass index in school-aged children. J. Pediatr. Health Care **26**(4), 276–282 (2012)
10. Clark, N.M., Becker, M.H., Janz, N.K., Lorig, K., Rakowski, W., Anderson, L.: Self-management of chronic disease by older adults: a review and questions for research. J. Aging Health **3**(1), 3–27 (1991)
11. Collins, R.L., et al.: Changes in health-promoting behavior following diagnosis with HIV: prevalence and correlates in a national probability sample. Health Psychol. **20**(5), 351 (2001)
12. De Ridder, D., Geenen, R., Kuijer, R., van Middendorp, H.: Psychological adjustment to chronic disease. The Lancet **372**(9634), 246–255 (2008)
13. Diaz, K.M., et al.: Fitbit®: an accurate and reliable device for wireless physical activity tracking. Int. J. Cardiol. **185**, 138–140 (2015)
14. Drake, C., Roehrs, T., Shambroom, J., Roth, T.: Caffeine effects on sleep taken 0, 3, or 6 hours before going to bed. J. Clin. Sleep Med. **9**(11), 1195–1200 (2013)
15. Endicott, J., Nee, J., Harrison, W., Blumenthal, R.: Quality of life enjoyment and satisfaction questionnaire: a new measure. Psychopharmacol. Bull. **29**(2), 321–326 (1993)
16. Feehan, L.M., et al.: Accuracy of Fitbit devices: systematic review and narrative syntheses of quantitative data. JMIR Mhealth Uhealth **6**(8), e10527 (2018)
17. Fernández, J.M., et al.: Towards argumentation-based recommendations for personalised patient empowerment. In: International Workshop on Health Recommender Systems, Co-Located with ACM RecSys 2017 (2017)
18. Hirshkowitz, M., et al.: National sleep foundation's sleep time duration recommendations: methodology and results summary. Sleep Health **1**(1), 40–43 (2015)

19. Hood, L., Friend, S.H.: Predictive, personalized, preventive, participatory (P4) cancer medicine. Nat. Rev. Clin. Oncol. **8**(3), 184–187 (2011)
20. Jaarsma, T., Halfens, R., Tan, F., Abu-Saad, H.H., Dracup, K., Diederiks, J.: Self-care and quality of life in patients with advanced heart failure: the effect of a supportive educational intervention. Heart Lung J. Acute Crit. Care **29**(5), 319–330 (2000)
21. Meyer, J., Boll, S.: Digital health devices for everyone! IEEE Pervasive Comput. **13**(2), 10–13 (2014)
22. Nakagawa-Kogan, H., Garber, A., Jarrett, M., Egan, K.J., Hendershot, S.: Self-management of hypertension: predictors of success in diastolic blood pressure reduction. Res. Nurs. Health **11**(2), 105–115 (1988)
23. Ohayon, M., et al.: National sleep foundation's sleep quality recommendations: first report. Sleep Health **3**(1), 6–19 (2017)
24. Riemsma, R.P., Taal, E., Kirwan, J.R., Rasker, J.J.: Systematic review of rheumatoid arthritis patient education. Arthritis Care Res. **51**(6), 1045–1059 (2004)
25. Ross, J., Stevenson, F., Lau, R., Murray, E.: Factors that influence the implementation of e-health: a systematic review of systematic reviews (an update). Implement. Sci. **11**(1) (2016). Article number: 146
26. Tabak, M., Op den Akker, H., Hermens, H.: Motivational cues as real-time feedback for changing daily activity behavior of patients with COPD. Patient Educ. Couns. **94**(3), 372–378 (2014)
27. Tomes, N.: Patient empowerment and the dilemmas of late-modern medicalisation. The Lancet **369**(9562), 698–700 (2007)
28. Vargiu, E.: From healthy to happy ageing: the power of self-management. In: AI*AAL.it 2017. Artificial Intelligence for Ambient Assisted Living. Proceedings of the Third Italian Workshop on Artificial Intelligence for Ambient Assisted Living, CEUR Proceedings, vol. 2061 (2018)
29. Vargiu, E., Fernández, J.M., Gonzales-Gonzales, M., Morales-Garzón, J.M., Prunera-Moreda, K., Miralles, F.: A self-management system for complex chronic patients. Int. J. Integr. Care (IJIC) **19**, 1–2 (2019)
30. Vargiu, E., Zambrana, C., Targa, A., Barbé, F.: Improving sleeping habits: preliminary experiments in Barcelona and Lleida. In: AI* AAL@ AI* IA, pp. 51–65 (2019)
31. Williams, G.C., McGregor, H.A., Zeldman, A., Freedman, Z.R., Deci, E.L.: Testing a self-determination theory process model for promoting glycemic control through diabetes self-management. Health Psychol. **23**(1), 58 (2004)

# Sharing Wearable Health Data Using User-Defined Blockchain Policies

Alan Colman[1]([✉]), Mohammad Jabed Morshed Chowdhury[2],
and Mohan Baruwal Chhetri[1,3]

[1] Swinburne University of Technology, Melbourne, Australia
acolman@swin.edu.au
[2] Latrobe University, Melbourne, Australia
m.chowdhury@latrobe.edu.au
[3] CSIRO Data61, Melbourne, Australia
mohan.baruwalchhetri@data61.csiro.au

**Abstract.** With recent advances in wearable technology and the rapid adoption of wearable devices, there are increased opportunities for setting up innovative data markets through which large amounts of user-generated physiological data can be made available to health researchers at relatively low costs. However, given the sensitive nature of such data, a major challenge associated with realizing a trusted wearable data marketplace is ensuring fine-grained access control and assuring conformance to it. In this paper, we propose a policy-based approach for facilitating the secure exchange of data between a wearable owner and a health researcher. User-defined data-sharing policies are translated into executable smart contracts that provide deterministic and transparent execution of transactions as per the terms and conditions of the data sharing agreement. To illustrate feasibility of the approach, we present a proof-of-concept implementation of the proposed policy-based access control mechanism using the open source Multichain platform.

**Keywords:** Wearable data · Blockchain · Data sharing policy

## 1 Introduction

With recent advances in wearable technology and the rapid adoption of wearable devices [1], we are witnessing a paradigm shift in the way personal physiological data is generated, stored and consumed. There are increased opportunities for setting up innovative markets where user-generated health data can be made available for consumption in real-time or batch mode, and at relatively low costs. However, given the sensitive nature of such data, there are several challenges associated with running wearable data markets while safeguarding the consent, security and privacy of all market participants. In particular, the owners of the wearables, referred to as *data subjects* in our terminology, should have full control over how their wearable data is shared with others, including which parts

P. Perego et al. (Eds.): ICWH 2020, LNICST 376, pp. 54–69, 2021.
https://doi.org/10.1007/978-3-030-76066-3_5

of the data is shared, under what context, and with whom. More importantly, they should have assurances that their data is shared in conformance with their data-sharing policies.

In our previous work [2], we presented an approach for building a consortium-based trusted marketplace for wearable data. In that paper we showed how blockchain technology can fulfil many of the requirements associated with creating trust between remote and unknown parties participating in a transaction. The requirements that we considered in that work include fairness, transparency, privacy, security and auditability. We further presented a high-level conceptual architecture showing how transactions related to the sharing of wearable data could be facilitated by a blockchain-based marketplace in accordance with the terms and conditions stipulated by the wearable user.

In this paper we extend our previous work on a general policy language for data sharing [3] that enables individuals to control access to their shared data based on context, device types and data types. In doing so, we make the following main contributions:

- We analyse various access modes provided by the main wearable device manufacturers that can enable third-party access to wearable data (Sect. 3).
- We show how data sharing policies can be applied to the sharing of wearable health data. User-defined data-sharing policies are translated into executable smart contracts on a blockchain that provide deterministic and transparent execution of transactions based on agreed terms (Sect. 4).
- We describe an architecture and protocols that enable researchers *(data consumers)* to securely access a wearable owner's *(data subject's)* bio-data from cloud storage provider's API *(data custodian)* in conformance with the owner's data sharing policy (Sect. 5.1).
- We present a proof-of-concept of the proposed system using the Multichain platform [4] and discuss the various trade-offs in implementing such systems (Sect. 5.2).

The rest of the paper is organized as follows. Section 2 provides background information on blockchain-based wearable data markets. Section 3 summarises the different access modes to wearable data while Sect. 4 provides an overview of the policy language for user-controlled wearable data sharing. It also provides a description of how the access control mechanisms work. Section 5 briefly describes the system design and implementation. Section 6 concludes the paper.

# 2  Background and Related Work

## 2.1  Wearable Devices in Medical Research

The use of wearable devices has proliferated in recent years. These devices include ubiquitous smartphones, smart watches and wrist bands that can monitor personal physiological data. Novel devices such as chest straps, electronic garments, skin patches, smart glasses, even smart jewellery are starting to emerge.

Seneviratne et al. [1] provide a recent survey of such devices. In the clinical medical domain, these devices are used to monitor vital signs such as heart rate, blood pressure, respiratory rate, blood oxygen saturation, and body temperature [5]. Personal monitoring devices are widely used in hospital settings. They are also being increasingly used for monitoring the condition of patients on discharge – in particular patients with chronic conditions such as diabetes and cardiovascular illness. Much work has been done to integrate such wearable Patient Care Devices (PCDs) with hospital information systems and electronic health records, and in developing interoperability standards for such integration [6]. Devices used in such clinical contexts typically tend to be expensive industry grade monitors.

The use of such devices in medical research, however, is a nascent field. These devices not only allow the researchers to collect and gather real-time data coming from individuals who can be profiled, but the fine-grained frequency of the data also makes it possible to reveal insights and correlations that were impossible or difficult to perceive previously. Of course, any inaccuracies in consumer devices used for research would affect the accuracy of the research results. However, given that the accuracy of sensor types can be characterized, it is established practice to model such inaccuracies and adjust for them in the interpretation of results. That being said, recent studies have shown that consumer wearable devices often have an accuracy compatible with clinical-grade devices [7]. As technology develops it can be expected that the accuracy of consumer devices will continue to improve.

However, while the use of wearables in health research studies may not pose any immediate clinical risk to the research subject's health, there are considerable risks to privacy through exposing identifiable personal data. Such devices are not only capable of recording physiological data but also typically record additional information such as the wearer's location. It is therefore paramount that any platform developed to acquire such data ensures that it is kept private by using anonymization [8] or encryption [9].

## 2.2   Blockchain

A blockchain is an immutable distributed ledger for recording transactions. Its transactions are called immutable because once inserted, they become permanent and cannot be modified retroactively, not even by the authors, without the alteration of all subsequent transactions. Having records added to the blockchain requires a consensus mechanism that ensures the transactions are confirmed as valid. A blockchain is secured by cryptographic techniques and managed by a decentralized community over a peer-to-peer network. These properties have made blockchain technology a suitable platform for enabling trust in transactions between parties who do not necessarily trust each other.

There are, however, many types of blockchain that vary according to the openness of the network, the type of transactions recorded, and the mechanism by which consensus is achieved. Blockchain technology gained prominence through Bitcoin which is an open system that records simple cryptocurrency transactions between untrusted participants. Participants are pseudo-anonymous in that their identity on the network is a public encryption key rather than a real-world identity. Consensus amongst participants in such open blockchains is reached through incentivized mechanisms such as proof-of-work [10].

Other types of blockchain platforms (e.g. Hyperledger[1]) enable blockchains to be formed by a consortium of participants. These *permissioned* blockchains are more common in facilitating cross-organisational collaboration between participants in an industry (e.g. supply chain tracking). Access to participation in the blockchain is defined by various roles. For example, certain members may be the only ones allowed to participate in consensus making while others may only have rights to participate in transactions. Depending on the level of trust between consortium members, consensus in permissioned blockchains can be typically realised through simpler mechanisms, such as simple majority voting. Depending on the implementation, participants may have pseudo or real-world identities visible to others on the blockchain. In general, if the blockchain is tracking activities in the real-world (rather than just virtual transactions between cryptocurrency accounts stored on the blockchain), real-world identities need to be able to be established for enforcement purposes (if not necessarily publicly visible).

The nature of transactions may also vary between types of blockchain. While crypto-currencies like BitCoin merely track the balances of accounts to establish if a transfer is valid, platforms like Ethereum[2] have generalised the mechanisms for making valid transactions in the form of *smart contracts*. Such contracts are immutable code stored on the blockchain that gets executed by the participants to a transaction. While there are various names for, and approaches to implementing such contracts, in this paper we use the term *smart contract* in the general rather than Ethereum-specific sense. Transactions on a blockchain can also be classified as *on-chain* or *off-chain*. In on-chain transactions, the validity of the transactions is only dependent on the state of the blockchain itself (e.g. does the payer have enough crypto-currency on the blockchain to make a transfer). In off-chain transactions, the blockchain facilitates and tracks the transfer typically through the exchange of encryption keys.

In terms of the above distinctions, the type of blockchain relevant to the data sharing platform we describe in this paper is a permissioned blockchain whose voting members are a consortium of research institutions. The blockchain stores access control agreements between data providers and data consumers as smart contracts. The blockchain is the decision point that controls and tracks data access, as well as facilitating payments from the data consumer to the data subject (wearable owner). While the blockchain creates a channel for the off-chain transfer of the wearable data, this data itself is not stored on the blockchain. It also gives participants in a sharing agreement visibility to the terms of the instance of the smart contract to which they are a party, along with a record of any transactions executed under that contract.

---

[1] https://www.hyperledger.org/.
[2] https://ethereum.org/.

## 2.3   Blockchain-Based Health Data Sharing

There has been a lot of work on blockchain based healthcare data sharing as evidenced by the numerous recent literature surveys [11–15]. Researchers have looked at using blockchain for a number of different data sharing scenarios including genomic data sharing [16], medical imaging data sharing [17], electronic medical record (EMR) sharing [18], clinical trial data sharing [19], and wearable data sharing [2].

In [16], the authors have proposed blockchain as the enabling technology for DNA brokerage. EncrypGen[3] is a commercial DNA data marketplace built on top of Multichain that gives individuals control over their personal DNA data and how it is sold to other users, researchers and companies. MedRec [18] is a blockchain based electronic medical record (EMR) management system proposed by researchers from MIT. It allows health care providers to share medical records amongst themselves and with their patients. Health care providers maintain control over the patient data which is stored on their servers, but provide controlled access to the data by entering into patient-provider relationships. The system is built on top of the Ethereum blockchain. [20] is another research proposal that proposes a consortium-led blockchain-based system for the secure sharing of medical big data between hospitals. Researchers from UCLA have proposed a private blockchain-based platform for sharing medical imaging data between data providers, physicians and personal health record vendors [17]. Similarly, Nugent et al. [19] have proposed a framework to improve data transparency in clinical trials using blockchain smart contracts. They have showed that smart contracts can act as trusted administrators, which can improve the transparency of data reporting in clinical trials. In [21], the authors propose a purpose-centric access model leveraging the blockchain to enables patients to own, control and share their healthcare data with untrusted third-parties without violating privacy. They also point out the secure multi-party computing is a promising solution to enable untrusted third-party to conduct computation over patient data without violating privacy. In [22], Benchoufi et al. explore the core functionalities of Blockchain that can be leveraged for conducting reliable clinical trials including patient enrolment, data collection, trial monitoring, data management and data analysis.

Our work differs from the above mentioned approaches in that we focus on continuously generated physiological data captured by data subject owned wearable devices as opposed to EMRs, medical images and one-off measured DNA data. We have previously proposed a blockchain based wearable data marketplace [2] where the main objective is to provide wearable owners complete control over how their physiological data is shared with unknown (and potentially untrusted) parties in an semi-trusted environment. We combine blockchain technology with policy-based management to address some of the issues associated with running a wearable data marketplace including fine-grained access control, privacy-preserving data sharing, confidentiality-preserving data sharing,

---

[3] https://encrypgen.com/.

auditable data sharing, integrity-preserving data sharing and fair and secure data exchange. The work in [23] is similar to our approach in that it proposes a blockchain based personal health data sharing system. However, the authors do not provide any details on (a) how the data consumers can achieve fine-grained access control over their data, (b) how data consumer requirements are matched with the available health data sets, and (c) how they address the issue of trust between untrusted data consumers and data owners.

## 3   Accessing Data from Wearable Devices

There are different types of wearable devices, however they largely follow the same steps in terms of flow of data. First, different types of sensors, such as motion, blood pressure, heart-rate continuously generate data. This data is temporarily stored on the wearable then typically transferred to a smart phone (unless of course the sensor is in the smart phone). User applications on these devices allow the owner to monitor the current or historical data.

At this point, approaches of vendors vary in terms of whether or not the data is uploaded to the vendor's cloud. Wearable device vendors usually provide SDKs to enable the development of apps for wearables to directly collect and send data. In the case of smartphones, tablets and PCs, SDKs are available to develop apps that collect data directly from wearable devices. Using these SDKs, third-parties can develop specific applications to collect data on wearables and send it to other applications. Cloud services usually provide REST APIs. These REST APIs allow third-parties to gain access to users' data stored in the cloud. Using these two options, it is possible to gain access to wearable data. Individuals can also delegate access to this data via these APIs. However, some of the wearable vendors provide both SDK and REST API and some only provide one option.

Below is the list of main wearable platforms and their data access methods:

- **Apple Health.** Apple Health is made up of both local storage and cloud services, an app, and a SDK (Health Kit). The Apple Health local storage and cloud services maintain all the data collected from users and provide some analytic services. Nevertheless, Apple Health does not provide any REST API for third-party systems.
- **Google Fit.** It provides both SDK and API to provide access to the stored data in the google cloud. It provides a SDK for app developers, a SDK to gain access to Google Fit local storage (device storage) and REST APIs for third-party systems. The Android app is needed to transfer the data from the wearable to the smartphone and then to the cloud servers.
- **S-Health.** Like Google fit, a mobile app is required to synchronize the data with the Samsung server. It also provides a SDK to support the development of apps by third-party developers, gaining access to collected data in the proprietary local storage (SDK-Warehouse). Nevertheless, this SDK does not enable the access to wearable data sensors directly. The S-Health platform does not include any REST API.

- **Fitbit.** It only provides REST API for third-party systems. This platform synchronizes data from Fitbit quantification bands and enables third-party developers to get such data through the REST API. Fitbit also provides SDK to allow the application developers to facilitate access to the fitbit cloud.
- **Microsoft Health.** It provides a SDK for app developers and a REST API for third-party systems. Using these two facilities it is possible to gain access to data available in the Microsoft cloud that has been collected from Microsoft Band devices.

In summary, there are two ways in which the data generated by the wearable devices can be accessed. Option 1 is to access the data via APIs and option 2 is to directly access the data from the devices via mobile apps.

### 3.1   Access to Wearable Data by Third Parties

In this paper we assume data from the wearable device has been uploaded to the vendor's or other cloud either automatically or via mobile app. We call the provider of this cloud the *data custodian*. To directly share access to their data with a third party the wearable owner (*data subject*) needs to provide credentials (e.g. access keys) to access that data. However, the data subject does not want to provide the data consumer access to *all* their wearable data on an ongoing basis. OAuth [24] is the de-facto access control mechanism for the REST APIs based data sharing. OAuth enables users to grant access to their data and process to third parties without disclosing the user's authentication data. Generally, OAuth provides to clients (used by data consumer) a "secure delegated access" to server resources (usually cloud service) on behalf of the individuals. Designed specifically to work with Hypertext Transfer Protocol (HTTP), OAuth essentially allows access tokens to be issued to third-party clients by an authorization server, with the approval of the resource owner. There are usually different types of APIs published by the vendors to share different types of data. OAuth token generated for any particular API works for that particular API only. For example, heart rate API by fitbit (https://api.fitbit.com/1/user/5Buser-id5D/activities/heart/date/5Bdate5D/5Bperiod5D.json) allows wearable owners to share their heart rate data and the OAuth token for this API can only be used to retrieve heart-rate data.

One of the major limitations of access delegation via mechanisms such as OAuth is that it is binary decision based access. That means either individuals have to give access to the resource or deny access. They do not have any fine-grained control over access. For instance, they cannot control access based on the context (e.g., time, location). In the next section we describe a policy schema that enables a data subject to define rules for fine-grained access to their data, and show how this schema can be incorporated into smart contracts that govern the sharing/sale of that data. We have described how the OAuth protocol can be combined with the user-defined data sharing policy to provide more fine grained control to the individuals over their data sharing in Sect. 5.1.

# 4    Data Sharing Policy Schema

We have proposed a general data sharing policy schema in our previous work in [3]. We have also defined the main roles involved in the trading of wearable data including the *Data Subject* who the data refers to, the *Data Consumer* who wants access to that data, and *Data Custodian* who holds the data on the Data Subject's behalf [2]. Below, we describe how the general data sharing policy schema can be applied to wearable data sharing.

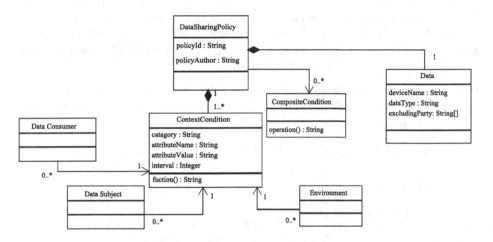

**Fig. 1.** Meta-model of data sharing policy.

The context and identity of the data consumer is captured by the attributes. For instance, location based access control is expressed as the location of either data subject or data consumer (e.g., dataSubject.location). Data is expressed using three attributes, namely deviceType, dataType and accessPoint. *device-Type* allows to define the types of device – in the case of wearables devices such as Apple Watch, Fitbit etc. *dataType* defines the types of data – in the case of wearable data parameters such as heart-rate, blood-pressure, sleeping pattern etc. *accessPoint* is the web address (e.g., URI) of the data access point often is the API end points. *excludingParty* defines if there is any party with whom the data subject does not want to share the data, such as military. Figure 1 shows the meta model of the data sharing schema, which consists of two elements, namely, context condition and data. *Context condition* allows the data subject to define different types of contextual requirements such as time context (e.g., 9 am to 5 pm). The *Data* element allows to define device types, data types, and excluding party (e.g., military). Listing 1.1 show the an example data-sharing policy.

## 4.1    Encoding Policy for Smart Contract Services on Blockchain

Blockchain ensures the immutability of the code or data. That means nobody can edit or delete any information from the blockchain network. In addition to that it ensures that what is written in the blockchain is always enforced in transactions on the blockchain. The way blockchain ensures that is typically through a *smart contract*. Depending upon the blockchain platform used, it can also be referred to as chain-code and smart filter. A smart contract is a self-executing contract with the terms of the agreement between buyer and seller being directly written into lines of code. The code and the agreements contained therein exist across a distributed, decentralized blockchain network. The code controls the execution, and transactions are trackable and irreversible.

In our mechanism, the user-defined policies giving consent to data access are a key part of the smart contract stored on the blockchain that ensures the consent defined by the data subject is always checked and enforced. The policy itself is encoded and stored in the blockchain as JSON format [25]. The following is a sample policy stored in the blockchain.

***Policy:*** *Share my blood-pressure data from fitbit from 10th of February to 15th of February excluding military purpose.* Listing 1.1 represents the JSON encoding of the above policy.

**Listing 1.1.** Policy Definition of Scenario Using Concrete Syntax

```
"dataSharingPolicy" : {
    "policyId" : "222",
    "author" : "Tanya",
        "ContextCondition" : {
        "function" : "greater-than-or-equal"
            "category" :  "environment"
            "attributeName" : "date"
            "attributeValue": "10-02-2020"  },{
            "function" : "less-than-or-equal"  {
            "category" :  "environment",
            "attributeName" : "date"},{
            "attributeValue": "15-02-2020"
    },
    "Data" : {
        "deviceName" : "fitbit",
        "dataType" : "blood-pressure",
        "excluding" : "military",
        }}
```

## 4.2   Data Sharing Contracts

A policy defines *what* wearable data the data subject is prepared to share and any context constraints they want imposed on that sharing – for example, *when* they are prepared to share and with what type of consumer. When the data subject makes an offer to sell their data, they also specify a price. When this offer is accepted by a data consumer it constitutes a contract of sale. The contract contains the agreement between the data subject and the data consumer and includes the asking price and the data sharing policy.

After a contract is created, it is linked with the data subject, broker and data consumer via their wallet id (which is the public key address in the blockchain).

Listing 1.2 shows the JSON encoding of a smart contract corresponding to the example data policy presented in Listing 1.1. The wallet id (public key) of the data subject is used to transfer payment from the data consumer to the data subject. Finally, the blockchain module namely, *"fetcher"* retrieves the individual's wearable data from the data custodian based on this contract. This contract is implemented as a *"smart contract"* or as we say a *"smart filter"* in terms of Multichain platform. As this is implemented as smart contract, blockchain always ensures that this contract is always enforced.

**Listing 1.2.** Template for Contract (Smart Contract)

```
"Contract" : {
    "subject-wallet-id"  :  "MIGfMA0GCSqGSIb3DQEBAQBgQCqGKuk",
    "broker-wallet-id"   :  "NMMafsdfhkhsdfSI4GNAkKBgQCqGKuk",
    "consumer-wallet-id" :  "Ikdfsakfhsadkjfhshhjfhsdkjdfd",
    "price" : "5",
    "policy" : {
            "function" : "greater-than-or-equal"
                "category" :  "environment"
                "attributeName" : "date"
                "attributeValue": "10-02-2020"    },{
                "function" : "less-than-or-equal"
                "category" :  "environment",
                "attributeName" : "date"},{
                "attributeValue": "15-02-2020"
                "deviceName" : "fitbit",
                "dataType" : "blood-pressure",
                "excluding" : "military"
            }}}
```

## 5   System Design and Implementation

A prototype of the system has been implemented using microservices and the MultiChain blockchain platform. In this section we will briefly describe the high level architecture of the system, and then discuss how this was implemented as a proof-of-concept prototype.

### 5.1   Architectural Design

Figure 2 shows a high-level view of the system run by a Consortium of research institutions, and how this system interacts with the wearable's owner, the APIs of the custodian (wearable manufacturer) who holds the data, and the health researcher who wants access to the data.

From Fig. 2, it can be seen there are two main data flows. The sequence of flow is indicated by the numbers in circles. The first data flow is that of the bio data itself as indicated by large brown arrows. Bio data is sent from the wearable device to the Data Custodian's cloud storage ① where such APIs are provided (as with FitBit and Google Fit), or third party storage that acquires the custom data through an app with appropriate SDKs (e.g. Apple Health) as discussed in Sect. 3. The Research Consortium's Fetcher service then securely accesses a user's data via an API provided by the Data Custodian ⑦. As we will discuss below, access to this data is controlled by a smart contract based on the Broker-mediated business agreement reached between the wearable Owner/user and the Health Researcher. The bio data is then anonymised and filtered if necessary ⑧ before being passed on to the Health Researchers ⑨.

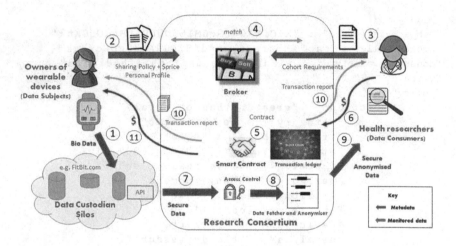

**Fig. 2.** A high level system architecture

The other main data flow represents the transactions that enable secure exchange of data according the smart contract agreement. This data flow is indicated by the large blue arrows in Fig. 2. Both the Owner and the Health Researcher interact with the system through client web apps. The Owner makes an offer to provide (or sell) their data using the provided web app ②. The Owner uses the form on the web app to specify an access consent policy that details what data they wish to sell, including the source, parameters (such as heart rate, BP, activity) and time window. To illustrate a screen shot from the prototype Owner Web App is shown in Fig. 3.

The user also provides a personal profile (age, sex, etc.), and nominates the price (if any) they want for their data. The Health Researcher uses a separate web app to specify the type of wearable data that they are interested in, the cohort from which they want this data, and the price if any they are prepared to pay ③. The Health Researcher can also specify the frequency with which they want the data from the Data Custodian. For much research, retrieving the data in large batch would be appropriate as the researcher is interested in historical data. However if the system is to be adapted to a clinical setting, then the data consumer could set the frequency of polling to a very short interval to achieve near real-time updates.

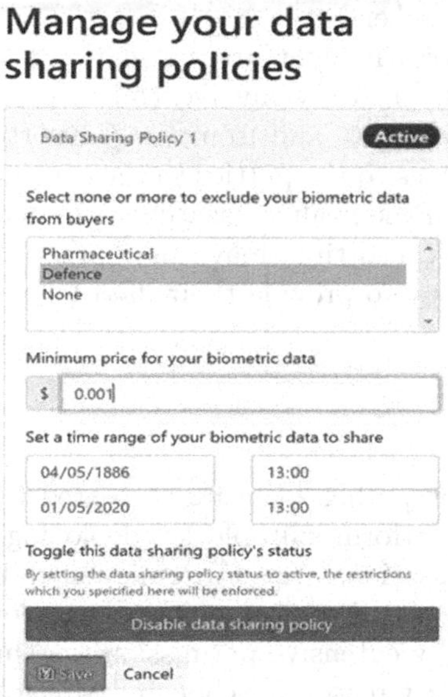

**Fig. 3.** Wearable owner web app: user-defined sharing policy and offer

The role of the Broker within the research consortium is to match buy offers from researchers with (multiple) sell offers for wearable health data ④. As well as matching data parameters the broker is, if required, matching the cohort requirements of the researcher with the personal profiles provided by the data subjects. This profile and cohort information is for matching purposes only and stays confidentially with the broker. The real identities of the participants also remain confidential to the broker with only the pseudo-identities (wallet ids) being exposed. When matches are found, the broker writes the policy, the wallet ids and the agreed price into a contract (as discussed in Sect. 4) onto the Consortium's blockchain ⑤ where they are visible to the parties to that contract for auditing.

These contracts are the control points that govern access to that data from the custodian's API. Once a contract is in place, a data channel is created by the Consortium's Fetcher service. This channel runs from the custodian's API, through the intermediate steps of anonymisation and filtering, to an end-point provided to the data consumer. The data consumer does not get direct access to the API. The data can then either be pulled by a consumer request, or pushed to the consumer.

While the Broker is assumed to be a trusted part of the Consortium in the above schema, in the more detailed design described below we have implemented the Broker as a separate service. This would enable the possibility of creating a marketplace with several competing for-profit brokers vying to match wearable data providers and consumers (although this then may create trust issue between the Consortium and the brokers).

The ancillary data flows in light arrows in Fig. 2 are directly handled by the Consortium's blockchain. They involve (micro)payments from the Health Researcher to the Consortium ⑥ and from the Consortium to the Owner (11), and reporting of transactions to the parties to the contract ⑩. The payment flow is optional. For example, if the health researcher works for a university that is a Consortium member, the consortium may not charge for that data. Similarly, a device owner may be happy to provide their data for gratis if they see it being used for the public good.

## 5.2 Implementation

A proof of concept prototype has been implemented using MultiChain [4], an open source blockchain platform suitable for deploying private (permissioned) blockchains across organisations. As a permissioned blockchain, MultiChain gives fine-grained access-control to users with various levels of authority within the blockchain using a very extensive permission system[4]. This fine-grain user-access control was a primary reason for choosing MultiChain over other permissioned blockchains such as the Ethereum-based Quorum[5]. In our case, owners, researchers and consortium members all have different level of access. Owners and researchers can only see contracts and transactions to which they are party. This allows parties to audit their own transactions without being able to breach the privacy of other participants. Being a permissioned system, consensus for confirming transactions does not need to rely on expensive mechanisms like proof-of-work. Rather, custom mechanisms for reaching consensus (e.g. simple majority) can be implemented amongst nodes with sufficient privileges, in this case the consortium institution members. Each member institution of the research consortium needs to configure a MultiChain node. In the prototype we have simulated these nodes running of separate VMs in a private cloud.

MultiChain uses 'smart filters' similar to the 'smart contracts' in Ethereum or 'chain code' as with HyperLedger. While the implementation of these contracts/filters varies depending on the platform, they all immutably define the transaction rules of a chain—in our case encoding the agreed policy contract. In this paper we have used the term 'smart contract' in a generic sense rather than referring to specific Ethereum concept. The Fetcher component of the Consortium system then uses this contract to securely retrieve the specified data. These transactions are recorded on the chain.

---

[4] https://www.multichain.com/developers/permissions-management/.
[5] https://www.goquorum.com/.

One limitation of blockchains is their limited ability to store large amounts of data. However, in our case this does not present a problem as the bio data and user profile data does not actually pass through the blockchain. Rather, the blockchain is controlling the access mechanism for that data. MultiChain also supports the transfer of assets enabling value exchange if that is required by the system. However, enabling crypto-currency transactions via the blockchain would require parties to have appropriate crypto-coin wallets. This may prove an impediment to the widespread adoption of the system. The alternative which we implemented in the prototype was to have the blockchain track a nominal asset value that maps to a fiat currency and externalise the payment mechanism.

As each custodian of wearable data is likely to have their own API for authenticate access and data retrieval, adaptors need to be added to mediate the interactions. In the prototype implementation we created adaptors for FitBit and Google Fit to successfully retrieve data as specified in policy contracts.

## 6    Conclusion

In this paper, we presented a policy-based approach for the secure, transparent and privacy-preserving exchange of wearable data between wearable device owners and health researchers. The data subjects can specify fine-grained access control over how their data is shared including which parts of the data is shared, under what context and with whom. When these policies are matched with the requirements specified by the data consumers, the resulting agreements get translated into executable smart contracts on the blockchain that ensure that consent as defined by the data subject is always checked and enforced thus facilitating data exchange between parties who are remote and potentially unknown to each other. We have implemented a proof-of-concept prototype of a wearable data marketplace using the open source Multichain platform in which smart filters are used to enforce data exchange in conformance with the data-sharing policies specified by the wearable owners.

As future work, we would like to explore some of the key challenges associated with realising wearable data marketplaces including ensuring the integrity and confidentiality of the wearable data. For example, how can data consumers be assured that the data they purchase is coming from *bona fide* wearables worn by subjects whose profile matches the cohort requirements. Similarly, how can data subjects be assured that the data consumer will not share their data with others without their explicit consent.

**Acknowledgement.** We acknowledge the contributions of our students, Paul Sarda and Andrew Davis from Swinburne University of Technology.

## References

1. Seneviratne, S., et al.: A survey of wearable devices and challenges. IEEE Commun. Surv. Tutor. **19**(4), 2573–2620 (2017)

2. Colman, A., Chowdhury, M.J.M., Chhetri, M.B.: Towards a trusted marketplace for wearable data. In: 2019 IEEE 5th International Conference on Collaboration and Internet Computing (CIC), pp. 314–321. IEEE (2019)
3. Chowdhury, M.J.M., Colman, A., Han, J., Kabir, M.A.: A policy framework for subject-driven data sharing. In: Proceedings of the 51st Hawaii International Conference on System Sciences (2018)
4. MultiChain: MultiChain—Open source blockchain platform (2019). https://www.multichain.com/
5. Dias, D., Cunha, J.P.S.: Wearable health devices–vital sign monitoring, systems and technologies. Sensors 18(8), 2414 (2018)
6. Rhoads, J.G., Cooper, T., Fuchs, K., Schluter, P., Zambuto, R.P.: Medical device interoperability and the integrating the healthcare enterprise (IHE) initiative. Biomed. Instrum. Technol. (Suppl), 21–27 (2010)
7. El-Amrawy, F., Nounou, M.I.: Are currently available wearable devices for activity tracking and heart rate monitoring accurate, precise, and medically beneficial? Healthc. Inform. Res. 21(4), 315–320 (2015)
8. Bayardo, R.J., Agrawal, R.: Data privacy through optimal k-anonymization. In: 21st International Conference on Data Engineering (ICDE 2005), pp. 217–228. IEEE (2005)
9. Chowdhury, M.J.M., Pal, T.: A new symmetric key encryption algorithm based on 2-d geometry. In: 2009 International Conference on Electronic Computer Technology, pp. 541–544. IEEE (2009)
10. Lo, S.K., et al.: Analysis of blockchain solutions for IoT: a systematic literature review. IEEE Access 7, 58822–58835 (2019)
11. Cyran, M.A.: Blockchain as a foundation for sharing healthcare data. Blockchain in Healthcare Today (2018)
12. Hathaliya, J.J., Tanwar, S.: An exhaustive survey on security and privacy issues in healthcare 4.0. Comput. Commun. 153, 311–335 (2020)
13. Khezr, S., Moniruzzaman, Md, Yassine, A.: Blockchain technology in healthcare: a comprehensive review and directions for future research. Appl. Sci. 9(9), 1736 (2019)
14. Mackey, T.K., et al.: 'Fit-for-purpose?'-challenges and opportunities for applications of blockchain technology in the future of healthcare. BMC Med. 17(1) (2019). Article number: 68
15. McGhin, T., Choo, K.-K.R., Liu, C.Z., He, D.: Blockchain in healthcare applications: research challenges and opportunities. J. Netw. Comput. Appl. 135, 62–75 (2019)
16. DeFrancesco, L., Klevecz, A.: Your DNA broker. Nat. Biotechnol. 37(8), 842 (2019)
17. Patel, V.: Secure and decentralized sharing of medical imaging data via blockchain consensus. Technical report, Department of Radiological Sciences, University of California, Los Angeles (2016)
18. Azaria, A., Ekblaw, A., Vieira, T., Lippmanm, A.: MedRec: using blockchain for medical data access and permission management. In: 2016 2nd International Conference on Open and Big Data (OBD), pp. 25–30. IEEE (2016)
19. Nugent, T., Upton, D., Cimpoesu, M.: Improving data transparency in clinical trials using blockchain smart contracts. F1000Research 5 (2016)
20. Cheng, X., Chen, F., Xie, D., Sun, H., Huang, C.: Design of a secure medical data sharing scheme based on blockchain. J. Med. Syst. 44(2) (2020). Article number: 52. https://doi.org/10.1007/s10916-019-1468-1

21. Yue, X., Wang, H., Jin, D., Li, M., Jiang, W.: Healthcare data gateways: found healthcare intelligence on blockchain with novel privacy risk control. J. Med. Syst. **40**(10) (2016). Article number: 218. https://doi.org/10.1007/s10916-016-0574-6
22. Angeletti, F., Chatzigiannakis, I., Vitaletti, A.: The role of blockchain and iot in recruiting participants for digital clinical trials. In: 2017 25th International Conference on Software, Telecommunications and Computer Networks (SoftCOM), pp. 1–5. IEEE (2017)
23. Zheng, X., Mukkamala, R.R., Vatrapu, R., Ordieres-Mere, J.: Blockchain-based personal health data sharing system using cloud storage. In: 2018 IEEE 20th International Conference on e-Health Networking, Applications and Services (Healthcom), pp. 1–6. IEEE (2018)
24. Hardt, D., et al.: The OAuth 2.0 authorization framework. Technical report, RFC 6749, October 2012
25. Shin, S.: Introduction to JSON (JavaScript object notation). Presentation (2010). www.javapassion.com

# Wearable Textile-Based Device for Human Lower-Limbs Kinematics and Muscle Activity Sensing

Liudmila Khokhlova(✉) ⓘ, Marco Belcastro ⓘ, Pasqualino Torchia ⓘ,
Brendan O'Flynn ⓘ, and Salvatore Tedesco ⓘ

Tyndall National Institute, University College Cork, Cork, Ireland
liudmila.khokhlova@tyndall.ie

**Abstract.** Lower-limbs kinematics and muscle electrical activity are typically adopted as feedback during rehabilitation sessions or athletes training to provide patients' progress evaluation or athletic performance information. However, the complexity of motion tracking and surface electromyography (sEMG) systems limits the use of such technologies to laboratory settings and requires special training and expertise to carry out accurate measurements. This paper presents a new wearable textile-based muscle activity and motion sensing device for human lower-limbs, which is capable of recording and wirelessly transmitting sEMG data for several specific muscles as well as kinematic parameters, allowing outdoor and at-home use without direct supervision by non-expert users. In particular, this work is focused on the development and analysis of textile electrodes and garment design, as well as the definition of a proof-of-concept study for sEMG data recording. Obtained values were compared against average rectified values (ARV) recorded using a gold-standard conventional wireless sEMG system. Apart from one muscle (vastus medialis), the developed device showed overall promising results in the muscle activity sensing for lower-limbs, highlighting its possible use in the rehabilitation and sport performance fields. In addition, a washing test was conducted on the electrodes, where it was shown that the proposed textile electrodes maintained structural integrity and showed an acceptable level of electrical parameters deterioration when comparing pre and post washing characteristics.

**Keywords:** Textile · Electrodes · Electromyography · Wearable · Smart Garments

## 1 Introduction

In the modern world, wearable devices permeate deeper and deeper into our lives. Personal health care and well-being are some of the fastest-growing areas for consumer electronics where these technologies are increasingly used. This can be seen by the pervasive adoption of next-generation smart watches, activity trackers and wearable heart rate monitors. The overall rise of connected devices is forecasted to increase from 593 million in 2018 to 929 million devices by 2021 [1].

© ICST Institute for Computer Sciences, Social Informatics and Telecommunications Engineering 2021
Published by Springer Nature Switzerland AG 2021. All Rights Reserved
P. Perego et al. (Eds.): ICWH 2020, LNICST 376, pp. 70–81, 2021.
https://doi.org/10.1007/978-3-030-76066-3_6

The current trend in the development of wearables relies on the technical advancements in systems integration. Up-to-date devices need to be discreet, easy-to-use, unobtrusive and able to perform continuous and remote monitoring in real time. Even though implantable devices seem to meet mentioned requirements, their development still poses numerous technical, medical and security issues [2, 3], making their use currently unfeasible in practice.

An alternative approach involves the integration of wirelessly connected technologies into items frequently used in everyday life (such as clothing). Thus, smart garments represent a potential solution for this problem. Research and development in this area in recent years is gaining wide popularity, as can be seen by the body of literature in the space, and by the large number of funded projects and an exponential increase in the number of associated publications [4].

One of the technologies whose development in this direction seems promising is surface electromyography (sEMG). Monitoring of muscle activity can be extremely useful in sports and medicine, especially physiotherapy and rehabilitation. However, the implementation of long-term regular monitoring has proven to be challenging using traditional sensing solutions (in particular, standard self-adhesive pre-gelled electrodes), due to these being relatively uncomfortable and possibly causing skin irritation and contact allergic dermatitis [5, 6].

Furthermore, the majority of commonly used devices utilize connecting copper wires which can restrict movement and cause motion artifacts in the recorded signal. Moreover the construction of adhesive electrodes makes the direct embedding of these into garments virtually impossible. An alternative solution for a wearable sensing solution which is compatible with daily regular use can be textile electrodes, which can be easily embedded into clothing and are comfortable and safe for long periods of use. In this work, the authors present an implementation of this concept: wearable device – smart leggings, which contain embedded textile electrodes as well as inertial sensors to measure lower-limbs kinematics. The following work will describe the technical process put in place for the development of the smart garments, as well as the functional performance testing procedure carried out for evaluation.

The manuscript is organized as follows: related work and current design challenges are briefly described in Sect. 2, while Sect. 3 is dedicated to addressing those issues in textile electrodes and garment design. In Sect. 4 descriptions and results of the washing test and proof-of-concept study are presented. Finally, Sect. 5 contains a discussion of the obtained results, overall conclusions and future perspectives.

## 2 Related Work

Several works investigating the development of smart garments with built-in sEMG for lower-limbs monitoring have been presented in recent years.

Catarino et al. [5] designed a swimsuit for monitoring biometric and performance parameters of athletes. The base of the suit is polyamide and elastane yarns using seamless knitting jacquard machine, while electrodes and connective paths are simultaneously knitted with conductive yarn. In other works, the authors used the same technology for manufacturing e-leggings with built-in sEMG functions [7]. Electrodes were knitted with silver-coated multifilament yarn and placed to record the electrical activity of the following muscles: vastus intermedius, rectus femoris, biceps femoris, tibialis anterior and gastrocnemius medialis. Electrodes placement and inter-electrode distance were chosen according to SENIAM recommendations. Authors also investigated two types of yarn, the Elitex, conductive yarn made of polyamide fibres with silver coating and Bekitex Mn 50/1 made of polyester and stainless steel. According to the authors, Elitex yarn showed better impedance stability under strain [8]. Despite the relatively low signal-to-noise ratio (SNR) values for knitted electrodes, the authors showed that it is possible to successfully register the electrical activity of muscles using knitted electrodes.

Jogging leggings with embroidered electrodes for recording quadriceps muscle electrical activity were presented by Manero et al. [9]. Stainless-steel thread-based (Sparkfun DEV-11791) sEMG electrodes were made using an embroidery machine and placed on pair of mass-produced jogging leggings. The areas underneath electrodes were thickened with an additional layer of felt fabric. Electrodes were placed according to SENIAM recommendations with 1 cm inter-electrode distance in unstretched state. The authors stated that this device was able to record the difference in muscle performance when running on various surfaces, such as sand, asphalt, and athletic track.

A prototype for recording upper leg muscle groups via sEMG was presented in [10], with authors using sewn-on textile electrodes, even though the type of fabric used was not disclosed in the work. Authors investigated agreement in average rectified values (ARV) of sEMG for their device and traditional Ag/AgCl electrodes and found it to be within 95%. This prototype was subsequently modified by the developers in the development of a commercially available product, e.g. the compression shorts Mbody by Myotec [11] that record cumulative sEMG data from different muscle groups: quadriceps, hamstrings, and gluteus. A similar device currently on the market is Athos [12], which is a wearable system with sEMG electrodes integrated into compression athletic apparel for the upper and lower body. Unlike Mbody, Athos compression shorts include separate sensors for outer quadriceps, inner quadriceps, hamstrings and gluteal muscles. Athos's electrodes are composed of conductive polymer ink applied to the fabric surface. A similar device was announced by B10nix (B10NIX Ltd., Milan, Italy) [13]. However, it is only available for pre-order and, to the best of the authors' knowledge, no information considering design or validation was disclosed.

Alternatively, beside the shorts and leggings solutions described, the implementation challenges associated with the development of a prototype of smart socks was also investigated in [14]. This device detects electrical activity of the gastrocnemius and tibialis muscles. Non-adhesive hybrid polymer electrolytes-based electrodes (polyvinyl alcohol and carboxymethyl cellulose blend complexed with 30 wt. % of $NH_4NO_3$) were used. In the case study, smart socks were used to detect the risk of falling.

While some promising results in wearable muscle activity tracking devices development have been shown, some shortcoming of smart garments are still present, such as motion artifacts, effects of fabric and electrodes stretching, unstable skin-electrode impedance, high cost for commercially available models, limited washability and, therefore, device lifetime. Those issues will be discussed and addressed in the presented solution in the following sections.

# 3 Implementation

A variety of methods have been considered as options for the development of the proposed textile electrodes with the ultimate goal being to ensure the suitable electrical properties and washability of appropriate wearable sensing systems. This includes for example poly (3,4-ethylenedioxythiophene): polystyrene sulfonate (PEDOT: PPS) electrodes that are actively gaining popularity recently due to their biocompatibility properties, as well as their electrochemical and thermal stability [15]. Such electrodes can be produced using a wide variety of methods, i.e., by soaking fabric in polymer solutions with subsequent treatment (drying, heating etc.), using screen printing or inkjet printing techniques. However, these electrodes need further improvement since they currently show inferior results in terms of washability and electrical parameters than textile electrodes made of silver-coated fibres [16]. Such textiles, woven, non-woven and knitted, are also widely available and inexpensive. While the electrical parameters of knitted conductive textile are unstable when worn due to stretching of the fabric [17], woven fabric, such as nylon ripstop, show better performance characteristics than knitted and non-woven [18], possibly due to tighter weave, relatively even surface of the fabric, and subsequent increase in the skin-electrode contact area. Thus, commercially available nylon silver-coated woven fabric Bremen RS (Statex, Bremen, Germany) was used for the textile electrodes. This fabric is suitable for medical applications and shows promising electrical properties [19].

The electrode-skin contact impedance is a major factor in obtaining good quality sEMG signals and this is highly dependent on the skin hydration levels; even though moistened textile electrodes proved to be comparable to traditional electrodes in terms of impedance and recording quality, however, drying of the electrode surface over time significantly worsens their electrical performance [20]. In practice, a sufficient level of moisture can be ensured by accumulating skin perspiration under electrodes over time and avoiding evaporation by using a polymer coating on the back of the textile electrode [21]. To avoid possible degradation of the conductive fabric electrical properties, instead of coating the back of the electrode with polymer solution, a thin polymer sheet was glued onto the base fabric, with a larger piece of conductive fabric placed on top (Fig. 1a), with the result that only the edges of the conductive fabric were glued to the base fabric and most of the electrode surface had a waterproof layer underneath.

Another technical challenge in the development of smart garments is ensuring robust, yet flexible electrical connections between the electrodes and associated integrated electronics. Thin multi-stranded wires with reinforcement thread were attached to the electrodes by sewing them with a conductive thread, with a technique similar to the one used in [22]. The wire core was twisted into a small loop and secured in place by 6–8 stitches, and afterwards stitches were placed along the edge of the conductive fabric and back to the loop (Fig. 1b).

This technique made the realization of a flexible connection both durable under mechanical strain and washable. For the current prototype, stitching was performed manually; however, sewing or embroidery machine can be also used in a manufacturing process. Manufactured textile electrodes shown in Fig. 2.

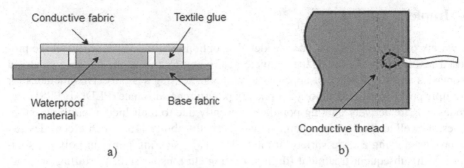

Conductive fabric          Textile glue

Waterproof          Base fabric
material

Conductive thread

a)                                        b)

**Fig. 1.** Construction of textile electrodes

**Fig. 2.** Textile electrodes: front and back view

Electrodes were sewn together in pairs with 2 cm inter-electrode distance and were additionally strengthen with several lines of machine stitching to prevent fabric stretching during movements, since it can result in changes in inter-electrode distance, affecting registered signal. Repetitive stretching can also lead to deterioration of glue seams and conductive fabric frying. It was previously reported in [23, 24] that soft padding can help reduce motion artifacts; therefore, an additional level of felt was added to the electrode pairs. Each pair was placed according to SENIAM guidelines on a base inner fabric for the following muscles: rectus femoris (RF), vastus medialis (VM), biceps femoris (BF), semitendinosus (ST), gastrocnemius medialis (GM) and lateralis (GL). The first four muscles are on the thigh, while the last two are on the calf. Connective wires were threaded through the fabric from the inner layer to improve user comfort and were attached to the fabric using zigzag stitches into respective places. A spare length was left to allow free stretching of fabric when worn (Fig. 3).

To simplify the next step of the prototyping process, mass-produced sports leggings were used as an outer layer. Light compression provided by such garment also ensures desired pressure on electrodes and the overall fit of the garment. Signals from the electrodes are transmitted to two electronic units, a slave unit for the calf muscles and a master unit for the thigh muscles. Registered sEMG then transformed into ARV envelopes by smoothing amplified and rectified signal with low pass filter. Using ARV allows lowering the sampling frequency and present sEMG signals in the conventional form [25].

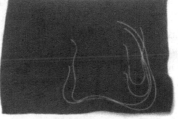

**Fig. 3.** Electrodes placement on the base fabric: front and back view

The device also obtains the body segments (lower and upper leg) orientation and transmit the collected data wirelessly to a smartphone, based on the system architecture described in [26]. The slave/master units' holders are attached to the outer layer fabric. The units can be easily removed from holders, thus leaving the leggings without any active electronics when needed to be washed. A general view of the device is shown in Fig. 4.

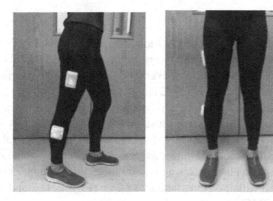

**Fig. 4.** General view of the designed device

## 4   Performance Tests

### 4.1   Proof-of-Concept Study

For this proof-of-concept, only two volunteers were recruited: female, height - 164, 167 cm, weight - 59.5, 56 kg, respectively. Each subject was informed about the nature of study, possible risks and the tasks given. Each subject completed the consent form and the Physical Activity Readiness Questionnaire (PAR-Q) and had no self-reported musculoskeletal and skin injuries or disorders. Clinical Research Ethics committee of the Cork Teaching hospitals approval was obtained to evaluate the device on human subjects.

Volunteers were initially asked to perform a set of exercises while wearing the designed device. Exercises were chosen in order to ensure the activation of separate muscle groups (Table 1). Participants wore the leggings under evaluation, and a 5-min pause was taken before the start of the experiment. No additional skin preparation was carried out. After 10 min rest, the same set of exercises was replicated in the same order with a gold-standard sEMG system (BTS FREEEMG, BTS Bioengineering, Italy with standard pre-gelled 24 mm adhesive electrodes from Covidien Kendall).

**Table 1.** Performed exercises

| Exercise | Major muscles engaged | No. repetitions |
|---|---|---|
| Sitting knee extension | Vastus medialis, rectus femoris | 5 |
| Standing hip flexion/extension | Rectus femoris, vastus medialis/bicepsfemoris, semitendinosus | 5 |
| Plantar flexion (standing on tip-toes) | Gastrocnemius medialis/lateralis | 5 |

MATLAB software was used to process all gathered data. The ARV of the sEMG activity signal was extrapolated. Raw data were exported from BTS EMG Analyzer and then rectified and averaged using a moving average by sliding a 200 ms window to obtain the ARV records, as recommended in [25, 27].

It is important to note that, due to the impossibility of placing the electrodes from the two systems simultaneously on the same muscles, the compared signals were recorded in different sessions, therefore differences between muscles activities evaluated in these initial trials can naturally occur. Despite this possibility, results obtained during the experiments are promising as the muscle activation times and sequences show a similar pattern to those obtained with the gold-standard system (Figs. 5, 6, 7 and 8). The amplitude of the obtained sEMG signals are also comparable, considering that the analog circuit of the wearable device contains an additional amplifier (factor of 10). For gastrocnemius muscles, however, current pre-set amplification of the signal led to saturation and a partial loss of the signal (Fig. 8). This issue does not affect the electrodes design and the circuit gain can be suitably adjusted in future trials.

Simultaneous recording of all major leg muscle made it possible to analyze the influence of motion on the quality of signal for each electrode pair. The VM muscle electrodes showed unsatisfactory results. The signal from this muscle was repeatedly lost. The proximity of the electrodes to the knee, when bending, results in an electrode displacement and consequent loss of the skin-electrode contact.

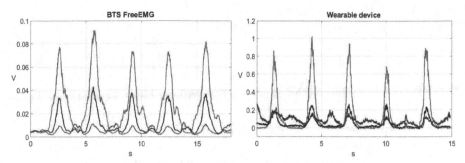

**Fig. 5.** Sitting knee extension: blue – RF, red – BF, yellow – ST

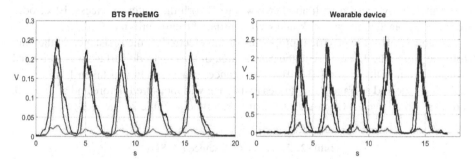

**Fig. 6.** Standing hip extension: blue – RF, red – BF, yellow – ST

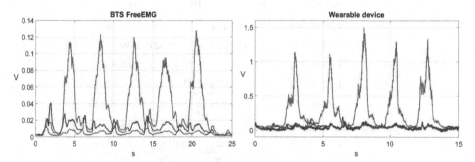

**Fig. 7.** Standing hip flexion: blue – RF, red – BF, yellow – ST

## 4.2 Washing Test

To assess the washability of the developed electrodes (shown in Fig. 1), a sample of 10 electrodes underwent 20 manual washing cycles. Five ml of mild detergent (liquid detergent for delicate fabrics) were diluted in 2 L of warm water at 33.8 °C (SD: 1.5 °C) as recommended by the manufacturer. Electrodes were allowed to soak for three minutes and then were gently "swished" through the water. Electrodes were then thoroughly rinsed three times in clean warm water 34.4 °C (SD: 1.2 °C) and placed flat on a thick

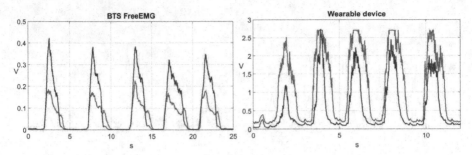

**Fig. 8.** Plantar flexion: blue – GM, red – GL

towel and gently pressed with another towel to absorb the water in excess. Electrodes were finally placed flat on a rack in a well-ventilated room until dry.

To characterize the electrical properties of the electrodes, the resistance in the path from the end of the 12 cm wire to the central area of the electrode surface was measured using a digital multimeter HP 34401A. Resistance measurement was taken 10 times for each electrode and averaged. Electrodes resistance was measured before and after 5, 10, and 20 washing cycles. Obtained values are presented in Table 2.

**Table 2.** Electrodes resistance ($\Omega$, SD)

| Electrode | Washing cycle | | | |
|---|---|---|---|---|
| | Before | 5 | 10 | 20 |
| 1 | 1.29 (0.18) | 1.71 (0.21) | 2.83 (0.13) | 4.10 (0.28) |
| 2 | 1.33 (0.13) | 1.25 (0.02) | 2.74 (0.32) | 2.49 (0.36) |
| 3 | 1.37 (0.17) | 0.91 (0.04) | 2.58 (0.32) | 2.88 (0.26) |
| 4 | 1.32 (0.11) | 1.61 (0.07) | 2.91 (0.14) | 2.97 (0.36) |
| 5 | 1.46 (0.25) | 1.62 (0.12) | 1.71 (0.13) | 2.33 (0.14) |
| 6 | 1.58 (0.15) | 1.78 (0.06) | 2.26 (0.22) | 2.19 (0.07) |
| 7 | 1.28 (0.03) | 1.24 (0.02) | 1.40 (0.09) | 1.70 (0.03) |
| 8 | 1.26 (0.13) | 0.93 (0.05) | 1.78 (0.07) | 1.57 (0.09) |
| 9 | 1.29 (0.24) | 1.62 (0.09) | 2.69 (0.19) | 3.18 (0.25) |
| 10 | 1.85 (0.34) | 4.11 (0.49) | 5.05 (0.76) | – |

Textile electrodes retained their performance throughout all 20 washing cycles. Figure 9 shows the sEMG obtained using washed electrodes. The observed increase in resistance after 20 cycles has not exceeded 3 $\Omega$ and averaged at 1.24 $\Omega$.

Sewn connections with conductive wires remained fully intact, apart from one electrode (10), most likely indicating an inconsistency in the manually performed wire insulation removal. Glued parts of conductive fabric started to peel off for a few electrodes,

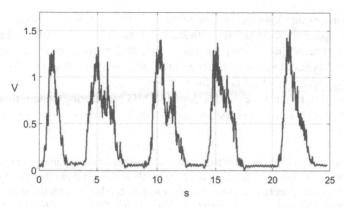

**Fig. 9.** Plantar flexion (GL), electrodes after 20 washing cycles

resulting in the slight fraying of the edges. This issue was observed in electrodes manufactured in one batch and while this has not affected the overall electrical properties of electrodes, this is a problem to be addressed in the future.

## 5 Conclusion

Wearable devices with embedded sEMG can open new opportunities in the field of rehabilitation and professional sports, which include a collection of data in real-world conditions, such as home-settings or athletes' outdoor practices. Ease-of-use of wearable devices can ensure that potential users will not need any training or previous knowledge related to sEMG, which would allow remote monitoring of patients and athletes without direct supervision from a medical professional in rehabilitation. The prototype of such a device was developed and presented in this paper and its potential applicability was evaluated in the proof-of-concept study and in the functional performance test. Furthermore, methodologies adopted for textile electrodes manufacturing were described in detail.

Preliminary results show that the presented device is capable of registering sEMG in form of ARV and obtained results are comparable to a gold-standard system. The study confirms previous findings that wearable sEMG technology is feasible and promising in research, medical, and sports applications. The washing test, conducted on a sample of electrodes, showed that conductive fabric and electrode-wire connections maintained their properties during 20 washing cycles. However further investigation of the gluing methods of conductive fabric to the base fabric is still needed. A possible solution to prevent frying of conductive fabric might be replacing adhesive with sewn connections entirely.

While the problem of motion artifacts was reported previously in the literature, the results of this study show that only VM signal was significantly affected during exercise performance. This information can provide insight into improvement of existing engineering solutions to ensure reliability for every muscle of interest, possible options include altering the sewing pattern of the leggings and/or the use of anti-slip materials. Further investigation on a bigger sample could shed light on the less prominent impact of motion artifacts on skin-electrode impedance. Long-term use is also a point of further investigation. Follow-up studies with sufficient sample size are planned to evaluate the validity and reliability of the proposed device and method for sEMG monitoring. Moreover, prototypes of various sizes need to be produced to reflect the diversity of the population and avoid possible bias in future trials.

The possibility to integrate the developed sEMG monitoring system in a real-time functional electrical stimulation system for feedback control is also a matter for future studies.

**Acknowledgements.** This publication has emanated from research supported by a research grant from the Enterprise Ireland (EI) funded project SKYRE under grant number CF-2015-0031-P. Aspects of this publication have emanated from research conducted with the financial support of Science Foundation Ireland under Grant number 12/RC/2289-P2, 13/RC/2077-CONNECT, 16/RC/3918-CONFIRM, 12/RC/2289-P2 INSIGHT which are co-funded under the European Regional Development Fund.

# References

1. Mück, J.E., Ünal, B., Butt, H., Yetisen, A.K.: Market and patent analyses of wearables in medicine. Trends Biotechnol. **37**(6), 563–566 (2019)
2. Hemapriya, D., Viswanath, P., Mithra, V.M., Nagalakshmi S., Umarani G.: Wearable medical devices - design challenges and issues. In: IEEE International Conference on Innovations in Green Energy and Healthcare Technologies, Coimbatore, pp. 1–6. IEEE (2017)
3. Zheng, G., Shankaran, R., Orgun, M.A., Qiao, L., Saleem, K.: Ideas and challenges for securing wireless implantable medical devices: a review. IEEE Sens. J. **17**(3), 562–576 (2017)
4. Pani, D., Achilli, A., Bonfiglio, A.: Survey on textile electrode technologies for electrocardiographic (ECG) monitoring, from metal wires to polymers. Adv. Mater. Technol. **3**, 1800008 (2018)
5. Avenel-Audran, M., Goossens, A., Zimerson, E., Bruze, M.: Contact dermatitis from electrocardiograph-monitoring electrodes: role of p-tert-butylphenol-formaldehyde resin. Contact Dermatitis **48**(2), 108–11 (2003)
6. Lyons, G., Nixon, R.: Allergic contact dermatitis to methacrylates in ECG electrode dots. Australas. J. Dermatol. **54**(1), 39–40 (2013)
7. Dias, R., da Silva, J.M.: A flexible wearable sensor network for bio-signals and human activity monitoring. In: 2014 11th International Conference on Wearable and Implantable Body Sensor Networks Workshops, Zurich, pp 17–22. IEEE (2014)
8. Catarino, A., Rocha, A., Carvalho, H.: Integration of biosignal monitoring in sports clothing. In: Proceedings of the TRS2012-The 41st Textile Research Symposium, Universidade Minho, Guimaraes (2012)
9. Manero, R.B.R., et al.: Wearable embroidered muscle activity sensing device for the human upper leg. In: 2016 38th Annual International Conference of the IEEE Engineering in Medicine and Biology Society (EMBC), Orlando, FL, pp. 6062–6065. IEEE (2016)
10. Finni, T., Hu, M., Kettunen, P., Vilavuo, T., Cheng, S.: Measurement of EMG activity with textile electrodes embedded into clothing. Physiol. Meas. **28**, 1405–1419 (2007)
11. Myontec - Muscle Activity Measuring Technology. https://www.myontec.com/. Accessed 05 Sept 2019
12. Athos. https://www.liveathos.com/. Accessed 05 Sept 2019

13. WISE - Wearable Interactive System. https://wise.b10nix.com/. Accessed 18 Nov 2019
14. Leone, A., Rescio, G., Giampetruzzi, L., Siciliano P.: Smart EMG-based socks for leg muscles contraction assessment. In: Proceedings of 2019 IEEE International Symposium on Measurements and Networking, Catania, Italy, pp. 1–6. IEEE (2019)
15. Pani, D., Dessi, A., Saenz-Cogollo, J.F., Barabino, G., Fraboni, B., Bonfiglio, A.: Fully textile, PEDOT: PSS based electrodes for wearable ECG monitoring systems. IEEE Trans. Biomed. Eng. **63**, 540–549 (2016)
16. Ankhili, A., Tao, X., Cochrane, C., Koncar, V., Coulon, D., Tarlet, J.-M.: Comparative study on conductive knitted fabric electrodes for long-term electrocardiography monitoring: silver-plated and PEDOT: PSS coated fabrics. Sensors **18**, 3890 (2018)
17. Catarino, A., Carvalho, H., Rocha, A.M., Montagna, G., Dias, M.J.: Biosignal monitoring implemented in a swimsuit for athlete performance evaluation. In: Proceedings of AUTEX 2011 Conference, Mulhouse, France, pp 807–813 (2011)
18. Beckmann, L., et al.: Characterization of textile electrodes and conductors using standardized measurement setups. Physiol. Meas. **31**(2), 233–247 (2010)
19. Fabrics – Shieldex Trading. https://www.shieldextrading.net/products/fabrics/. Accessed 10 Oct 2019
20. Pylatiuk, C., et al.: Comparison of surface EMG monitoring electrodes for long-term use in rehabilitation device control. In: 2009 IEEE International Conference on Rehabilitation Robotics, Kyoto, pp. 300–304. IEEE (2009)
21. Soroudi, A., Hernández, N., Wipenmyr, J., Nierstrasz, V.: Surface modification of textile electrodes to improve electrocardiography signals in wearable smart garment. J. Mater. Sci. Mater. Electron. **30**(17), 16666–16675 (2019). https://doi.org/10.1007/s10854-019-02047-9
22. Chen, W., Oetomo, S.B., Feijs, L., Bouwstra, S., Ayoola, I., Dols, S.: Design of an integrated sensor platform for vital sign monitoring of newborn infants at neonatal intensive care units. J. Healthc. Eng. **1**(1), 535–554 (2010)
23. Cömert, A., Honkala, M., Hyttinen, J.: Effect of pressure and padding on motion artifact of textile electrodes. Biomed. Eng. Online **12**, 26 (2013). https://doi.org/10.1186/1475-925X-12-26
24. Cömert, A., Hyttinen, J.: Investigating the possible effect of electrode support structure on motion artifact in wearable bioelectric signal monitoring. Biomed. Eng. Online **14**(44), 1–18 (2015)
25. Konrad, P.: The ABC of EMG a Practical Introduction to Kinesiological Electromyography. Noraxon INC., USA (2005)
26. Tedesco, S., et al.: A multi-sensors wearable system for remote assessment of physiotherapy exercises during ACL rehabilitation. In: Proceedings of 26th IEEE International Conference on Electronics Circuits and Systems, Genova. IEEE (2019)
27. Farfán, F.D., Politti, J.C., Felice, C.J.: Evaluation of EMG processing techniques using information theory. Biomed. Eng. Online **9**, 72 (2010). https://doi.org/10.1186/1475-925X-9-72

# Integration of Wearable Inertial Sensors and Mobile Technology for Outpatient Functional Assessment: A Paradigmatic Application to Evaluate Shoulder Stability

Paolo Mosna[1]([📧]) [iD], Roberto Luongo[2], Manuela Morghen[2],
and Nicola Francesco Lopomo[1] [iD]

[1] Dipartimento di Ingegneria dell'Informazione, Via Branze 38, 25123 Brescia, BS, Italy
{p.mosna,nicola.lopomo}@unibs.it
[2] Independent Clinical Researcher at Genetica Amica Association, Via Pola 6,
38066 Riva del Garda, TN, Italy

**Abstract.** Wearable devices based on inertial measurement units (IMUs) are now-a-days a *de facto* standard in the field of human motion analysis. Lower costs, improved quality and enhanced accuracy promote a very fast and diffused adoption of such devices in healthcare and wellness areas. In clinical settings, these technological solutions allow for a quantitative evaluation of functional and clinical tests. This article aimed to present a practical and feasible approach using IMU-based wearable devices and mobile applications to rapidly collect 3D motion information coming from different body segments. The proposed solution was specifically designed for a rapid and precise monitoring of the patient's status both outdoor and indoor, including home and clinical contexts. The modularity concept in designing the application allows to easily plug specific and customized modules addressing data analysis and patient status assessment. The acquired data are always available to the user to be archived or re-processed. Without loss of generality, the developed system was tested in a real clinical context, addressing the need for assessing the shoulder mobility in order to automatically identify the presence of symptomatic or asymptomatic humerus-scapular dyskinesis. This approach allowed to define a kinematic-based set of novels metrics - called Shoulder Primary Key Indicators. The proposed system demonstrated to be a practical and effective solution in the most clinical context, giving room to the adoption of this kind of approach to a wider range of applications related to the functional assessment of different body segments and joints, such as the knee, the spine or the elbow.

**Keywords:** Healthcare · Mobile apps · Inertial sensors · Motion analysis · Shoulder dyskinesis

## 1 Introduction

In the last decade, the evolution of inertial measurement units (IMUs) and magneto-inertial measurement units (MIMUs) have been leading to enormous improvements in

P. Perego et al. (Eds.): ICWH 2020, LNICST 376, pp. 82–98, 2021.
https://doi.org/10.1007/978-3-030-76066-3_7

term of precision and hardware quality, with a progressive size and cost reduction. This new wearable technology is slowly spreading around due to several competitive advantages related to other technologies, including lower costs, good quality, easy to setup, waterproof and possibility to be used indoor or outdoor, even in unstructured environment [1–3]. Moreover, inertial and magnetic sensors can be used almost everywhere, thus they can be easily employed in the fields of rehabilitation, wellness and sports [4–6].

The huge success behind this type of "smart" technology is mainly due to their design. A wearable device is basically a tiny computer with sensing, processing, storage and communication capabilities [6]. Improvements in LiPo battery technology, reduced sensor consumption and thanks to the latest Bluetooth Low Energy (BLE) technologies even small devices can provide a long-lasting duration in between two consecutive charge. Wearable inertial devices (WID) can be considered indeed small elaborators integrating a set of Micro-Electro-Mechanical-Systems (MEMS) and magnetic sensors and a wireless communication channel. High performance micro-processors can collect data from sensors up to 1 kHz data rate and directly process on-board data, by applying data-fusion algorithm in order to estimate the device spatial orientation. Processed data and results can be stored locally or can be transmitted in real time over wireless channels.

Developing healthcare application for clinical fields supporting motion-data analysis paradigm requires to face several critical aspects [7, 8]; in particular, when considering outpatient visits, application requirements are mainly related to the context itself, the management of the patients and the overall logistics of the clinical structure. These issues implied the need for portable, low-cost and rapid setup-time applications. This work aimed to report the design, the development and the clinical results of a modular android-based application specifically addressing – but not limited to – the body functional assessment. The system was designed to run on mobile devices and to provide immediate assessment outcomes to the clinicians thus, to complementarily support the clinical assessment. With this work we also aimed to underline the key aspects and critical factors involved in a possible wide adoption of such technology in clinical setting.

## 2    Materials and Methods

### 2.1    System Requirements

At design stage, various hypotheses were made in order to obtain a reliable and easy-to-use system. In particular - after having evaluated the use cases in agreement with several opinion leaders - we defined a basic set of functional requirements (FR):

- run on mobile devices (tablet or smartphone) (FR1);
- be easy to use (FR2);
- be easy to acquire data (FR3);
- be easy to setup (FR4);
- provide "general purpose" data analysis (FR5);
- support multiple motion data acquisition devices (FR6);
- provide data storage (FR7).

FR1 means that the application must be able to run on mobile phones and tablets. Mobile phones and tablets are inexpensive and portable devices that can be easily moved around. We initially targeted Android-based devices which are less expensive and more diffused with respect to solutions based on different OS. FR2 and FR3 imply that the application must let the user do not spend much time to manage patient's data and acquisition phase; from the design point of view, specific attention was given to the user interface (GUI), thus to allow the physicians to quickly go through data entry and data acquisition. FR4 stands for the ability to easily and rapidly positioning and calibrating of wearable sensors; subject calibration must not take more than few seconds, indeed. FR5 allows to use the system for different types of acquisition, including – for instance - gait analysis, shoulder assessment, upper and lower limb functional testing, etc. The possibility to support multiple device vendors (FR6) allows to support both low-quality inexpensive devices such as high-quality expensive devices depending on the economic availability. Finally, FR7 provides the ability to store acquired motion data in local database or in XML files. Stored data can be used for a deeper analysis if required; cloud storage was also envisaged.

Furthermore, application's modularity represents a key aspect of the overall project. In general, approaching human motion analysis, setup and data acquisition are common phases in all the considered possible use cases. Usually, common phases (CP) include: (CP1) subject identification, (CP2) setup, (CP3) calibration, (CP4) data acquisition. Data analysis is indeed specific for each type of acquisition; therefore, data processing and visualization specifically require a "plug-and-play" approach. Thence, the application was designed to have a generic core architecture which can be used in various type of data acquisition applications, whereas several modules were thought to be customized in order to interface to specific device vendor, to provide dedicated data processing and to provide detailed representation of the clinical outcomes.

## 2.2 Hardware Selection

Following FR1, the application was designed to run on any Android device that support at least Android Oreo (i.e. 8.0), which corresponds to API level 26. For the validation of the system, the developed application was tested on the Motorola One mobile phone.

The selection of the WID vendor for clinical trials implied the definition of specific requirements, since on the market there are several different manufacturers, each one providing a product with its own advantages and disadvantages. Basic requirements were identified as:

– Low-cost;
– In a minimal set of 3 devices;
– Bluetooth communication;
– Rechargeable;
– 9DoF sensors data.

Browsing the market, the following available products were found and evaluated: DOT by Xsens [9] and Wearnotch by Notch Interfaces [10]. Other systems were excluded due to costs, number of devices or need for dedicated base station.

Between DOT and Wearnotch, we finally decided for the second one for the following reasons:

- Support for Android devices (a very complete SDK is provided);
- Software already available with clear practical examples;
- Set of 6 devices;
- Practical case;
- Waterproof;
- Easy to calibrate.

Among several features provided by the Notch SDK, there are a couple of interest: 1) an already available calibration process with respect a base subject position and 2) a graphical representation of the subject activity, that can be used to show – even in real time – the body posture and movements. Moreover, the subject's base-position (also called "steady position") for initial calibration can be easily personalized. Finally notch devices have a multi-color led that can be used to identify each single device thus, to support an easy positioning of the sensors on the correct body segment.

## 2.3 Software Design and Development

The mobile application was developed using Android Studio®, exploiting the SDK provided by Notch Interfaces.

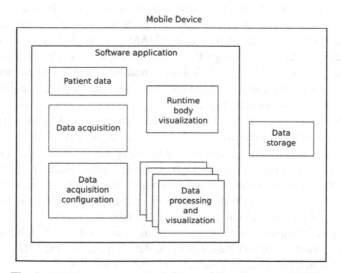

**Fig. 1.** Modular representation of the mobile software application.

Considering the modular structure of the application (Fig. 1), we identified 7 main modules, including:

– Patient Data Service (PD);
– Data Acquisition (DA);
– Data Acquisition Configuration (DAC);
– Runtime Body Visualization (RBV);
– Data Processing and Visualization (DPV);
– Data Storage (DS);
– Communication Bus (CB).

The PD, DA, DAC and RMV modules are part of the core application; this implies that, regardless of any body segments you aim to analyze and any assessment you want to perform, this set of modules and their interaction never change.

The DPV module may change depending by the specific application or functional analysis; this module must be designed to processes the acquired data in order to infer the results and represent the data, considering their clinical meaning and importance.

PD module takes care of the management of the patient's data and information. Connects directly to the persistence service to retrieve already profiled patients. Moreover, to speed up the process the physician can proceed with data acquisition without validating the patient's data.

DA module allows for data acquisition, connecting with the hardware devices interface. This interface provides a generic callback-based interface framework to abstract the physical hardware and to provide transparences with respect the specific hardware vendor solution. All the information related to each acquisition session are saved as XML files or entered in a dedicated database. DAM is supported by the DAC module which has been conceived to manage the device configuration. This means that DAC component must perform two tasks: 1) define the number of sensors to use and 2) define the position of each device on the body segments. This information is controlled by a json-formatted configuration file (Fig. 2(b)).

The RBV module was conceived to receive data from DAM and to apply them to the skeleton to provide a real-time feedback of the movement to the user. Real-time feedback is important in order to check both the running status of the system, the sensors configuration and the avatar calibration. During runtime body visualization, the user can ask the patient to perform some preliminary simple movements in order to verify the correctness of the setup. If calibration is wrong or the device configuration is not the right one, the user can go back and fix any possible issue.

Figure 2(a) reported an example of the standard avatar given by Notch Interfaces, in a specific pose. After the opportune calibration, data acquired by the WIDs are directly applied to the avatar's body segment to reflect subject's position.

The DPV module processes acquired motion data in order to perform the user's data analysis. Processed data are then shown to the user adopting specific visualization depending on the analysis performed. For sake of clarity, in the next sections we present the "Shoulder Stability Assessment" module (SSAM). The SSAM basically uses two WIDs, one applied to the humerus and one to the scapula in order to identify dyskinesis in the scapulo-humeral rhythm.

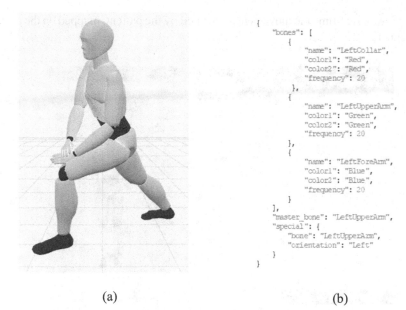

```
{
    "bones": [
        {
            "name": "LeftCollar",
            "color1": "Red",
            "color2": "Red",
            "frequency": 20
        },
        {
            "name": "LeftUpperArm",
            "color1": "Green",
            "color2": "Green",
            "frequency": 20
        },
        {
            "name": "LeftForeArm",
            "color1": "Blue",
            "color2": "Blue",
            "frequency": 20
        }
    ],
    "master_bone": "LeftUpperArm",
    "special": {
        "bone": "LeftUpperArm",
        "orientation": "Left"
    }
}
```

(a)                                            (b)

**Fig. 2.** (a) Example of avatar graphical representation (image published on Wearnotch's website at https://wearnotch.com/). (b) Example of the configuration file for the Data Acquisition Configuration (DAC) module.

The DS module was designed to handle the access to the database providing transparent access to various persistence solutions: SQLite and Cloud to cite two of them. Cloud based persistence allows the storage of the data in the cloud where can be accessed from other applications to outperform further and more detailed analyses.

Finally, all the modules relate to an event driven communication bus used, for example, by the data acquisition module to share the acquired data among other modules such as the DMV. The CB is basically an event bus with the subscriber-dispatcher paradigm. Whenever an event is dispatched all the registered listener gets automatically notified. The CB allows for a transparent pluggable mechanism for the custom modules DPV to receive notification of events or the motion data in real-time without a direct interface binding easing module integration.

### 2.4 "Shoulder Stability Assessment" Application: Development and Validation

Without loss of generality, we declined the system into a specific application to assess the shoulder stability, we called the "Shoulder Stability Assessment" (SSA) application. This app included a specific DPV module able to display all the information concerning the clinical assessment.

**Application Modules**
The application presents an initial GUI, where the user can set the patient's information (Fig. 3 Left), a main interface with the possibility to connect the sensors and calibrate the avatar (Fig. 3 Center), and a runtime visualization and acquisition interface, which

allow the view in real-time the movement performed by the patient, mapped on the avatar (Fig. 3 Right).

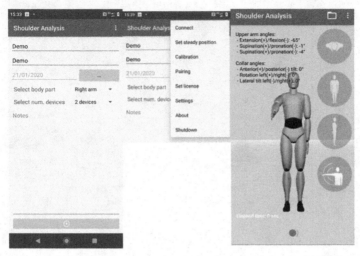

**Fig. 3.** App initial interface (left), main interface (center) and runtime visualization interface (right).

The mobile application was tested on-field with a dedicate DPV module to assess the shoulder stability in order to discover presence of dyskinesis in the scapula-humeral joint. The DPV module, for this specific use case, was addressed to the possibility to identify asymptomatic shoulder dyskinesis by using a set of shoulder primary key indicators (SPKIs), as hereinafter reported. The role of the system was to extract these specific SPKIs from the motion data acquired during the execution of defined tasks and report them to the user to support clinical decision.

**The Shoulder**
The shoulder articular complex is made of synovial articulations and functional articulations [11]. This means the shoulder is a complex structure characterized by wide mobility at the expense of overall instability. The shoulder consists of four distinct articulations: the glenohumeral joint, the chromium clavicular joint, the sternoclavicular joint, and the scapulothoracic articulation [12]. These biomechanics characteristics gives to the shoulder articular complex a huge sensibility to a various pathological dis-order: acute disorders (such as subluxations, dislocations, instability, bunions etc.) and chronic disorders (such as tendinitis-tendinosis, broken tendons due to over-load or over-work). Lesions of soft tissue of the shoulder are seconds only to the vertebral spine lesions in term of disability costs [13].

The application has been tested to acquire shoulder data in the initial phase of the abduction movement. Given the shoulder biomechanical characteristic [14–18], we consider the micro-modification of the scapulo-humeral joint dynamics, in the initial abduction movement, significative in the identification of the presence of shoulder kinesis and impingements. The shoulder dynamic in the initial phase of the movement has been describe a set of SPKIs.

**Subject Selection and Group Definition**

In order to validate the system, a preliminary pilot study was performed on voluntary subjects. Each subject was asked to report the presence of any pathology at the shoulder level, including (1) tendinitis-tendinosis of the rotator cuff, (2) tenosynovitis of the biceps caput longum, (3) subacromion-deltoidea bursitis, (4) partial or total lesion of the rotator cuff, (5) frozen shoulder and (6) articular movement limitation associated or not with muscle hypostemia. All the subjects were previously informed on the main aim of the study and they gave to the experimenter their open consent. The following groups were identified:

1. **Group HF (GHF)** included all the female subjects with no shoulder pathology.
2. **Group PF (GPF)** included all the female subjects with any reported shoulder pathologies,
3. **Group HM (GHM)** contains all the male subjects with no shoulder pathologies and normal shoulder functionalities.
4. **Group D (GDP)** contains all the male subject with shoulder pathologies.

**Validation Setup**

All the data were acquired on the subject standardizing the setup. Specifically, the subject was seated on a stool, with standing vertebral column and both arms laying down along the side of the body. The height of the stool was set in order to have a proximal 90° angle on the knee. With the subject in this position, three WIDs were specifically positioned on the acromion, the humerus and the radio, as reported in Fig. 4 (left). For all the sessions, all the WIDs were placed by the same person, who was previously trained in this operation. The device on the scapula was placed on the postero-lateral side of the acromion, whereas the device on the humerus was positioned on the distal lateral side. The device on the radio was used to check the configuration, communication and real-time features. In this work, we did not take into consideration the thorax movements of the subject while executing the required task, since we empirically verified that the thorax compensation was almost negligible.

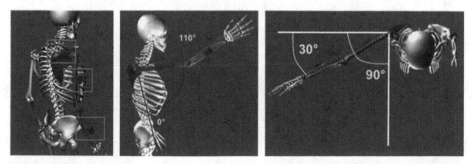

**Fig. 4.** WDIs positioning on the scapula and upper limb (left) and required movement in the sagittal (center) and coronal (right) planes.

The steady calibration was performed with the targeted arm relaxed; lying on his side. Overall calibration takes no more than 2/3 s. Then, each subject was specifically asked to execute an abduction movement of the upper limb (ULA) starting from the steady position up, rising the upper limb and maintaining it within the scapular plane, with a normal speed, up to reach the maximum abduction level without feeling pain, and back (Fig. 4, center and right). Before recording the data, the subject was asked to simulate the movement thus, to verify the task and train for the exercise. In order to test the reliability of the approach, the subject was required to execute a minimum of three to a maximum of five movements. Between each ULA, a pause of 5 s was applied to not induce muscular fatigue. The rhythm of the movement execution was manually driven by an external trigger. Motion data acquired by the WIDs were used to compute the following planar angle rotations:

– Scapula frontal plane rotation (SFPR);
– Scapula sagittal plane rotation (SSPR);
– Humerus abduction (HA);
– Humerus axial rotation (HR);
– Humerus extra-rotation (HE).

In the definition of these SKPIs, we kept into account the functional relationship that is present among different rotation angles (e.g. between HA and SFPR and between HA and HR). Each SPKI was extracted from the angular values, by performing several hypotheses on their progress in time. Considering the graphs reported in Fig. 5, we can define the following parameters:

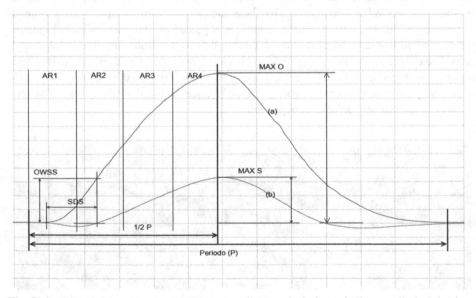

**Fig. 5.** Details of HR (red line) and SFPR (yellow line) angle during a single upper limb abduction (ULA). (Color figure online)

– **P** as the overall period of a single ULA;
– **P′** is the instant of the period P, when the humerus reaches the maximum abduction value;
– **MAXS** is the maximum scapular rotation on the frontal plane;
– **MAXO** is the maximum humerus abduction value;
– "Scapula delta start segment" (**SDSs**), as the segment identified by the initial abduction movement to the moment in which the scapular rotation crosses the zero line (which is considered the steady position of the humerus);
– "Humerus when scapula starts" (**OWSS**), is the value of abduction (in degrees) of the humerus when scapula starts, so when scapula cross the zero axis.
– "Humerus when scapula is 5°" (**OWSS5**) is the value of abduction (in degrees) of the humerus when scapula rotation reaches 5°.
– "Area ratios" (**AR1p, AR2p, AR3p** and **AR4p**) are 4 areas obtained dividing the whole P′ range in 4 equal parts; in this analysis only AR1p was considered.

From all these parameters, several SPKIs were identified, including:

– **OWSS** and **OWSS5** identified the humerus abduction when scapula start moving and when scapula reaches the 5° of rotation respectively.
– **SDS** defined as reported in Eq. (1):

$$SDS = (SDSs/P) * 100 \tag{1}$$

– **AR1** defined starting from the corresponded AR1p value, applying the Eq. (2):

$$AR1 = (AR1_S/AR1_O) * 100 \tag{2}$$

where: $AR1_S$ is the area of the scapula time series in zone AR1;
$AR1_O$ is the area of the humerus time series in zone AR1.

– **MOAR** defined as the maximum humerus axial rotation normalized with respect the main humerus abduction value considering graphs reported in Fig. 6 and using the Eq. (3):

$$MOAR = (M2/M1) * 100 \tag{3}$$

where: M1 is the maximum humerus abduction value;
M2 is the maximum humerus axial rotation.

All SPKIs were computed for each ULA movement and a mean value was evaluated considering all the ULA movements acquired by the system. In order to clearly report the data to the final user, we decided to introduce a discretization of the values obtained for each SPKIs by introducing a score with 4 grades:

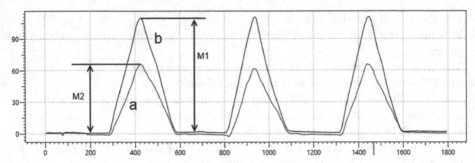

**Fig. 6.** Humerus abduction (b) vs. humerus main-axis rotation (a) during three ULA movement.

- S1: when the SPKI is in the range [0–6);
- S2: when the SPKI is in the range [6–11);
- S3: when the SPKI is in the range [11–16);
- S4: when the SPKI is ≥16

These grades consider the distribution of the SPKIs, obtained during the acquisition sessions. Furthermore, we verified the reliability of the system in the clinical context by qualitatively analyzing its inherent usability through unstructured interview performed involving two opinion leaders.

## 3 Results

This work presented a twofold aim. The first objective was to experiment the possibility to adopt inertial sensors and mobile applications in clinical settings, in order to acquire motion data on subject, thus, to assess his/her functional state. The second objective was to try to apply the developed system in a paradigmatic context and therefore verify the possibility to assess the presence scapula-humeral dyskinesis. Hereinafter, the main results obtained and related to both the aims are presented and discussed.

### 3.1 Wearable Inertial Devices and Mobile Application

The first objective was verified by evaluating the overall usability of the system. We provided the system – consisting in a mobile phone and WIDs - to two clinicians, who performed some test on voluntary subjects. A training was executed with all the clinicians involved in the experimentation. During the training we showed the clinicians how to apply the sensors and how to use the mobile application to acquire data and save them. With the experts, we also designed the overall protocol to use to acquire the motion data. Further, clinicians were followed during the use of the system in order to provide support if needed and to verify how they were able to handle the overall solution.

The results obtained for this aspect of the work, were very interesting. The clinicians involved in the experiment resulted to be very comfortable with the adoption of this technology. Mobile phones are indeed very diffuse in their environment and they were very keen in using the phone normally during their daily work (e.g. to communicate with their patients and coworkers). They were very pleased of the provided commodity and of the possibility to have the entire system "in pockets of their medical gown". No difficulties nor critical events where encountered during WID positioning or system use. Further analysis will include the possibility to perform a pilot study quantitatively addressing the usability of the system, by introducing proper scores and questionnaires.

## 3.2 Humerus-Scapular Dyskinesis Assessment

The second objective of this work was to verify the possibility to identify symptomatic or asymptomatic humerus-scapular dyskinesis by exploiting motion information acquired by using two WIDs and a dedicated module for the analysis.

In particular, the validation included 82 subjects of age ranging between 19 and 80 years. Demography and pathology presence are reported in Table 1.

**Table 1.** Demography data.

| Subjects | Pathological | Non-pathological |
|----------|--------------|------------------|
| 45 females | 18 | 27 |
| 37 males | 15 | 22 |

This section presents the final SPKIs analysis, performed on a total of 52 subjects. Without loss of generality, in this discussion we reported the results obtained on OWSS, SDS and AR1 parameters. In order to limit any possible difference due to gender characteristics, we divided the analysis considering separately males and females. In Table 2 we report SPKIs for female subjects, considering those who reported a joint pathology and those who did not.

In the same way, Table 3 shows the characteristic SPKIs data for male subjects grouped into "Pathology" and "NO-Pathology".

Focusing on females, OWSS, SDS and AR1 well demonstrated to be the extremely significant indicators in the identification of specific pathology of the scapulo-humeral joint. Considering OWSS, more than 81% of non-pathologic female subjects reported an index value OWSS larger than 16. On the other hand, 100% of the pathologic female subjects presented an OWSS value lower than 16. Furthermore, SDS well discriminated for the presence of pathology, where 100% of the female subjects presented a value lower than 11. In this case, SDS was not so significant in identifying non-pathological subjects. In this group around 63% of the subjects presented an SDS value lower than 11 and 37% of the subjects remain in the range S2. In this case, the identified thresholds resulted to be not the optimal selection. We discuss this point hereinafter, in the Discussion. Eventually, also AR1 index was quite a good indicator for the identification of the presence of a dyskinesis in the humerus-scapular joint. With this SPKI 100% of the female subjects in PFG presented a value above 6 and only 11% reported an index below 11. Among the "No-Pathology" subjects, 70% presented a value of AR1 below 11. Similar evidences are present in the male groups; focus - for instance - on OWSS index.

**Table 2.** Characteristic SPKIs for female subjects divided into "NO-Pathology" and "Pathology" groups.

| Data | NO-Pathology | Pathology |
|---|---|---|
| **Quantity** | 27 | 18 |
| **Age** | | |
| MIN | 30 | 25 |
| MAX | 86 | 80 |
| MEAN | 56 | 59 |
| **OWSS** | | |
| From [0–6) | 0 | 1 |
| From [6–11) | 0 | 11 |
| From [11–16) | 5 | 6 |
| Above 16 | 22 | 0 |
| **SDS** | | |
| From [0–6) | 0 | 7 |
| From [6–11) | 10 | 11 |
| From [11–16) | 14 | 0 |
| Above 16 | 3 | 0 |
| **AR1** | | |
| From [0–6) | 13 | 0 |
| From [6–11) | 6 | 2 |
| From [11–16) | 5 | 5 |
| Above 16 | 3 | 11 |

**Table 3.** Characteristic PKIs for male subjects divided into "NO-Pathology" and "Pathology" groups.

| Data | NO-Pathology | Pathology |
|---|---|---|
| **Quantity** | 22 | 15 |
| **Age** | | |
| MIN | 19 | 44 |
| MAX | 72 | 77 |
| MEAN | 46 | 62 |

*(continued)*

**Table 3.** (*continued*)

| Data | NO-Pathology | Pathology |
|---|---|---|
| **OWSS** | | |
| From [0–6) | 0 | 0 |
| From [6–11) | 0 | 9 |
| From [11–16) | 2 | 2 |
| Above 16 | 20 | 4 |
| **SDS** | | |
| From [0–6) | 0 | 5 |
| From [6–11) | 2 | 8 |
| From [11–16) | 8 | 2 |
| Above 16 | 12 | 0 |
| **AR1** | | |
| From [0–6) | 12 | 1 |
| From [6–11) | 7 | 1 |
| From [11–16) | 1 | 5 |
| Above 16 | 2 | 8 |

## 4 Discussion

This preliminary work is mainly focused on the design and development of a system integrating a mobile application and WIDs addressing the clinical field. From the usability point of view, we demonstrated that these tools were very appreciated by the clinicians and that functional assessment in real-time is possible. In our experimentation we sought to keep all things as simple as possible. In this context, we must investigate what could happen if the number of WID increase and the WID setup get more complex. In this case, the adoption of the presented solution will not be immediate, since the scalability of the technology should be well evaluated for each specific application. However, one of the points where application engineering must put attention is the possibility to optimize the number of WIDs to use for a given analysis, keeping it as low as possible. From the use case analysis, the subject preparation must be comfortable and rapid, movement to execute must be easy and short to complete. The key points, which worth for the clinicians - after the patient's health-, are time, simplicity and result. Applications which provide short set-up time, easy movement execution and provide reliable results would have a good spread in the clinical environment.

The second objective of this work was to apply the developed solution to the assessment of humerus-scapular dyskinesis. The target of this work was only to verify the possibility to functionally asses the joint by using the 3D motion data acquired by using the developed system. In our work we analyzed the shoulder behavior in the very first dynamic of humerus abduction executed on scapular plane, were we specifically defined several SPKIs to characterize the shoulder status. Many works were dedicated to the shoulder assessment [19–22] but none of them concentrate research in the specific initial phase of the shoulder movement as key aspect in dyskinesis identification. As explained in [23], in a non-pathological subject, the scapula start moving when the humerus reaches the 30° of abduction on scapular plane. Always in [23] they high-lighted the fact that the kinematics of the humerus-scapular joint in the first 30° of humerus abduction is very difficult to measure and that the same kinematic behavior is very difficult to standardize. This means that the kinematic behavior of the humerus-scapular joint in the initial motion is very subjective and that would change from subject to subject. On the contrary, the humerus-scapular joint, when humerus abduction is over the 30°, manifests common behavior among all subjects with a constant ratio of around 1-to-2 between the rotation of humerus and scapula [23]. The basic idea is to characterize a similar behavior by using a wide set of SPKIs in order to better address the investigated kinematics. In non-pathological subjects we specifically expected that OWSS and OWSS5 was like those reported in [23] (scapula start moving when the humerus reached the 30° of abduction on scapular plane). On the other hand, in pathological subject we expected that the scapula started mowing just before the humerus reaches 30° of abduction. Moreover, we expect that the humerus-scapular joint kinematics, de-spite the high variability among non-pathological subjects, showed characteristic patterns among pathological subjects. In this work, we marginally considered the behavior of the humerus-scapular joint when the humerus abduction reached values above 30° of abduction. This choice is since, above this value, the kinematic patterns are quite simple, with a maximum static value which identify the overall range of motion. Besides the humerus abduction value with respect to the scapular rotation, this work took also into consideration the relationship between humerus abduction value and the humerus axial rotation. Also, in this case we expected a wide and variable kinematic pattern for non-pathological subjects and a characteristic behavior for pathological subjects, thus giving us the possibility of introducing similar and classifiable behavioral patterns. The problematic relative to the Intraclass Correlation Coefficients (ICC) [24–29] has not been considered in this work and will be subject of future investigation. Herein, to reduce the ICC effects on measured data all the WID setup has been performed by the same person. The results obtained are interesting and demonstrated the feasibility of the proposed solution. From the data discussed in previous sections, these results were somehow unexpected. When we started this work, we were not sure that SPKIs would be able to classify pathological subjects. The asymmetric patterns defined by the SPKIs between pathological and non-pathological sub-jects are extremely evident in the acquired data.

In order to automatically identify the presence of the pathology, by considering at the same time several SPKIs, we are strongly working on the possibility to introduce AI solutions. We recently performed a first and preliminary test using a basic Perceptron based Neural Network (NN) with 5 inputs and a single output (pathologic or non-pathologic subject). The results were extremely promising. Using half of the samples for NN training and half of the sample for the test, we obtained a correct classification score of 90% which means one single error on a set of 22 subjects processed.

# 5  Conclusion

The presented work highlighted how a rapid, comfortable and easy-to-use system can be used in the most clinical setting. The integration of inertial sensors and dedicated mobile app were able to provide reliable information related to the functional assessment of a joint. A paradigmatic application was indeed realized considering the possibility to assess the humerus-scapular joint kinematics and allowing for dyskinesis identification in both symptomatic and asymptomatic cases. The provided system allowed us to design a set of specific kinematic-based parameters, which were extremely discriminative in identifying the presence of any joint pathology. This approach can be easily generalized to further applications and assessments. Future developments will mandatorily focus on the necessity of introducing automatic classification solutions.

# References

1. Roetenberg, D.: Inertial and magnetic sensing of human motion [s.n.], S.l. (2006)
2. Krüger, A., Edelmann-Nusser, J.: Application of a full body inertial measurement system in alpine skiing: a comparison with an optical video based system. J. Appl. Biomech. **26**(4), 516–521 (2010). https://doi.org/10.1123/jab.26.4.516
3. Deppe, O., Dorner, G., König, S., Martin, T., Voigt, S., Zimmermann, S.: MEMS and FOG technologies for tactical and navigation grade inertial sensors-recent improvements and comparison. Sensors **17**(3) (2017). https://doi.org/10.3390/s17030567
4. Avci, A., Bosch, S., Marin Perianu, M., Marin Perianu, R., Havinga, P.J.M.: Activity recognition using inertial sensing for healthcare, wellbeing and sports applications: a survey, pp. 167–176, February 2010
5. Patel, S., Park, H., Bonato, P., Chan, L., Rodgers, M.: A review of wearable sensors and systems with application in rehabilitation. BioMed. Cent. (2012). https://doi.org/10.1186/1743-0003-9-21
6. Sazonov, E., Neuman, M.R. (eds.): Wearable Sensors: Fundamentals, Implementation and Applications. Academic Press is an imprint of Elsevier, Amsterdam (2014)
7. Leonard, K.: Critical success factors relating to healthcare's adoption of new technology: a guide to increasing the likelihood of successful implementation. Electron. Healthc. **2**(4), 72–81 (2004)
8. Ventola, C.L.: Mobile devices and apps for health care professionals: uses and benefits. P T Peer-Rev. J. Formul. Manag. **39**(5), 356–364 (2014)
9. XSENSE DOT, 07 February 2020. https://www.xsens.com/xsens-dot
10. Wearnotch, 07 February 2020. https://wearnotch.com
11. Bencardino, J.T. (ed.): The Shoulder: Imaging Diagnosis with Clinical Implications. Springer, Cham (2019). https://doi.org/10.1007/978-3-030-06240-8
12. Bronzino, J.D., Peterson, D.R.: Biomedical Engineering Fundamentals. CRC Press (2017)
13. Rockwood, C.A.: The shoulder. Saunders/Elsevier, Philadelphia (2009)
14. Ludewig, P.M., Braman, J.P.: Shoulder impingement: biomechanical considerations in rehabilitation. Man. Ther. **16**(1), 33–39 (2011). https://doi.org/10.1016/j.math.2010.08.004
15. Watson, L., Balster, S.M., Finch, C., Dalziel, R.: Measurement of scapula upward rotation: a reliable clinical procedure. Br. J. Sports Med. **39**(9), 599–603 (2005). https://doi.org/10.1136/bjsm.2004.013243
16. McCluskey, G.M., Getz, B.A.: Pathophysiology of anterior shoulder instability. J. Athl. Train. **35**(3), 268–272 (2000)

17. Tate, A.R., McClure, P., Kareha, S., Irwin, D., Barbe, M.F.: A clinical method for identifying scapular dyskinesis, part 2: validity. J. Athl. Train. **44**(2), 165–173 (2009). https://doi.org/10.4085/1062-6050-44.2.165
18. McClure, P., Tate, A.R., Kareha, S., Irwin, D., Zlupko, E.: A clinical method for identifying scapular dyskinesis, part 1: reliability. J. Athl. Train. **44**(2), 160–164 (2009). https://doi.org/10.4085/1062-6050-44.2.160
19. Garofalo, P.: Development of Motion Analysis Protocols Based on Inertial Sensors Healthcare Applications. Lambert Academic Publishing, Saarbrücken (2011)
20. Körver, R.J.P., Senden, R., Heyligers, I.C., Grimm, B.: Objective outcome evaluation using inertial sensors in subacromial impingement syndrome: a five-year follow-up study. Physiol. Measur. **35**(4), 677–686 (2014). https://doi.org/10.1088/0967-3334/35/4/677
21. Hsu, Y.-L., et al.: A wearable inertial-sensing-based body sensor network for shoulder range of motion assessment. In: 2013 1st International Conference on Orange Technologies (ICOT), Tainan, pp. 328–331, March 2013. https://doi.org/10.1109/ICOT.2013.6521225
22. van den Noort, J.C., Wiertsema, S.H., Hekman, K.M.C., Schönhuth, C.P., Dekker, J., Harlaar, J.: Measurement of scapular dyskinesis using wireless inertial and magnetic sensors: importance of scapula calibration. J. Biomech. **48**(12), 3460–3468 (2015). https://doi.org/10.1016/j.jbiomech.2015.05.036
23. Inman, V.T., Saunders, J.B., Abbott, L.C.: Observations of the function of the shoulder joint. Clin. Orthop. (330), 3–12 (1996). https://doi.org/10.1097/00003086-199609000-00002
24. Koo, T.K., Li, M.Y.: A guideline of selecting and reporting intraclass correlation coefficients for reliability research. J. Chiropr. Med. **15**(2), 155–163 (2016). https://doi.org/10.1016/j.jcm.2016.02.012
25. Gallin, J.I., Ognibene, F.P., Johnson, L.L. (eds.): Principles and Practice of Clinical Research, 4th edn. Academic Press, London (2018)
26. Liu, L.: Biostatistical basis of inference in heart failure study. In: Heart Failure: Epidemiology and Research Methods, pp. 43–82. Elsevier (2018)
27. Riffenburgh, R.H.: Statistics in Medicine, 3rd edn. Elsevier/AP, Amsterdam (2012)
28. Hoffman, J.I.E.: Biostatistics for Medical and Biomedical Practitioners. Academic Press, Amsterdam (2015)
29. Laboratory statistics. Elsevier, Waltham (2017)

# Multimodal Wearable System for Motor Rehabilitation - Design Perspective and Development

Paolo Perego[1(✉)], Roberto Sironi[1], Martina Scagnoli[1], Marcello Fusca[1], Emanuele Gruppioni[2], and Angelo Davalli[2]

[1] Design Department, Politecnico di Milano,
via Durando 38/A, 20157 Milan, MI, Italy
paolo.perego@polimi.it

[2] Centro Protesi INAIL, Via Rabuina 14, 40054 Vigorso di Budrio, BO, Italy

**Abstract.** Wearables can ease the transition towards personalized medicine, bringing healthcare to anyone, anytime and anywhere. For wearable devices, human factors are essential; from conception to subsequent design phase. Current solutions are cumbersome and, despite they are designed according to standardized guidelines, they are developed for skilled users (physicians or engineers), without taking into consideration the real actors who will use and wear them: the patients. This paper aims to describe the application of a new methodology for integrating design and technology requirements in the development of wearable systems.

**Keywords:** Wearable devices · Pervasive healthcare · Human-centered design

## 1 Introduction

Population ageing is leading society to rethink and reshaping the healthcare system, bringing care and rehabilitation directly into patient's home, in order to reduce healthcare costs.

Nowadays, wearable devices can offer not intrusive ecological solutions for monitoring people anywhere. Wearable devices can ease the transition from today medicine to a more personalized one, for healthcare to anyone, anytime and anywhere by removing location, time and other restraints, while increasing its coverage, customization and quality [1]. Considering devices which are wearables, the human factors are essential in the entire development process; from conception to subsequent design and finally to the test and production phase.

This paper aims to analyze the different design requirements of a wearable system for personalizing rehabilitation at home, in order to define and apply a new design methodology for developing a modular textile sensing platform suitable to fit a wide range of people. The research outcome is the implementation of a multimodal wearable system for motor rehabilitation based on co-design

P. Perego et al. (Eds.): ICWH 2020, LNICST 376, pp. 99–106, 2021.
https://doi.org/10.1007/978-3-030-76066-3_8

methodology and User-Centred Design principles (e.g. wearability, usability and acceptability) following all the requirements and indications which come from the User Research process.

## 2    Design Methodology for Wearable

### 2.1    User-Centered Design

User-Centred Design (UCD) is an approach commonly used to develop products and solutions by involving human perspective (the users) in all the steps of the process [2].

UCD does not simply force to considers desires, wants and needs of the users, but targets the studies to satisfy needs onto two different levels: functional and emotional.

In order to better investigate the functional and emotional level, UCD defines three general principles:

- *Collaboration*: all the user are involved in all the process.
- *Empathy*: deeply understand desires and motivation which drive the users.
- *Experimentation*: hypothesize and verify this hypothesis experimenting with the users.

These three principles need to be approached using five different interactive stages schematized in Fig. 1.

- Planning: drawing up the entire design process in order to guide developers and users interaction.
- Context of use: collecting information about the intended user (user characteristics, tasks, equipment, interaction, physical and social environment);
- Usage requirements: extracting task which the user perform or should perform while using the product/system;
- Design: developing a first draft of the product/system by means of prototypes;
- Evaluation: involving the user with the prototype in order to understand the strengths and weaknesses of the products/system and re-calibrate the development step.

For each of these stages, Maguire et al. [3] underline specific design methods in order to collect qualitative and quantitative data. Nevertheless, the design methods to be used are strictly related to the product/system topology and purpose. Wearable devices and systems require an ad-hoc method which includes both user and technological aspects, also analyzing connectivity, data analysis and data management aspects.

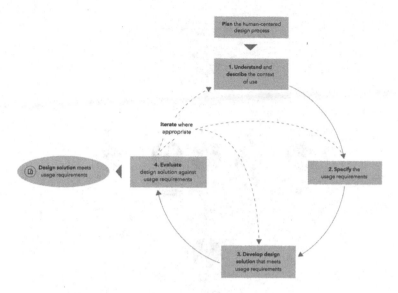

**Fig. 1.** User-centered design process study (ISO/TC 159/SC 4 Ergonomics of human-system interaction [4]

## 2.2 Octopus Methodology

One of the first try in wearable design methodology is Octopus presented by Martin et al. [5].

Octopus methodology is the result of an ad-hoc study which involved different disciplinary actors intending to create an optimal strategy for motion capture (MoCap) wearable product development. Figure 2 shows the representation of the MoCap wearable product/system structure and its ecosystem. Octopus consists into three main areas:

- context: strictly related to UCD first two stages; in this area, environment and users are analysed to extract characteristics and needs both from the technical and emotional sphere.
- device: it consists of the study and development of the material part of the project. Here it is the evaluation of technological aspects, the prototyping and the evaluation of the product/system.
- software: it is the "fluid" part of the product/system, but often the most valuable. It consists of all the algorithm for data analysis and the program for data visualization.

Designing wearable involves different disciplinary actors from medical to engineer and designer. Design methodology for wearable needs to include all these subjects in order to optimize the product/system not only for the user but also for all the actors which intervene in the use of the system, even if only marginally. This is especially true for medical wearable systems in which the

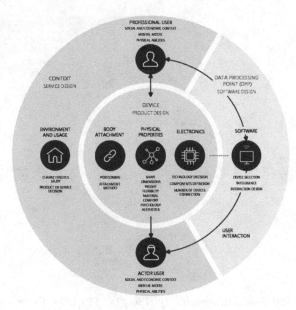

**Fig. 2.** The Octopus methodology [5]

actors related to the use are both patient, physicians and also relatives. Aiming to create a more personalised medicine, removing location, time and other restraints, modern wearable system make use of transmission technologies and internet connection that allow the sharing f medical data and the constant connection with the physician. Moreover, these technologies add some degrees of complexity to the system which, although on the one hand increase the performance of the system [6], on the other it can cause a decrease in usability due to a lack of interaction and experience evaluation. These two main factors have been found during focus groups, during which some subjects highlighted difficulties of daily used connected equipment, due to loss of connection or lack of status feedback. For this reason, Octopus methodology, developed for MoCap wearable product/service design, is not enough and needs and add-ons.

## 3   Evolving Design Methodology and In-Vivo Application

This paper is based on the project Multimodal Wearable (MW), funded by "Centro Protesi" INAIL, one of the research centres of the National Institute for Insurance against Accidents at Work.

The project goal is the design of a wearable system for monitoring and evaluating motor rehabilitation activities in post-stroke patients, with the aim of reintegrating them into the work environment. The core strength of the project is the migration from the classic hospital rehabilitation, to a more personal and personalized at-home rehabilitation, with the aim to improve both the well-being and effectiveness of the treatment.

One of the most import parts of the project has been the design methodology development. Starting from Octopus methodology, MW project evolves it, based on information gathered through focus groups and interviews, adding two other main areas: the communication and the human factor. The evolved methodology has then five main areas:

- users and environment;
- wearable device/s;
- communication and network
- software;
- human factor;

All of these areas, as described below, has been studied by means of specific tools, in order to extract information that have been then applied for the development of the system. Next paragraphs summarise the application of these tools.

## 3.1   User/s and Environment

Wearable itself define a piece of technology which are in close contact with the user's body. For this reason, it seems quite easy to define the context of the study of a system like this, but this applies only to simple commercial devices such as fitness trackers, which do not deal with medical data. Wearable contextualized within telemedicine or pervasive health (in terms of medicine for everyone, regardless of geo-location, timing and personalizing), the context of the study and any servitization became more complex due to the presence of multiple actors which operates with the product/system. For a multi-modal wearable system for motor rehabilitation, two types of users can be defined: professional users and everyday users. Each of these types can contain different sub-categories of users. In order to study all the users and actors, the environment variables and their interaction, the most used methods, suggested by the handbook of human-centred design [2] are Personas and Scenarios. The definition of personas and scenarios allow for the first technologies skimming and the definition of all the users/actors. Thanks to the concrete application of these methods, our approach for wearable devices allow to define two main actors typology:

- Expert or Professional users: who does not directly use the system, but it is involved in the prescription, configuration and installation (e.g. physicians, health workers, engineers...).
- Common users: who really use the system but also relatives which can help using it.

## 3.2   Wearable Device/s

After defining users' types and environment, one of the following steps is the definition of technology. Technologies are strictly related to the interaction with the user and for this reason, choosing which technology to put in place is related to user studies. Ones of the best methods for collecting this information are the focus groups and questionnaires [2]. Applying the method, three design interactions were carried out:

1. two focus groups with all the actors (30 peoples) found during the context study, followed by an ad-hoc paper questionnaire administered of the end-users;
2. design and technical analysis followed by a validation of "fake products" with a panel of users;
3. prototyping and final standardised questionnaires (SUS - QUIS) for acceptability and usability study.

Information gathered by means of focus groups and questionnaires is then used for selecting both proper technologies and interaction methods. In the in-vivo application of the methodology, we divided the technological study into two parts: wearable devices development and smart garment.

Wearable devices development consist in the design of electronics, enclosure and connection with the smart garments; smart garment consists in the design of the garments (based on activities to be analyzed), connection with electronics and embedded sensors. Figure 3 shows the output obtained from the information collected during the activities described above.

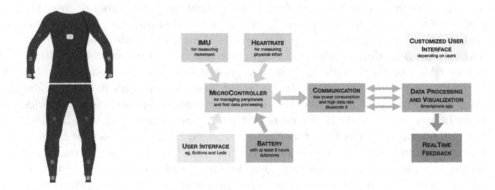

**Fig. 3.** On the left, the sensorised suit structure: the colored squares are the wearable devices; on the right, block diagram of the wearable device

### 3.3   Communication and Network

Figure 3 shows the block diagram of the wearable device. It consists of nine main parts: from the micro-controller to battery management circuit. Ones of the most important parts of the system, related to how user interact with the product, are the communication part and the networking part. The communication encapsulates all the aspects related to user communication of system state, alert, error and data. A product usually implement displays, LEDs, sound, but also wireless communication which allow for product interaction by means of other instrumentation (e.g. personal computer, smartphone...). Moreover, wireless communication can be also used for data communication and recording, both with other wearable device or smartphone/tablet, without user intervention. Although the user is very often marginally involved in the design of these aspects, due to the fact that they are seen as unrelated to the actual use of the system, it is important to consider the analysis of user data and user's feedback in the technological development. In fact, the choice of the technological component and the communication standard can largely influence the usability of the entire system, as underlined by Yaakop et al. [7] who study the usability of Bluetooth 5 technology in the IoT field.

The in-vivo application of this methodology, thanks to information collected from engineers and users during the first phase of the focus group, sees these two parts composed by:

- Communication: devices show status and error by means of one multi-color LED. The only input methods is instead a button (which include the previous LED). Data are shown on the smartphone and tablet. A most accurate status visualization and error management can be done using the smartphone application.
- Network: multiple devices are connected to the same smartphone or tablet via Bluetooth 5. This allows for high speed and compliance, without compromising the normal use of the system forcing the user to long and tedious connection procedures.

### 3.4 Software

Another fundamental part of a wearable system is the software. Software means both the data collection and processing component (the algorithms), and the part of the graphic interface and visualization. User takes part especially in the design of the front-end graphical interface. This is the most sensitive point of the whole system: it is the one with which the user will interact most. For this reason, it is very important to design a stable, minimal and understandable UI: Nielsen heuristics [8] are good practice for this. In our in-vivo application, the software has been tested with users by means of an A/B test [9].

### 3.5 Human Factor

The human factor for wearable devices and system is essential both in terms of wearable device size and position. Size of the devices are highly dependent on the technologies used and the battery; smaller is better, in terms of wearability but too small dimensions can cause usability issue. Moreover, the position of sensors on the human body can cause discomfort under multiple aspects, as described by Zeagler [11]. For this aspect, our in-vivo solution takes into consideration both Zeagler consideration but also biomechanical aspects, studying the best positioning that can optimize both wearability and the biomechanical model performances.

# 4   Conclusion

The promising application of an expanded octopus methodology for the wearable device allows obtaining a system with a good level of acceptance by the users. In-vivo application of the methodology allows developing a new multi-modal suit composed by a sensorised suit and 14 wireless sensors. The results emerged from the qualitative analysis (interviews with users) show that the system has excellent approval ratings from all the actors involved in the rehabilitation process: from users to caregivers and clinicians. The design process, based both on Octopus and User Centred Design, has a continuous iteration between users and designer in order to create an high-level product/system. The next step will be the standardization of the described method and its application to a big scale production wearable system.

# References

1. Varshney, U.: Pervasive Healthcare: Applications, Challenges And Wireless Solutions. Communications of the Association for Information Systems, vol. 16 (2005). https://doi.org/10.17705/1CAIS.01603
2. LUMA Institute: Innovating for People Handbook of Human-Centered Design Methods (2012)
3. Magurie, M.: Methods to support human-centred design. Int. J. Hum. Comput. Stud. **55**(4), 587–634 (2001). https://doi.org/10.1006/ijhc.2001.0503
4. ISO/TC 159/SC 4 Ergonomics of human-system interaction. ISO 9241–210:2019 - Ergonomics of Human-System Interaction - Part 210: Human-Centred Design for Interactive System (2019)
5. Marin, J., Blanco, T., Marin, J.: Octopus: a design methodology for motion capture wearables. Sensors **17**(8), 1875 (2017). https://doi.org/10.3390/s17081875
6. Ho, B.-J.: Modeling Human Engagement State to Lower Cognitive Burden and Increase User Interaction Responsiveness, (Doctoral dissertation, UCLA) (2019)
7. Yaakop, M.B., Malik, I.A.A., Bin Suboh, Z., Ramli, A.F., Abu, M.A.: Bluetooth 5.0 throughput comparison for internet of thing usability a survey. In: 2017 International Conference on Engineering Technology and Technopreneurship (ICE2T), Kuala Lumpur, pp. 1–6 (2017)
8. Nielsen, J.: 10 usability heuristics for user interface design. Nielsen Norman Group, vol. 1, no. 1 (1995)
9. Siroker, D., Koomen, P.: A/B Testing: The Most Powerful way to Turn Clicks into Customers. John Wiley & Sons, Hoboken (2013)
10. Pingel, T.J., Clarke, K.C.: Assessing the usability of a wearable computer system for outdoor pedestrian navigation. Autocarto ACSM **805** (2005)
11. Zeagler, C.: Where to wear it: functional, technical, and social considerations in on-body location for wearable technology 20 years of designing for wearability. In: Proceedings of the 2017 ACM International Symposium on Wearable Computers, pp. 150–157 (2017)

# Innovation by Design

# Quality-by-Design Development of a Patient Mobility e-Monitoring System

Yaël Kolasa[1,2]($\boxtimes$), Eliott Gandiole[1,4], and Thierry Bastogne[1,2,3]

[1] Université de Lorraine, CNRS, CRAN, 54000 Nancy, France
[2] CYBERnano, 54600 Villers-lès-Nancy, France
ykolasa@cybernano.eu
[3] INRIA SIMBA, 54000 Nancy, France
[4] Université de Lorraine, 54000 Nancy, France
https://www.cybernano.eu/

**Abstract.** Wearable sensors are a growing trend within the Internet-of-Things. Their use within many fields, such as e-Health, is more and more common and with such versatility and constraints due to their portable nature, it is important to achieve the best fine-tuning possible for the desired application. To this end, the application of the Quality-by-Design good practices of development could drastically ease the process. This study aims to apply the Quality-by-Design approach to the development of an e-monitoring solution of patient mobility. After defining the profiles of the targeted system, three critical quality attributes: autonomy, data upload duration and data integrity are defined. A criticality assessment study, based on the implementation of specific designs of experiments, is carried out to identify the most impacting process parameters. Finally, suitable operating modalities of the sampling rate, number of sensors, as well as uploading mode and period are determined to comply with the specifications on the three critical quality attributes.

**Keywords:** Quality-by-Design · Internet of Things · Wearable sensors · e-Health

## 1 Introduction

The ever growing use of Internet of Things nowadays has shed light on its potential for healthcare applications. Such versatility also comes with significant downsides that need to be monitored in order to produce an adequate solution. To help define and fine tune a solution to remain within specifications, the Quality by Design development guidelines (ICH Q8-Q12)[1], can be used. Quality by Design (QbD) is a data-driven engineering approach made to assess and control risks of development (being out-of-specifications) at the earliest steps by using appropriate statistical modeling methods. Since mid-2000, QbD has become the main good practices guidelines recommended by ICH (International Council for

---

[1] https://www.ich.org/.

© ICST Institute for Computer Sciences, Social Informatics and Telecommunications Engineering 2021
Published by Springer Nature Switzerland AG 2021. All Rights Reserved
P. Perego et al. (Eds.): ICWH 2020, LNICST 376, pp. 109–121, 2021.
https://doi.org/10.1007/978-3-030-76066-3_9

Harmonisation of technical requirements for pharmaceuticals for human use) for drug development [1,2]. Similar risk-based development approaches was previously applied to control quality and safety during the whole product lifecycle such as the Total Quality Management in the United States Navy [3] and Six Sigma used by Motorola [4] in mid-1980, but also Lean Management [5] in mid-1990. QbD has introduced the concept of "Design Space": a probabilistic map of quality and safety risks in the space of process parameters, which allows developers (i) to identify which are the most critical parameters to be controlled and (ii) to determine which are the normal operating regions in which critical parameters have to belong.

In this study, we assess the applicability of the first steps of the QbD workflow to the safe development of a patient mobility e-monitoring solution based on wearable inertial motion units. Indeed the QbD concept was initially proposed for drug development and our objective is to examine its applicability to implement a rational design of medical devices and more particularly e-Health systems. We firstly present the Quality-by-Design cycle before applying the first steps to our study case, and finally presenting and discussing the application results.

## 2    Method

### 2.1    Quality-by-Design Approach

Quality by Design (QbD) is a risk-based engineering approach that aims at reducing cost and time of development by minimizing additional unexpected resources not already allocated. The QbD workflow can be sum up by a cycle decomposed into eight key steps but only the first five ones were implemented in this study case.

1. The first step of QbD is to define the Quality Target Product Profile (QTPP): a dynamic summary of the expected quality features regarding the future product [6]. This proactive document can include the technical and economical characteristics of the future product. This document has to be updated throughout the development process. It is intended for all the stakeholders: management, board members, advisors, investors, regulatory authorities and strategic partners.
2. The second step aims at defining the Critical Quality Attributes (CQA) of the product. A CQA is a physical, chemical, biological or microbiological property or characteristics that should be within an appropriate range to ensure the desired product "quality" [6]. Multiple methods can be used to assess criticality of quality attributes. For instance, Summary Risk Chart can allow the identification of CQA with a simple traffic light color indicating the rank of the criticality (red for critical, amber for potentially critical and green for non-critical). The FMEA method (Failure Mode & Effects Analysis) is another possible method to evaluate criticality of quality attribute.
3. In the third step, critical Material Attributes and Process Parameters are identified. They correspond to design and manufacturing factors, which have

a significant effect on the critical quality attributes. They should be monitored or controlled to ensure that CQA specifications are fulfilled. A common tool used to enumerate all risk factors is the Ishikawa diagram.

4. A criticality assessment of process parameters is performed in a fourth step to identify the main active system parameters to focus on. Screening design of experiments such a Taguchi or Plackett-Burman designs are often implemented to that aim [6]. They allow to reduce a lot the number of experiments to be carried out and to rank their effects in a Pareto diagram as illustrated in Fig. 1.

5. The mathematical relationship between critical quality attributes (outputs) and critical process parameters (inputs) is identified in a fifth step in which specific experimental designs such as central composite, Box-Behnken and Doehlert are implemented to collect informative data with a parsimonious number of trials. In practice, response surface models are used to describe those relationships. This type of model allows us to perform prediction, optimization and to compute a Design Space, *i.e.* a diagram composed of four regions of probability:
   - the Out Of Specification (OOS) region - outlines the region where the quality product is not acceptable and thus necessitates investigations in order to highlight the reasons of unacceptance;
   - the Proven Acceptance Region (PAR) – depicts the region where an acceptable product can be produced but where some adjustments should be done to access the NOR;
   - the Normal Operating Region (NOR) – represents the desired region where the quality product has a high degree of probability to comply with the quality specifications;
   - the Control Operating Region (COR) - a subregion of NOR in which a control strategy has to maintain the operating point.

   A design space can be regarded as a map locating the operating region of quality.

6. The sixth step introduces process analytical technology (PAT) to measure on-line critical attributes and process parameters. PAT often relies on process analyzers and sensors to inform in real-time about the location of the operating point within the Design Space.

7. The feedback information provided by PAT is necessary to implement a control strategy able to maintain the operating point within the COR region of the design space whatever the fluctuation of background variables. Statistical Process Control and Bayesian Process Control are two examples of strategy often used in practice to solve that technical issue [6].

8. The last step of QbD concerns the Data Management. All the manufacturing data can be stored in a large database, which can be used *a posteriori* to refine the working hypothesis and help to continuously improve the product quality.

In this application, only the first five steps are implemented since our objective is firstly to establish the proof of concept for the e-monitoring system. Moreover, since most of the system parameters are categorical, the determination of

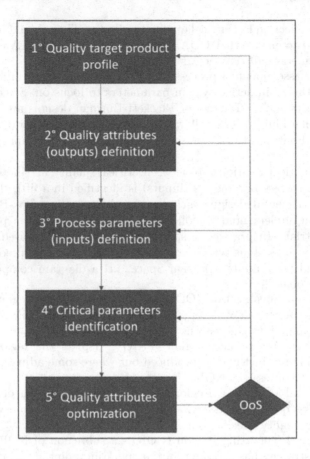

**Fig. 1.** Quality-by-Design methodology (OoS: Out of Specification)

a Design Space is not necessary since we can directly identify their optimal modalities.

## 2.2  Quality Target Product Profile

**Intended Application.** The system to be developed aims at collecting, monitoring and characterizing the mobility of patients for targeted applications such as electronic Clinical Outcome Assessment (eCOA), Adapted Physical Activity (APA) or homecare monitoring. Targeted patients can be involved in clinical studies, or people with chronic conditions as well as elderly persons. The wearable sensor can be worn on the waist (belt), the wrist (bracelet), the foot (shoes) or on the ankle. The environment in which the device shall be used is the patient's home but could also be used in an hospital, a clinic or a retirement residence.

**Materials.** The test subject was equipped with one wearable inertial sensor at his belt. We used a MetaMotionR sensor developed by Mbientlab Inc, as seen in

Fig. 2. This technology is composed of a BMI160 6-axis Accelerometer + Gyroscope, a BMM150 3-axis Magnetometer, a BOSCH 9-axis Sensor Fusion, a 8 MB Flash Memory and a lithium-ion rechargeable battery. 9 signals (accelerometry, gyrometry and magnetometry) were measured during each run. The Metabase mobile application proposed by Mbientlab was used to collect the experimental data. The design of experiments and the data analysis were performed in the R statistical computing environment.

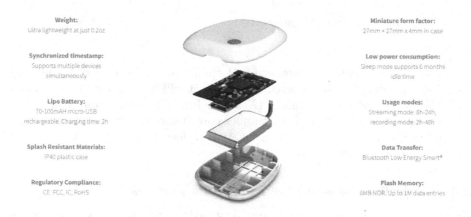

**Fig. 2.** MetaMotionR sensor (Mbientlab)

## 2.3   Critical Quality Attributes

To make such a patient mobility e-monitoring possible, some technical properties are critical such as the memory of the wearable sensor, and its autonomy. Another important quality criterion deals with the data integrity. Indeed, for a good monitoring of the patient mobility, it is critical to minimize data loss. Since no measurement is possible during the data uploading process, the duration of data transfer is also identified as a critical quality attribute. As a consequence, six critical quality attributes noted $Y_1$ to $Y_6$, have been defined in the Table 1 with their desired specifications. The memory should hold up to at least 30 min of data, the battery must power up the sensor for at least 16 h, the data uploading duration shall not exceed 30% of the data uploading period and the data integrity shall be greater than 80%.

## 2.4   Identification of Process Parameters

The definition of Process Parameters is done in the third items of Fig. 1. A cause-effect (Ishikawa) diagram is used for each CQA to list all the potential causes that could affect the quality attributes of the medical device [7]. Causes are usually grouped into major categories to identify and classify these sources of variation.

**Table 1.** Critical quality attributes

| Variable | Factor | Unit | Specification |
|----------|--------|------|---------------|
| $Y_1$ | Memory | Time | >30 min |
| $Y_2$ | Autonomy | Time | >16 h |
| $Y_3$ | Data uploading duration/Data uploading period | % | <30 |
| $Y_4$ | Data integrity (Accelerometry) | % | >80 |
| $Y_5$ | Data integrity (Gyrometry) | % | >80 |
| $Y_6$ | Data integrity (Magnetometry) | % | >80 |

Among all the listed factors, some of them cannot be controlled and are therefore considered as disturbances. Their effect will be described by a random variable in the risk analysis model ($E(k)$) in Eq. 1. The remaining factors are split up into two groups: the factors under consideration will be gathered to be studied in the next step while the estimated irrelevant parameters will be kept constant during the experiments.

## 2.5   Criticality Assessment of Process Parameters

The parameters under consideration identified at the previous step are all involved in a criticality assessment process involving both a full factorial design of experiments and t-tests [6,8]. This analysis relies on an ANOVA model described as follows:

$$Y_i(k) = b_0 + b_{1B}u_{1B}(k) + \cdots + b_{pB}u_{pB}(k) + E(k), \tag{1}$$

with:

- $Y_i(k)$: measured value of the $i - th$ CQA during trial $k$
- each factor $u$ takes two modalities: $A$ and $B$.
- $b_0$: mean response when all factors takes their reference level (A).
- $b_{1B}$: additive effect of factor 1 when it takes its level B.
- $b_{pB}$: additive effect of factor $p$ when it takes its level B.
- $E(k) \sim \mathcal{E}(0, \sigma^2)$: random variable describing the experimental modeling residuals.
- Variance $\sigma^2$ represents the inter-assay variability.

An ANOVA estimator was used to determine the model coefficients: $b$ (factor effects) from the collected data on the response: $Y_i$. After the estimation step, a t-test is applied to each model coefficient to assess its statistical relevance, *i.e.* the criticality of the associated factor effect:

$$\begin{cases} H_0: & b_i = 0 \\ H_1: & b_i \neq 0. \end{cases} \tag{2}$$

At total seven factors were tested in this study:

**Table 2.** Factors under consideration in the different tests carried out in this study. AGM: Accelerometer/Gyrometer/Magnetometer. STR: streaming and STO: data storage on sensor.

| Notation | Factor | Unit | Level 1 | Level 2 | Level 3 |
|---|---|---|---|---|---|
| $u_1$ | Sampling rate | Hz | Low frequency | High frequency | |
| $u_2$ | Nb of sensors | – | AG | AGM | |
| $u_3$ | Data upload mode | – | STR | STO | |
| $u_4$ | Data uploading period | min | 15 | 60 | |
| $u_5$ | Bluetooth mode | – | ON | OFF during 1 h | |
| $u_6$ | Sensor/mobile phone distance | m | <5 m | >10 m | |
| $u_7$ | Wall type | – | None | Thin | Thick |

**Tests on Autonomy and Memory Operating Duration.** The risks of having the autonomy of the sensor and the memory duration not meeting the expectation would be the loss of data collected by the device and therefore a lesser quality of diagnostic afterwards. Factors under consideration for the criticality assessement associated with the memory operating time are $u_1$, $u_2$ and $u_3$. The implemented experimental protocol consists in testing the most extreme combination of factors, *i.e.* $u_1$: high frequency, $u_2$: three sensors AGM and $u_3$ in storage mode.

**Tests on Upload Time.** Factors under consideration for the criticality assessement associated with the upload time are presented in Table 2. The $2^3$ full factorial design of Memory tests is composed of eight different experimental conditions, each one duplicated once, and is presented in Table 3. We can see in the Table 3 the three critical parameters that are to be tested, with the first being the sampling frequency of the sensors: $u_1$. This parameter is thought to heavily impact the autonomy and the memory availability of the device. The second is the number of sensors: $u_2$. We can see in the Table 2 the characteristics of the different sensors available on the chip. Each one of them have a minimum and a maximum frequency which will also determine the electric consumption of the sensor, and the volume of data generated. Furthermore, the accelerometer and gyrometer (AG) are either both set to work, or the additional magnetometer (AGM) can be added. The accelerometer and the gyrometer are both needed to have coherent data, the magnetometer adds useful but optional data. A third sensor will also add to the electric consumption and data generation of the system. The last parameter is the data uploading period: either 1 or 4 upload sessions every hour.

**Tests on Data Integrity.** Factors under consideration for the criticality assessement associated with data integrity are: $u_5$, $u_6$ and $u_7$ defined in Table 2. They are involved in a $2^3$ full factorial design composed of eight different experimental conditions and is presented in Table 4.

# 3   Results

## 3.1   Criticality Assessment of the Sensor Autonomy (Battery Duration)

The Ishikawa diagram of the battery duration is presented in Fig. 3(a). It shows the potential factors that may affect the sensor autonomy. Among them, three parameters, given in Table 2 were selected. One experiment was carried out in extreme condition, *i.e.* by using three sensors (Accelerometer + Gyrometer + Magnetometer), each at high sampling frequency (25 Hz, 50 Hz, 25 Hz) and with a local data recording on the inertial motion unit. After 22 h of operation, the battery charge level was still at 53%. In other terms, even in this critical configuration, the battery duration is enough to comply with the desired application.

**Table 3.** Full factorial design applied to the data upload duration

| $u_1$ | $u_2$ | $u_4$ | $Y_3(\%)$ |
|-------|-------|-------|-----------|
| BF | AGM | 15 | 41.67 |
| BF | AG | 60 | 25.56 |
| HF | AGM | 15 | 39.78 |
| HF | AG | 15 | 36.00 |
| HF | AGM | 60 | 26.00 |
| HF | AG | 60 | 25.28 |
| BF | AG | 60 | 23.25 |
| BF | AGM | 60 | 24.58 |
| BF | AG | 15 | 32.22 |
| HF | AG | 60 | 26.67 |
| BF | AGM | 60 | 26.61 |
| BF | AG | 15 | 37.33 |
| BF | AGM | 15 | 53.78 |
| HF | AG | 15 | 48.11 |
| HF | AGM | 15 | 36.44 |
| HF | AGM | 60 | 23.17 |

## 3.2   Criticality Assessment of the Memory Operating Duration

If storage capacity cannot withhold all data generated within a session, the oldest data would be lost to the newest ones, thus lowering the quality of the data analysis once they are transferred. New data could also partially replace some old data, thus giving unreadable data that are still stored and taking place on the storage. The Ishikawa diagram of the Memory Operating duration is presented in Fig. 3(b). It shows the potential factors that may affect this quality operating attribute. As previously, the three parameters; $u_1$, $u_2$ and $u_3$ were

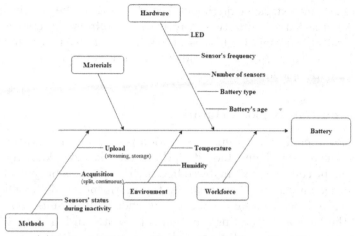

*(a)* List of Factors affecting the Battery Duration

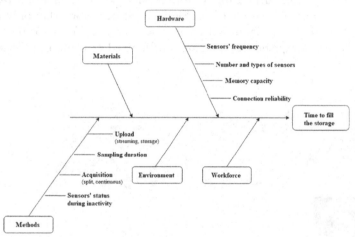

*(b)* List of Factors affecting the Memory Storage

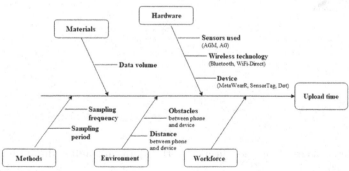

*(c)* List of Factors affecting the Data Uploading Duration

**Fig. 3.** Ishikawa diagrams of three critical quality attributes.

tested and the same extreme experimental condition than the one implemented before to test the battery duration were used to address the question of the memory operating duration. In this case, the sensor memory was saturated after 1 h 26. As a consequence, we have decided to fix the duration upload period to 30 min (i.e. 2 data upload session/h).

## 3.3   Risks on Data Upload Duration

The risks encountered on data upload duration is to miss an important motion event during the period of time. Indeed, the longer it takes to upload the data, the fewer data can be collected and analyzed because the device is busy sending them instead of collecting them. Thus, lowering the pertinence and the efficiency of the analysis algorithm. This can, at the end, provide faulty results. The Ishikawa diagram of the Memory Operating duration is presented in Fig. 3(c). Three specific factors were more particularly tested: $u_1$, $u_2$ and $u_4$. To that aim, the full factorial design presented in Table 3, were implemented. Estimation results are presented in the Pareto diagram of the Fig. 4. It clearly shows that only $u_4$ (Data Uploading Period) has a significant effect. Increasing $u_4$ from 15 min to 60 min lowers $Y_3$. As a consequence, this factor will be fixed at 60 min in the sequel.

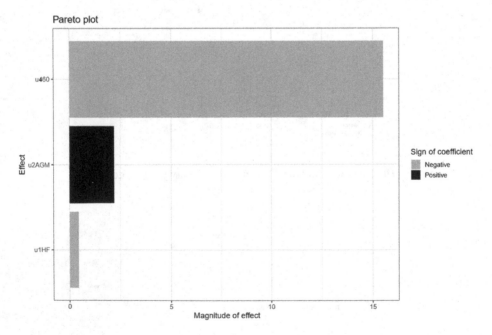

**Fig. 4.** Pareto diagram of the effects on the data uploading duration. P-values: 8.51e−05; 0.427; 0.871.

## 3.4   Risks on Data Integrity

If data integrity is not ensured, because of a lack of battery life or storage capacity, the analysis cannot take place, or could produce erroneous results. Nevertheless, four experimental conditions were not able to be carried out in the environment we had to conduct the trials. The observation dataset is given in Table 4. Responses can be greater than 100%, in that case, it means that the sensor saved several times some pieces of data after transmissions interruptions. 100% corresponds to a perfect continuous communication without loss. Three specific factors were tested to estimate their effect on Data Integrity: $u_5$, $u_6$ and $u_7$. To that aim, the fractional factorial design presented in Table 4, were implemented.

## 3.5   Integrity of Accelerometer Data

The estimated effects of each factor are presented in Fig. 5(a). Only the first two effects were significant (t-test: $p = 0.0077$ and $p = 0.042$ respectively). We can see that the most impacting factor is $u_6$, which implies that the further the smartphone is from the sensor, the lesser the communication is. We can also see that when the factor $u_5$ is OFF, $i.e.$ when the Bluetooth mode is inactive, the response is better. $u_7$ has no significant effect on the integrity of accelerometric data.

## 3.6   Integrity of Gyrometer Data

The estimated effects of each factor are presented in Fig. 5(b). The first two effects were almost significant (t-test: $p = 0.071$ and $p = 0.078$ respectively). We

**Table 4.** Full Factorial Design and experimental data for the Data Integrity Test. $u_5$: bluetooth mode (ON: normal/OFF: no bluebooth at the first connection but switched on and re-connection after 1 h). $u_6$: sensor/mobile phone distance (<5 m; >10 m). $u_7$: wall type (no wall, "Cloison" = thin wall, "Porteur" = thick concrete wall) $Y_4$: % data for accelerometer. $Y_5$: % data for gyrometer. $Y_6$: % data for magnetometer.

| $u_5$ | $u_6$ | $u_7$ | $Y_4$ | $Y_5$ | $Y_6$ |
|-------|-------|-------|----------|-----------|----------|
| ON | L5 | None | 188.4077 | 26.427058 | 195.5040 |
| ON | L5 | Thin | 195.5083 | 25.893829 | 195.4962 |
| OFF | L5 | None | 333.3137 | 43.178598 | 333.4007 |
| ON | L5 | Thick | 196.6234 | 7.207227 | 196.5224 |
| ON | G10 | Thick | 0.0000 | 0.000000 | 0.0000 |
| ON | G10 | Thick | 0.0000 | 0.000000 | 0.0000 |
| OFF | L5 | Thin | 378.3933 | 51.097817 | 378.3866 |
| OFF | L5 | Thick | 378.3481 | 51.059389 | 378.1941 |
| OFF | G10 | Thick | 0.0000 | 0.000000 | 0.0000 |

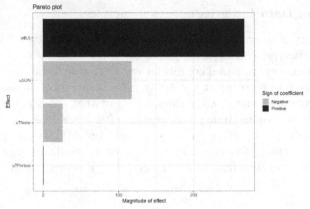

*(a)* Effects on the accelerometry response

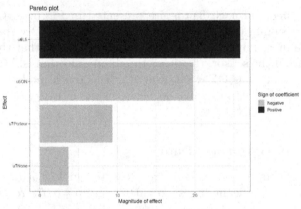

*(b)* Effects on the gyrometry response

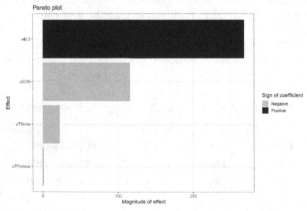

*(c)* Effects on the magnetometry response

**Fig. 5.** Pareto diagrams of the effects of three factors ($u_5$: bluetooth mode; $u_6$ sensor/mobile phone distance; $u_7$: wall type) on the three motion responses.

can see that, as for the accelerometer, the most impacting factor is $u_6$, which implies that the farther the smartphone is from the sensor, the lesser the communication is. We can also see that when the factor $u_5$ is inactive, the response is better. As previously, $u_7$ has no significant impact on the integrity of gyrometric data.

### 3.7 Integrity of Magnetometer Data

The estimated effects of each factor are presented in Fig. 5(c). Only the first two effects were significant (t-test: $p = 0.0075$ and $p = 0.043$ respectively). Conclusions are the same than the ones already drawn in the two previous sections.

## 4 Conclusion

This study confirms the relevance of the Quality by Design approach to identify critical factors of development and to analyze their effect on the quality responses of a medical device. In this application, QbD allowed us to find suitable operating modalities such as: sampling frequency, uploading mode and period as well as the possible number of sensors to activate. It also emphasized the possibility to work in an environment composed of several types of wall within a 5-m radius from the mobile phone. This test also stressed the ability of the proposed solution to recover data after a long (>1 h) period of connection loss.

Further studies on the performances of this application with the integration of a Blockchain solution for greater data integrity are on the way, to completely analyze and fine tune the solution using Quality-by-Design. It will then help to define sturdy Blockchain solutions for e-health innovative solutions.

## References

1. European Medicines Agency, ICH Q8 (r2) pharmaceutical development (2009)
2. Bastogne, T.: Quality-by-design of nanopharmaceuticals - a state of the art. Nanomed. Nanotechnol. Biol. Med. **13**(7), 2151–2157 (2017)
3. McDaniel, D.M., Doherty, L.M.: Total quality management case study in a navy headquarters organization (1990)
4. Pyzdek, T.: The Six Sigma. McGraw-Hill Education, New York (2003)
5. Womack, J.P., Jones, D.T., Roos, D.: The Machine that Changed the World: The Story of Lean Production-Toyota's Secret Weapon in the Global Car Wars that is Now Revolutionizing World Industry. Simon and Schuster, New York (2007)
6. Lewis, G.A., Mathieu, D., Phan-Tan-Luu, R.: Pharmaceutical Experimental Design. Marcel Dekker, New York (2005)
7. Wong, K.C.: Using an Ishikawa diagram as a tool to assist memory and retrieval of relevant medical cases from the medical literature (2011)
8. Lawson, J.: Design and Analysis of Experiments with R. CRC Press, Boca Raton (2015)

# Wear-to-Care. Co-designing the Next Wave of Open Wearables in the Healthcare Sector

Massimo Bianchini[1], Patrizia Bolzan[1(✉)], Barbaras Parini[1], Stefano Maffei[1], and Filippo Cipriani[2]

[1] Department of Design, Politecnico di Milano, Milan, Italy
patrizia.bolzan@polimi.it
[2] Sanofi Genzyme, Milan, Italy

**Abstract.** The paper explores the topic of design, materialization and release of open source wearables that can increase awareness about the mental, behavioral and physical conditions of people with health impairments. The first part, which is based on literature review, investigates the design of healthcare wearables connected to the emerging phenomena of open and user innovation. The second part describes the whole process of design and materialization of DermAware, an open source "experiential" wearable developed within the project Distributed Design Market Platform (Creative Europe Programme) and specifically conceived to increase the social awareness on a pathology such as Atopic Dermatitis. The final part defines an operational framework to design open source wearables, evidencing the process - from design to materialization – and the main critical aspects and opportunities related to the development of "experiential" devices. The conclusions of the paper identify a possible field for designing healthcare wearables called "Wear-to-Care".

**Keywords:** Open innovation · Interaction design · Smart wearables · Atopic dermatitis · Disease awareness · Patient advocacy

## 1 Introduction

Nowadays, wearables such as smartbands, wristbands, and smartwatches are designed to capture and monitor human activity parameters and to display such data and information. Characterized by a rapidly accelerating technological evolution, the market of smart wearables is constantly growing, and their fields of application are constantly expanding (Fig. 1). Within this emerging global market, the market share represented by smart devices dedicated to diagnostics and medical treatment is also growing. Finally, a specific segment dedicated to healthcare consumer wearables is beginning to appear.

On an industrial level, design and production of consumer and specialized wearables is currently characterized by three main aspects. Firstly, the majority of these smart devices are conceived with a top-down design logic and therefore not designed through explicit co-design and user processes. These tools are designed to enable personal use

© ICST Institute for Computer Sciences, Social Informatics and Telecommunications Engineering 2021
Published by Springer Nature Switzerland AG 2021. All Rights Reserved
P. Perego et al. (Eds.): ICWH 2020, LNICST 376, pp. 122–138, 2021.
https://doi.org/10.1007/978-3-030-76066-3_10

but cannot be customized according to personal needs, different from those for which they are conceived. Secondly, these devices are equipped with industrial components and "proprietary" software far from open source logic applied to design, hardware and software. In practice for these products there is no release of digital files and code. Finally, the majority of consumer wearables can record data to provide basic diagnostics (e.g. heartbeat, pressure, temperature, sleep cycles,…) while medical wearables are mainly conceived for a professional use. On the contrary, are not so common cases of wearables designed to release physical inputs, enabling and stimulating users to have alternative sensorial experiences. Irrespective of the prevalence of the disease, there is the need for new experiences enabling new forms of health literacy, disease awareness, and patient advocacy. Currently, this need is weakly satisfied by smart wearables on the market since they are not co-designed with patients.

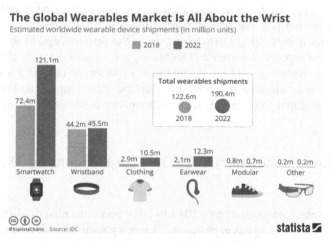

**Fig. 1.** The global wearables market is all about the wrist (source: Statista)

Starting from this assumption, the paper aims to explore wearables designed to improve physical and social interactivity needs of people with disabilities or health impairment - which are influenced by *open* and *user innovation* cultures - developed through a co-design approach, manufactured through open and distributed production processes.

Through the design perspective, the paper defines as "Wear-to-Care" this area of participatory and bottom-up innovation for the development of smart wearables, proposing to address to the following research questions:

1. *What are the key elements that define Wear-to-Care as an approach and innovation process?*
2. *What functional, performance and perceptive characteristics do Wear-to-care wearables have or must have?*
3. *What is the process of design-production and distribution that characterizes Wear-To-Care devices?*

The paper aims to create an initial framework on the design of open source "Wear-to-Care" wearables, focus on a specific case study related to a pilot research initiative: DermAware, an open source device specifically designed to increase the social awareness about the mental, behavioral and physical conditions of people with Atopic Dermatitis (AD), still underestimated today [9]. DermAware has been developed in 2018 within FabCare, an experimental initiative part of the Distributed Design Market[1] project (Creative Europe Platform Programme), thanks to the collaboration, in Italy, between Sanofi Genzyme[2] and Polifactory, respectively the specialty care unit of Sanofi and the Fab Lab of the Politecnico di Milano. DermAware is an open source wearable device that does not track or capture information but, on the contrary, faithfully simulates the uncontrolled sensation of constant itching that is the hallmark of AD. The first part of this paper combines literature review and a short selection of case studies in order to explore the evolution in the design of healthcare wearables connected to the phenomenon of patient innovation and supported by the democratization of open source design and distributed digital manufacturing [2]. The second part of the paper describes the whole process of designing and materializing DermAware, from the first concept, to the subsequent reflections on the aspects of design and technology, up to the usability characteristics connected to the pathology and the desired user experience. The third and final part attempts to elaborate a framework highlighting all the critical aspects and opportunities related to the development of devices such as DermAware, within the emerging field of "Wear-to-Care".

## 2    Healthcare Evolutionary Paths and Implications for Wearables Design

A multiyear research conducted from 2017 to 2019 by Politecnico di Milano[3] entitled MakeToCare[4] (MTC) [3, 4] has explored the emerging socio-technical transformations within the healthcare sector. MTC describes an area of convergence that begins from the interaction between the official healthcare sector, making and new manufacturing and patients as carriers of innovation needs. The research, in fact, begins from the assumption of a deep transformation of the contemporary healthcare sector. A preliminary literature review highlighted the following research topics:

---

[1] distributeddesign.eu.

[2] www.sanofigenzyme.com.

[3] The research has been promoted by Fondazione Politecnico and Sanofi Genzyme and coordinated and developed by Polifactory the makerspace FabLab of Politecnico di Milano (www.polifactory.polimi.it).

[4] MakeToCare (www.maketocare.it) is a research initiative that was born as a spin-off of the first edition of the homonymous contest organized in 2016 by Sanofi Genzyme, on the occasion of the European Maker Faire in Rome. MakeToCare aims to identify, map and represent an emerging ecosystem made up of innovative patients, independent researchers, research institutions, startups and new entrepreneurs, makers, and laboratories for digital manufacturing that work on the development of concrete design solutions capable of improving daily life and the health of people living with disabilities. The research, still ongoing, has mapped 180 subjects and 150 solutions developed in Italy.

- *healthcare tailored to an aging population.* It analyzes aging from the perspective of its social implications on an individual and collective levels (impact on patient and caregivers and social sustainability of welfare);
- *healthcare for the new generations (between prevention and prediction).* It concerns the digital transformation of healthcare, the virtualization of medicine, new forms of health literacy, and new levels of knowledge and awareness of the human body from external manifestations to genetic structures;
- *healthcare on a metropolitan scale.* It concerns the increasing concentration of population in the cities seen from the new perspectives of citizens-patients and the perspective of the healthcare system;
- *technologically enabled and enhanced healthcare.* It concerns the technological development that 'enhance/augment' persons and products-service systems for care changing the body's limits and barriers, and extensions of the objects and care environments. In that sense, disability can be 'simply' considered as a gap between the person and the environment, a situation that can be reduced or closed with design-focused interventions.

Starting to consider this general framework of transformation, a relevant aspect can be considered: the role of the patient and the impact generated by his engagement in an extended and inclusive way. It is the patient (r)evolution: from *human factor* to *human actor* within innovation processes. Starting from this statement, we can identify grassroots innovation models where the patient is the activator or where there is an open and participatory activity between patients and other subjects with different expertise. Moreover, these evolved forms of user participation foster the rise of the *patient-innovator* and *user-driven healthcare* [5–7]. Platforms like patientlikeme.com, patientinnovation.org, and careables.org are initiatives that operationally and socially support patient innovation. Patients were for a long time considered primarily the passive recipients of the processes of innovation proposed by public and private healthcare systems or by healthcare sector companies, i.e. the providers of products and services.

Nowadays, cultural globalization and democratization of enabling technologies make people increasingly informed and socially connected to assert themselves in different fields and sectors. A greater knowledge, combined with growing awareness and supported by the new production possibilities offered by digital manufacturing such as personal fabrication, have gradually transformed the patient not only into an element at the center of the innovation process, but often the trigger of the whole process. This is the so-called Patient Innovator (PI), an actor who actively works in the field of designing and materializing products and services to solve a personal problem, often self-producing solutions to improve his condition. Often the new wearables are born precisely in similar contexts. It is undeniable that the development of wearable devices in the healthcare sector is following two parallel directions that are destined to converge. On one hand, there are devices designed and used for purely medical purposes, with functions ranging from pharmacological therapies to specialized biometric monitoring (such as insulin pump, artificial pancreas, cardiac holter), whose purposes from diagnostics to tests to postoperative follow-up. On the other hand, there is an evolution of wearables for digital well-being, equipped with a number of sensors capable of performing an increasingly accurate biometric monitoring on the state of health and well-being of the person, then returning it in the form of raw data or aggregated information (even alerts) thanks to dedicated smartphone applications. A clear example in this direction is represented by the evolution of the Apple Watch [8].

Next to "top-down" wearables, born in the industrial sector with declared commercial purposes or within research centers as tools of investigation and analysis, we are witnessing the progressive appearance of wearables that we might better define as "bottom-up". These are often devices born from the intuition of subjects (individuals or small design teams) in response to specific needs (own or others), as shown by the MTC research, which since 2017 has investigated open and user innovation (especially bottom-up) within the healthcare sector in Italy. The MTC research shows how more and more often we are witnessing the development and implementation of wearables capable of supporting users in better managing pathology and/or disability. Two specific cases (on a total of 150 initially mapped) have been extracted from MakeToCare to support this analysis: ABBI K and Sensewear. Although these two wearables are very different in terms of design process, scopes and subjects involved, in both cases they have been designed to release data and information not only in visual form, but also through physical inputs, providing a sensory experience to the user. On the one hand, the Italian Institute of Technology (IIT) project developed starting from a European research aimed at developing devices for the rehabilitation of subjects with visual impairment. On the other hand, the project developed by a young startup, Witsense, born from the union of the technological skills of a company specialized in wearable biomedical systems with the vision of a design studio.

ABBI K[5] is a kit for the assessment and rehabilitation of children with visual impairments. Thanks to a sound bracelet, kids can associate movements with acoustic feedback, which provides them with the opportunity to perceive their movements in a more appropriate way and develop skills to move and play within the space. Sensewear is an inclusive collection of garments and accessories that emphasize the use of senses. It is in fact a sensitized set of garments clothing line that, reacting to changes in some vital parameters, allows children with autism and/or communicative-relational difficulties to communicate their moods and reach a condition of comfort. The Sensewear collection is inspired by therapies applied to Sensory Processing Disorders and developed with the technical support of therapists assisting people affected with autism.

---

[5] ABBI K is developed by Unit for Visually Impaired People of IIT (www.iit.it/research/lines/unit-for-visually-impaired-people); the main aim of the Unit is to early identify spatial impairments that impact life of visually disabled people and build innovative solutions to prevent the risk of developmental delays.

In terms of maturity, ABBI K has completed the testing, verification and final implementation phases and is preparing to become a commercial product in all respects, distributed via spin off by the Italian Institute of Technology itself; Sensewear has concluded the second phase of prototyping. The last version of the collection includes SenseMe, a smart t-shirt that monitors heartbeat, breath rate and movement, sending data to an application that records sessions and triggers other garments' functionality according to adjustable values. Two pieces from the previous collection have been further developed and upgraded with tech.

Within this scenario is precisely placed the DermAware project, a wearable device which integrates an unprecedented concept. In fact, DermAware combines the common capability of many wearables in providing feedback to better manage a pathology with a new dimension related to the awareness and communication of the pathology, not only by the "user-patient" but also and above all by the entire formal and informal caregiving system surrounding him (Fig. 2 and 3).

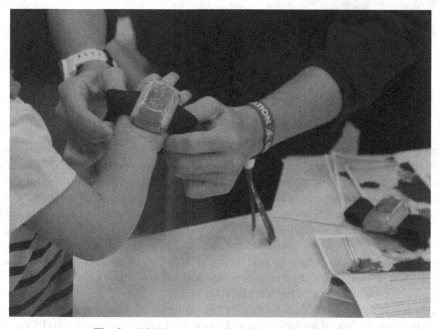

**Fig. 2.** *Abbi K* (photo credit: L. Taverna © 2017IIT)

**Fig. 3.** *Sensewear* (photo credit: Witsense srl).

## 3  The DermAware Project

### 3.1  Designing for the Atopic Dermatitis

General definitions provided by national patient association like Associazione Nazionale Dermatite Atopica (ANDeA, Italy) and National Eczema Association (NEA, US) describe Atopic Dermatitis as the most common type of eczema. AD is a chronic skin disease characterized by intense itching, dry skin, the appearance of diffuse redness and blisters on different areas of the body. It is a non-contagious chronic-frequent inflammatory dermatosis that alternates periods of exacerbation and remission, mainly affecting hands, feet, inner fold of the elbow and the rear fold of the knees, wrists, ankles, face, neck and chest, but also present around the eyes. Although its onset is often associated with the first years of life, with an incidence that is around 10–20% of children and 2–8% of adults (in most countries of the world) [10–12].

AD has a strong impact on quality of life in terms of recurrent skin infections, sleep disturbances, social relationships and work productivity. According to literature, children with AD present emotional-relational difficulties: low self-esteem, behavioral and attachment disorders. Adolescents and adults with AD present severe difficulties in interpersonal relationships (also caused by bullying phenomena), personal insecurity, and increasing stress levels, anxiety and depressive symptoms [12–14]. To date there is no definitive cure capable of leading to a complete recovery from AD. Patients must therefore "learn" to coexist with this pathology and manage it with daily tricks that can help alleviate its symptoms and prolong the phases of remission. Special soap-free products, appropriate clothing and the systematic use of emollient creams formulated specifically for sensitive skin are all elements that can mitigate the discomfort of those living with AD.

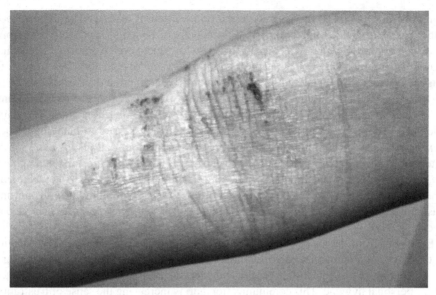

**Fig. 4.** Patient with Atopic Dermatitis of the inside crease of the elbow (source en.wikipedia.org/wiki/Atopic_dermatitis)

Born in Boston as a pioneering biotech in the early '80s, Sanofi Genzyme (SGZ) became in 2011 the specialty care division of Sanofi group and is conducting research and development in many therapeutic areas, including Atopic Dermatitis. Sanofi Genzyme has developed over the years a patient-centric approach which also combines Open Innovation and Responsible Research Innovation. For this reason, SGZ is very active in co-designing pilot initiatives with patient associations, patients, caregivers and independent innovators, universities and Fab Labs to empower knowledge and capabilities of patients affected by AD and other diseases. The goal of these initiatives is to increase the level of awareness about this pathology and to find new solutions, even beyond the pill, that can improve the quality of life. With that goal in mind, Sanofi Genzyme Italian affiliate took part to ICARO UNIMORE[6], an entrepreneurial education program promoted by University of Modena and Reggio Emilia. ICARO UNIMORE is an experimental project focused on entrepreneurial education in which multidisciplinary teams collaborate with researchers to develop six-months project-works aimed to provide innovative solutions to real challenges. In 2018, a multidisciplinary group of young student and innovators - Nicolò Bisi, Nur Eral, Mattia Fantoni, Volodymir Hladysh, and Maria Benedetta Maffezzoni[7] - supported by researchers, medical specialists and patients collaborated with SGZ to develop a workstream for rediscovering AD and empower patients. The DermaTrack concept was conceived to understand AD experience in order to develop a new generation of Patient Support Program (PSP) aimed at ameliorating the relationship between patients and dermatologists. Patients complained about the difficulties to

---

[6] See www.unimore.it/ICARO/.

[7] Nicolò Bisi, Nur Eral, Mattia Fantoni, starting from the results of the preliminary analysis have actively participated in designing and prototyping the first version of the DermaTrack.

summarize during check-up visits about the real burden of disease. The DermaTrack project has been divided into two parts: (i.) analysis of patients' needs and behaviors, (ii.) design and prototyping of a concept for a new product-service. Patients' needs and behaviors were initially documented through interviews of 50 patients[8]. 70% of respondents are under 35 years old and 60% are women. Regarding the degree of severity of the disease: 20% declared mild AD, 50% moderate AD, 30% a severe AD. The sample has later been expanded to 159 patients, though online questionnaires. The daily difficulties encountered were partly physiological, closely related to pathology (such as excessive itching, burning sensation, difficulty in sleeping and resting) and partly related to its social stigma, both in the private-family and public-professional sphere, with repercussions on the emotional wellbeing. Itching turns out to be a key element. Although it represents one of the main symptoms of this pathology, it is in fact not measured according to objective criteria. Patients describe the itch intensity using a 0 to 10 scale.

Emerging from the survey, itching and scratching were often the cause of misunderstandings and communication difficulties between the patient and their formal and informal caregivers (medical staff, family and friends). Itching was often misinterpreted as poor personal hygiene. This communication gap is increasing the sense of frustration and inadequacy in the patient himself. Through the interpretation of this analysis it is possible to outline some key points necessary to (co)design feasible solutions: (i.) helping the patient to feel understood and accepted; (ii.) assist the patient in effectively communicating the severity of symptoms to doctors/family members/friends; (iii.) increase the knowledge of AD in the population (Population Awareness).

In addition, through this interpretation, the relationships between the various stakeholders (doctors, institutions, caregivers and general population) and patients can improve, leaving room for empathy, better collaboration and, ultimately, acceptance. Moreover, the analysis evidenced the importance of active listening and sharing. And it is mainly thanks to the re-evaluation of soft skills that we have understood how fundamental it is to give a voice to the patient with AD, whose disorder is often not considered severe enough and not impacting in daily life. We believe patients feel not included because the disorder is not objectively transferable: an objective measuring system must be created that can measure and transmit the impact of the pathology. This is true for AD but can be applied to many other conditions.

Nowadays, dermatologists measure the multidimensional impact of AD by assessing: lesions (EASI Index- Eczema Area and Severity Index), pain (VAS), itching and sleep disturbances (NSR scale - Numeric Rating Scale), quality of life (DLQI - Dermatology Life Quality Index), anxiety and depression level (HADS) and the patient benefit index (PBI). However, patients do not have immediate tools to self-evaluate the severity of their pathology which has a dynamic nature. Therefore, dynamic and objective measurement of itching is a topic that is taking on a relevant dimension even among dermatologists who might be interested in monitoring disease activity through longitudinal quantification of the itch (Fig. 4).

---

[8] 60% of the sample interviewed by telephone and 40% interviewed in person.

## 3.2   Origins and Development of DemaTrack

Starting from patient quotes, the students further investigated living with AD. For 84% of all respondents (89% in moderate and severe cases) itching is the most problematic aspect of AD, more than the extent and severity of the lesions. The data on the frequency of scratching (Fig. 5) is emblematic. 42% are not even able to make a hypothesis while 22% report to scratch more than 120 times/hour or more than 2880 times per day. Itch is responsible for sleep difficulties (more than 120 days in 30% of responders) as well as disturbance in daily activities (more than 120 days in 98% of responders).

This shows how it is impossible for a patient to keep a diary updated manually (and how it is necessary to automate the process) and how the pathology generates a compulsory and uncontrollable scratching that is difficult to hide in public and be ignored by other people. 65% of respondents complain that it is very difficult to transfer effectively the impact of the disease to their doctor. About 40% of patients said they were very interested in solutions for itch monitoring while 34% already tried in the past to keep a diary to monitor the course of symptoms.

All these aspects generate problems in terms of communication, trust, and self-esteem with those around you: not only doctors but also family and friends. The first prototype of the DermaTrack wearable has been developed by hacking and reprogramming an existing *smart band*, and connecting it to an app, allowing patients and specialists to visualize data and information. Basically, the bracelet allows the patient to quantify the itch in an indirect way: counting the frequency and the intensity applied by patients to seek itch relief through the action to scratch.

Together with other parameters such as degree of skin hydration hours of sleep, UV index, weather, humidity, quantity of pollen/allergens in the air will support dermatologists in a multidimensional monitoring, extending the observation beyond the test itself. DermaTrack is conceived to be a discreet personal wearable, indistinguishable from other devices, both for users and observers. The manually adjustable parameters are instead the self-reported daily mood, foods ingested, if different from standard diet, and a space for personal notes.

Another key point missing with respect to the needs analysis is solved: through DermaTrack, a person affected by AD will in the future have a more accurate detection system that will improve individual knowledge of the pathology as well as the relationship with the dermatologist. The students also thought about social acceptance aspects of pathology: to make everyone experience what it means to live for a while with AD. The idea was to have a "play" function: AD patients can borrow their DermaTrack to a healthy individual. DermaTrack will then faithfully reproduce itch intensity and frequency recorded in the AD Patient.

However, due to the complexity to develop simultaneously all these functionalities, it took form the idea of developing a second, simpler and stand alone, device capable of generating this type of experience together with the makerspace of Politecnico di Milano (Polifactory), in an open innovation approach: the *DermAware* project.

The opportunity to study the broader implications of leveraging itch as disease awareness came up by participating in a call for ideas promoted by Polifactory, the Fab Lab and makerspace of Politecnico di Milano, as part of the first year of the FabCare initiative, within the *Distributed Design Market Platform* (DDMP), that is a project funded by

In the most intense periods, how many times do you scratch yourself in an hour?

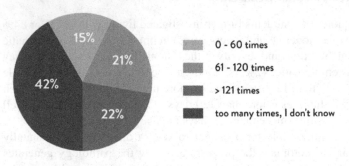

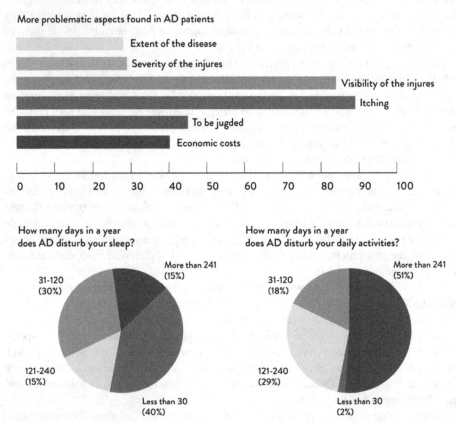

**Fig. 5.** Data on aspects connected to *Atopic Dermatitis* (base: 159 answers; source: DermaTrack project Report)

Creative Europe Program to implement the global network of Fab Lab promoting and improving the connection between makers and designers with the European market. The premise behind FabCare [1] is that nowadays, types of products such as aids and prostheses can be designed using open source knowledge, software and hardware, and then be materialized in Fab Labs combining makers' skills with digital manufacturing technologies. Starting from this logic, a multiplicity of different solutions can be conceived, intertwined and implemented answering the needs of prevention or care for everyone. FabCare is an experimental initiative created to stimulate designers, makers and independent innovators to design open source products for healthcare that can be distributed through digital platforms and materialized in Fab Labs. Therefore, FabCare's challenge aims to demonstrate how designers, makers and independent innovators – also interacting with patients, caregivers and their associations – can concretely design, produce and distribute open source healthcare solutions with a real market potential.

The challenge of FabCare is to demonstrate how an open source approach concretely offers advantages for the patient, for the health care system and stimulates the production system, digital manufacturing in particular.

This challenge is based on an emerging discussion both in the scientific world and in communities of independent innovators (e.g. makers) about the effectiveness of the current approach to the development of consumer wearables, ranging from sports to healthcare. An emerging and diversified scientific literature is studying comparative models on the accuracy of consumer wearables [17], verify the effectiveness of the sensors used [16] reflect on privacy and security aspects in relation to shared use of biometric data [18], identify the limits on human empowerment achievable through these devices [15]. Independent innovators not only think and work on how to democratize design and fabrication of the consumer wearables but are also thinking out-of-the box on how to design "anti-wearables" trying to move tracking functions from wearable devices to common objects that interact everyday with the people.

Taking into account these emerging opportunities and critical issues, the advantages offered by open source in the development of consumer wearables on which the development of DermaTrack and DermaWare projects is based are:

- to develop totally customized solutions that do not constitute an alternative to the existing consumer wearables market but create an additional market option;
- to develop different versions of the same solutions in order to satisfy simultaneously several purposes related to a pathology such as diagnosis, monitoring, treatment, learning, awareness, etc.;
- to build peer-to-peer design and production platforms, where patients, specialists, designers and manufacturers can collaborate in the design and implementation and overall management of design solutions (hardware, software, design and usability);
- to use design and manufacturing resources and tools that allow patients and specialists to access these solutions locally (one-off or small series parts, specific components to repair, modify or upgrade existing versions) while taking advantage of the possibilities offered by digital fabrication and at the same time respecting its limits;
- to enable the replicability, transferability and possible scalability of a solution if it is useful for multiple patients affected by the same pathology, if it is useful for patients

affected by other pathologies, if it needs to be produced on a large scale by engineering it for industrial production.

### 3.3 Design, Materialization and Showcase of DermAware

The new project of the digital bracelet has been named DermAware, just to emphasize the desire to shift the focus more on the phase of awareness of the disease experienced by people with atopic dermatitis. It is an educational digital device conceived to make people aware of the effects generated by the co-existence with atopic dermatitis. It simulates the annoyance generated by pruritus, typical of this pathology, at variable intervals and with different levels of intensity. Likewise, the presence of LED lights on the wearable that light up randomly, serves to attract people's attention by simulating what happens to a patient with AD when scratching in public, unintentionally.

In this way, DermAware can be used by patient associations, such as ANDeA, or in schools and workplaces (where there is a compelling body of evidence of bullying and discrimination versus AD patients) to organize sensibilization and educational initiatives. Therefore, the choice has been made to develop a hardware from scratch, which can be realized with the machines typically present inside the Fab Lab, made up by: a custom electronic board[9], a chassis made with Stereolithography (SLA) 3D printing technology and a bracelet created with Fused Deposition Modeling (FDM) 3D printing technology (Fig. 6).

The authors, Nicolò Bisi, Nur Eral, and Mattia Fantoni, were in charge of developing a new open-source code, while Polifactory's contribution was to design and build the whole performing hardware, and to support the development of the user experience that DermAware was supposed to offer. Instructions and files to create your DermaAware can be downloaded from the distributeddesign.eu platform and the Polifactory's website[10]. Thanks to the development provided by Polifactory in terms of usability and product design, and by a research group from the Department of Electronics, Information and Bioengineering (DEIB, Politecnico di Milano)[11] concerning the electronic design and debugging of a custom PCB, it is remarkable how the idea behind the project has finally had the strength to be communicated in an effective and coherent way. In fact, from the point of view of electronic hardware production, it has been possible to obtain an open-source electronic board of very small dimensions - which is essential when working in the wearable field. As far as the formal design of the device is concerned, it has been chosen to work in a complementary way: the electronics has been completely incorporated into a smoothly sculpted body, with a surface texture whose function is to amplify the punctiform perception of the vibration on the user's skin. DermAware is an object designed without display and buttons - except for the power-on one - just to not distract the user from the haptic dimension of the experience. Thanks to the support

---

[9] Designed and made thanks to the collaboration with Angelo Geraci, Nicola Corna, Fabio Garzetti, Nicola Lusardi belonging to the Department of Electronics, Information and Bioengineering (DEIB).

[10] Direct link: www.polifactory.polimi.it/polifactory_progetti/ddmp-fabcare?lang=en.

[11] PCB designed by Angelo Geraci, Nicola Corna, Fabio Garzetti, Nicola Lusardi (DEIB Department, Politecnico di Milano).

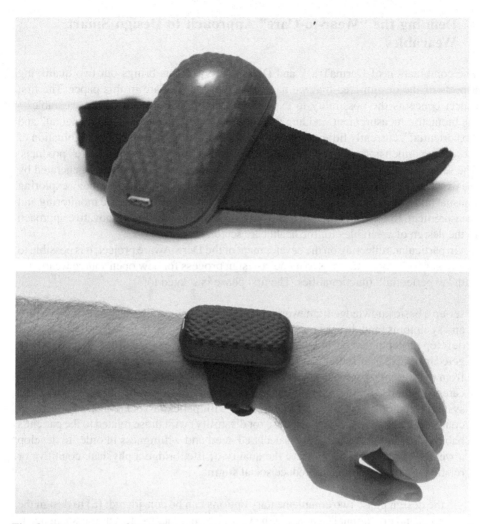

**Fig. 6.** The prototype of DermAware (open source project downloadable at: www.polifactory.pol imi.it/polifactory/fabcare/ and distributeddesign.eu)

provided through the Fabcare initiative, DermAware has become a functioning prototype, presented to the public at the Sanofi Genzyme booth during the European Maker Faire in Rome in 2018[12] where the most promising open source healthcare solutions on the Italian scene of the moment were shown.

---

[12] Every year, the European Maker Faire Rome registers more than 120.000 visitors.

## 4 Defining the "Wear-to-Care" Approach to Design Smart Wearables

The combination of DermaTrack and DermAware projects brings out two qualifying aspects of the design area that we have named Wear-To-Care in this paper. The first aspect concerns the possibility to expand the "functional" dimension of wearables - the biometric measurement - adding the open source dimension of "experimental" and "experiential", currently little explored by wearables on the market. The combination of these three dimensions is what characterizes the originality of "Wear-to-care" products. The second aspect - strongly related to the first - concerns the innovation generated by the experiential dimension of wearables that allows to think "out-of-the-box" exploring unusual and unexplored functions or purposes that go beyond biometric monitoring and measurement. In this way the "Wear-to-Care" is characterized as an innovative approach to the design of wearables for the healthcare sector.

In particular, reflecting on the development of the DermAware project, it is possible to extrapolate some general rules to model a design process for new open source wearables with "experiential" functionalities. The first phase is related to:

- set-up a basic knowledge framework on the pathology through the acquisition of signs and symptoms. and disease management by healthcare specialists;
- develop in-depth and on-field knowledge related to the change of life dynamics triggered by illness at an individual, family and social level. This knowledge can be derived from the patient's personal experience, from the interaction with family members and caregivers and with the relevant environment. Such data can be later integrated and systematized on a larger scale by interacting with patient associations;
- combine the knowledge on the disease (or disability) with those related to the patient's habits and condition, and with his declared need and willingness in order to develop a wearable that works to improve the quality of life, bridge a physical, cognitive or relational gap and ultimately reduce social stigma.

In the design phase two complementary options can be considered: (i.) to design the "functional and operational" version of the wearable, in order to meet the personal needs of the patient (or a group of patients); (ii.) to design the "experimental and experiential" version of the wearable in order to allow people who do not have the pathology to understand or share what the patient feels or to interact with him.

These devices can be designed and materialized through a co-design and open design process that involves the patient, his family and healthcare specialists. The devices can be materialized collaborating with professionals who have design and technical skills (makers, hackers, engineers, etc.) and accessing digital fabrication technologies and enabling places such as makerspaces and Fab Labs. Finally, wearables are open source and codified projects, therefore customizable and (re) producible in a distributed way.

More precisely, it is observable the development of two distinct approaches in the product and user-driven/user-centered design of wear-to-care products: "operational" wearables are characterized by the "anonymity" of the design (to be a technical or technological object of recurrent use) and the guarantee of full effectiveness and control of the object. Therefore, they are not devices designed to show or emphasize functions related to specific aspects of a disease (unless it is necessary, vital or functional to communicate them) but on the contrary they work to normalize the patient's life condition. On the contrary, "experiential" devices are designed to exaggerate emphasize all visual, tactile, olfactory, sound aspects that simulate physical, mental or behavioral states related to a specific disease. This is to make the experience "memorable".

The last phase concerns the adoption and scalability of projects at a social and entrepreneurial level. The "operational and functional" versions of the wearable can be materialized in a personalized way by patients with the support of patient associations and the verification of healthcare specialists. In this way, errors and risks are eliminated and patients are fully accepted. In parallel, these devices can be implemented at an entrepreneurial or industrial level by designers and manufacturers who have participated in the co-design phase. In this case, they would populate market niches that still lack dedicated solutions. On the other hand, thanks to the integrated support provided by companies, patient associations and other stakeholders, "experimental/experiential" wearables can be developed and disseminated on a larger scale by organizing awareness raising initiatives that aim to decontextualize the context of use of these solutions, stimulate or "normalize" the use of these devices, encourage fundraising for the production of "operational/functional" wearables.

Lessons learnt from the DermAware project, contextualized in a wider framework of innovations within the healthcare sector, highlights some key steps:

– design of wearables should go beyond the pure technical and functional dimension and must work on a more extensive, open, inclusive and participatory concept of "care";
– design of wearables with a dual nature – "operational and functional" and "experimental and experiential" - can provide useful elements and indications to improve the quality and effectiveness of the interactions between patients, formal and informal caregivers and the inclusion of patients in society;
– design of open and adaptable wearables for different utilities can be a real possibility for populating niches still lacking dedicated solutions.

Summarizing experiences and reflections we can propose a first general definition of "Wear-to-Care" as an area of potential innovation characterized by the development of open and collaborative design and materialization processes aims to produce interactive wearable devices that improve the effectiveness in the personal disease monitoring and increase the level of understanding and social awareness of the effects these pathologies have on patients' lives.

Starting from the experience gained through the prototyping of DermaTrack first and then DermAware, it emerges that we are still witnessing an experimental phase in the conception of new types of wearables. However, it is precisely the design openings that these experiments still present that can be considered as a testimony of how the concept and approach of Wear-to-Care can be further explored, until a stabilization is achieved. Further experimentation and collaborations with technological partners are currently underway to further ameliorate both DermaTrack and DermAware. The real challenge in this sense will be to transform an entire experiment into a certifiable and distributable product on the market.

# References

1. Bianchini, M., Maffei, S., Bolzan, P.: Distributed design for Distributed Care. In Armstorng, K., Diez, T., Goldapple, L., Schmidt, A., Villum, C. (eds.) Design Remix Share Repeat. How distributed design is changing the way makers and designers approach collaboration, tools and the market. Institute for Advanced Architecture of Catalonia (2019)
2. DeMonaco, H., Oliveira, P., Torrance, A., Von Hippel, C., Von Hippel, E.: When Patients Become Innovators. MIT Sloan Management Review, Spring 2019 IssueResearch (2019). https://sloanreview.mit.edu/article/when-patients-become-innovators/. Accessed 31 Jan 2020
3. Maffei, S., Bianchini, M., Parini, B., Delli Zotti, E.: MakeToCare. An Ecosystem of user-centered actors and solutions for innovation in the healthcare sector. 1st edn. Libraccio Editore (2017)
4. Maffei, S., Bianchini, M., Parini, B., Cipriani, L.: MakeToCare2. Patient innovation in Italy between project and market. 1st edn. Libraccio Editore (2019)
5. Kanstrup, A.M., Bertelsen, P., Nøhr, C.: Patient innovation: an analysis of patients' designs of digital technology support for everyday living with diabetes. Health Inf. Manag. J. 44(1), 12–20 (2015)
6. Krummel, T.M.: The Rise of Wearable Technology in Healthcare. JAMA Network Open Health Inf. 2(2) (2019)
7. Oliveira, P., Zejnilovic, L., Canhão, H., Von Hippel, E.: Innovation by patients with rare diseases and chronic needs. Orphanet J. Rare Diseases 10(1), 41 (2015). https://ojrd.biomed central.com/articles/10.1186/s13023-015-0257-2. Accessed 31 Jan 2020
8. Sienkiewicz, D., van Lingen, C., e Bedlington, N., Bullot, C., Immonen, K.: The added value of patient organizations. www.eu-patient.eu/globalassets/library/publications/epf_added_value_report_final.pdf. Accessed 10 Feb 2020
9. Senra, M.S., Wollenberg, A.: Psychodermatological aspects of atopic dermatitis. Br. J. Dermatol. 170(1), 38–43 (2014)
10. Slattery, M.J., Essex, M.J., Paletz, E.M., Vanness, E.R., Infante, M., Rogers, G.M., Gern, J.E.: Depression, anxiety, and dermatologic quality of life in adolescents with atopic dermatitis. J. Allergy Clin. Immunol. 128, 668 (2011)
11. Wollenberg, A., Barbarot, S., Bieber, T., Chriten-Zaech, S., et al.: Consensus-based European guidelines for treatment of atopic eczema (atopic dermatitis) in adults and children: part I. J. Eur. Acad. Dermatol. Venereol. 32(5), 657–682 (2018)
12. Rønnstad, A.T.M., Halling-Overgaard, A.S., Hamann, C.R., Skov, L., Egeberg, A., Thyssen, J.P.: Association of atopic dermatitis with depression, anxiety, and suicidal ideation in children and adults: a systematic review and meta-analysis. J. Am. Acad. Dermatol. 79(3), 448–456.e30 (2018)
13. Silverberg, J.I.: Atopic dermatitis in adults. Med. Clin. North Am. 104(1), 157–176 (2020)
14. Zuberbier, T., Orlow, S.J., Paller, A.S., Taïeb, A., Allen, R., Hernanz-Hermosa, J.M., Ocampo-Candiani, J., Coxh, M., Langeraari, J., Simon, J.C.: Patient perspectives on the management of atopic dermatitis. J. Allergy Clin. Immunol. 118(1), 226–232 (2006)
15. Morley, J., Floridi, L.: The limits of empowerment: how to reframe the role of mhealth tools in the healthcare ecosystem. Sci. Eng. Ethics 26, 1159–1183 (2020)
16. Pardameana, H., Soeparnoa, B., Budiartoa, A., Baurley, J.: Comparing the accuracy of multiple commercial wearable devices. In: 4th International Conference on Computer Science and Computational Intelligence 2019 (ICCSCI) (2019)
17. Aroganam, G., Manivannan, N., Harrison, D.: Review on wearable technology sensors used in consumer sport applications. Sensors (Basel). 19(9), 1983 (2019)
18. Banerjee, S., Hemphill, T., Longstreet, P.: Wearable devices and healthcare: data sharing and privacy. Inf. Soc. 34 (2018)

# Parametric Design and Data Visualization for Orthopedic Devices

Gabriele Pontillo[1]($\boxtimes$) (iD), Roberta Angari[2] (iD), and Carla Langella[2] (iD)

[1] Università degli Studi della Campania "Luigi Vanvitelli", Via Roma 29, 81031 Aversa, Italy
gabriele.pontillo@unicampania.it

[2] Università degli Studi della Campania "Luigi Vanvitelli", Via San Lorenzo 31, 81031 Aversa, Italy
{roberta.angari,carla.langella}@unicampania.it

**Abstract.** The paper aims to illustrate the ongoing research based on the development of orthopedic devices, characterized by the integration between parametric design and data visualization, for the product customization on specific morphologies and needs of users, and the return of information of the course and therapeutic advancement made readable for both, patients and doctors.

As highlighted by the scientific literature and by the state of arts, nowadays always more the convergence between design, medicine, and data analysis/mining, is the experimental field for the research and develop of innovative biomedical devices, which integrate users as proactive part of the design and treatment processes, thanks to the integration of different methods and techniques of design: as Sabine and Dietrich affirm, design of orthopedics devices based on systems of parametric and generative prototyping, let's get a high level of personalization of medical devices (2017), which can be enriched by the integration of different kind of sensors which returns complex and scientific information. The extraction, analysis, and translation of these data, make it possible to represent this complexity in visual form making it readable not only for the scientific community of reference but for a wider range of users (Stoll 2014).

**Keywords:** Parametric design · Biomedical design · Data visualization · Orthopedic devices

## 1 Introduction: Traces of Interdisciplinary Convergence for the Development of Innovative Devices

In recent years, the rapid evolution of science and technology has led to the emergence of a new scenario based on the collaboration between design and science (Ito 2016) whose products have a deep effect on people's way of life, on their opinions and choices (Langella 2019). The increasingly fitting innovation of science and technology is therefore transferred to society through images, objects, communication devices, services, or tangible and intangible artifacts, which through the relationship established with individuals allow conveying knowledge by offering, moreover, the possibility of metabolizing and use it consciously (Olson 2000).

© ICST Institute for Computer Sciences, Social Informatics and Telecommunications Engineering 2021
Published by Springer Nature Switzerland AG 2021. All Rights Reserved
P. Perego et al. (Eds.): ICWH 2020, LNICST 376, pp. 139–153, 2021.
https://doi.org/10.1007/978-3-030-76066-3_11

Such a scenario leads design to become more than ever a strategic choice, as it is not only a *trait d'union* between individual technical/scientific disciplines but also a medium for the enjoyment of individuals. In this sense, hybridizing the research and development process with different methods and techniques of the project and above all with different knowledge and professions, allows design to translate the complexity and technicality of the scientific community of reference into artifacts that enable people to relate with these devices - whether tangible or intangible - which thus become in all respects part of everyday life.

To arrive at the creation of artifacts similar to those described above, designers cannot ignore a fundamental question, linked to ethical responsibility (Chan 2018) and beyond. Designers are in a position to give shape to objects related to the universe of scientific disciplines, and for this reason, they must fully understand their methods and contents, interpret them, assimilate them and translate them (Langella, ibidem), ensuring a faithful and effective and efficient use. What has been said requires designers not only to always keep direct comparison and dialogue with the scientific community of reference open but above all to acquire the skills necessary to be considered proactive part of the process of joint definition of common and shared languages and of the process of research and development.

When this process converges towards the realization of medical devices, designers are called to intertwine their research and experimentation activity with the method and results of science, actively collaborating with scientists and research centers, sometimes physically entering chemistry laboratories, physics and biomedical, to develop innovations with a high content of design thought, as well as science. It is these dynamics that favor the creation of contact points, intersections and opportunities for contamination between designers and scientists, which allow them to cooperate to derive mutual benefits in their research activities (Ito 2016) and prefigure together possible futures: in this optics scientists provide designers with the theoretical foundations on which to develop innovative products characterized by the scientific method - therefore constituted by the rigor in observing protocols and verifications -, at the same time designers can provide science with indications on new directions and research topics to be undertaken that respond to the needs of society and the market and cultural changes, or to stimulate the creative capacity of science with points of view and design-matrix approaches.

An example of what has been said, as it will be articulated in detail in the following paragraphs, is the ever-greater integration of digital environments and tools in the design processes of medical and therapeutic devices, as well as interaction with them, in which the possibilities offered from parametric design, from additive production and finally from data analysis and visualization, it allows to reach levels of innovation that not only facilitate and optimize treatment but above all make available, in open format, the data that in this way become the basic element for the verification and dissemination of technical/scientific knowledge related to the medical field of reference.

## 2 Biomedical Design: Open Issues and Unsolved Needs

The last decade has led to a significant advancement in medical research concerning the testing of new techniques that allow achieving a form of improvement in the quality of life, both for patients undergoing transitive treatment and for those reporting permanent trauma. This advancement, made possible also by the constant research activity carried out on techniques and materials for the production of medical devices, still leaves open some questions and, consequently, unsolved needs related to various stages of development, production, and use of devices such as orthoses, braces, and prostheses.

In particular, for the research conducted, are considered as open issues those related to:

- Acquisition techniques. To date, the method used still requires that the parts of the body to be subjected to therapeutic medical treatment are examined and detected in an artisanal way, for example through the creation of a plaster cast used as a mold for plastic casting. This produces an inaccurate result, as it is subject to human error by the health worker who takes care of the realization of the survey, easily improved with the integration of modern survey technologies and acquisition of three-dimensional digital images through, for example, 3D scanning or photogrammetry.
- Production techniques. As a direct consequence of the deficits of the acquisition phase, the production of immobilization devices, such as plaster, through the artisanal method implies many limitations, among which we highlight those relating to the production time and human errors of the operator – don't forget that these devices are commonly produced by hand, and for this reason the production phase may also require several revisions and modifications.
- Costs. If you look at the context of the market for orthoses, braces, and prostheses, it is easy to understand why these products are considered excessively expensive: first of all, this kind of devices can be for transitive or permanent use, in variable term, subjected to the modifications due to the change of patient's treatments or physique. The high cost is not even due to the materials used, because those most commonly used are extremely inexpensive. So neither the duration nor the materials directly impact on the cost, but the latter mainly depends on the workforce, that is, on the manual skills and the time that the health worker will spend in making the product, aware of the critical issues highlighted above.
- Comfort. Always starting from the analysis of the devices currently on the market, it is possible to notice and understand what are the reasons that lead patients to complain about numerous inconveniences due to the use of therapeutic devices: they, first of all, have shown - in most cases - to be uncomfortable, cumbersome for carrying out daily movements and actions, produced with heavy and not very breathable materials that often cause redness and irritation due to the heat and the low washability of the materials used. These critical factors only worsen the psychophysical condition of the patients, who in this way also feel uncomfortable because of the device worn.
- Aesthetics. If we consider the traditional production methods of orthoses, braces, and prostheses, the customization possibilities are somewhat limited. The resolution of this deficit through the use of additive production technologies would facilitate the psychological acceptance of the patient, who in this way will not see the therapeutic device only as an imposition by his doctor, who once integrated into the decision-making process and the realization it will feel part of it.

## 2.1  Clinical Efficacy

Clinical efficacy is a central aspect that must be taken into account by designers in the development and production phase of products dedicated to medical treatments, as it directly impacts all phases of the design and use process of medical devices.

In the first phase, relating to the detection of the part to be subjected to treatment, the digital acquisition of the geometry of the anatomical part would allow obtaining a greater correspondence to the real morphology, perfectly shaped, therefore, on the patient. This phase, as seen previously, could be improved, through the integration of innovative detection methods, which provide for the use of 3D scanners or photogrammetry for 4 or more points that return as output clouds of points or photographic shots attributable, in both cases, with three-dimensional models perfectly faithful to the detected part.

After the detection phase, if one of the aforementioned methods has been used, it is possible to proceed with the development of the device through specific three-dimensional modeling software, which allows obtaining optimal results especially if implemented by the parametric approach, through which automate the project phases. The tools offered by 3D modeling software allow to circumvent the problems deriving from artisanal modeling by eliminating the critical issues due to the health worker's workforce.

Finally, adopting additive manufacturing as a production technology would make it possible to obtain artifacts characterized not only by specific performance properties but also by the possibility of customizing them according to the tastes of the patient, who in this way becomes involved in the decision-making process.

All the previously mentioned elements converge strategically in the development of a device that is not only therapeutic, as orthoses, braces, and prostheses that patients consider more comfortable and conform to their tastes, are worn more continuously, consequently having a direct effect on the clinical efficacy, without leading to patients' refusal of treatment.

This is even more emphasized if sensors are integrated in the devices that allow returning exact measurements on the progress of the treatment, as evidenced by the ever-increasing diffusion of medical e-health products in which tools based on information and communication technologies allow to monitor the treatment of pathologies and consequently manage their lifestyle, in order to pursue optimal clinical efficacy.

As highlighted by the scientific literature and the state of the art of reference, choose, in the development and design of medical devices, to make use of the methods and techniques outlined, to achieve the creation of orthoses, braces, and prostheses characterized by better wearability, greater patient participation and awareness and, therefore, greater rehabilitation capacity.

## 2.2  Psychological Acceptance

A further open question, which the ongoing research has highlighted and to which it tries to answer, is that relating to psychological acceptance, as it is believed that to ensure that patients are aware of the importance of wearing products for orthopedic rehabilitation it is necessary to convey to them how much the use of these devices is fundamental in order to achieve complete recovery of mobility in the shortest possible time.

Acceptance of treatment is one of the main issues to be taken into consideration for the pursuit of an optimal outcome of orthopedic therapies that involve the use of specific devices, numerous studies have underlined how patient compliance is closely related to final results so that the good outcome of the treatment appears to retrospectively influence the patient's judgment (Katz and Durrani 2001; Landauer et al. 2003; Sifert et al. 2009).

Therefore, the acceptance of orthotic treatment is a matter strictly related to the quality of life and the psychological factors of the patients who derive it (Rivett et al. 2009; MacLean et al. 1989). Therefore, alongside the clinical efficacy of short and/or medium-term treatment, it becomes fundamental to succeed in the realization of devices that can be accepted more easily, that is, less bulky, with less aesthetic and functional impact on the subject's life, for the same effectiveness of the final result.

The importance of these aspects makes the collaboration between medicine and design particularly significant since the design is able to provide design solutions that considerably improve many of the aspects related to compliance, such as the aesthetic aspect, comfort, acceptability, wearability, and lightness.

## 3 Biomedical Design and Digital Technologies

Based on what has been previously reported, it is possible to affirm that the scenario outlined by the interdisciplinary convergence between design and science, and more particularly between parametric design and medicine, today finds a consistent response in the design of biomedical devices, focus of increasing interest and field experimentation for designers who draw from the scientific method the analysis models as well as the ability to follow rigorous protocols and verifications and from the design methods the task of translating these models into forms which, aligned with patient compliance, return highly effective devices from the clinical point of view and at the same time acceptable from a psychological point of view. With this in mind, it is specified that biomedical design is characterized by many constraints linked above all to the need to integrate with the physical, physiological and psychological factors of patients, to which medical research tries to respond thanks to continuous research and rapid evolution of methods and techniques. This implies that this rapidly expanding sector will increasingly need to integrate designers into the research and development process.

The particularly incisive role of design can be found in all phases of the project, which offers as final output objects that directly impact on the quality of life of users and, more generally, on society. Think, for example, of the pharmaceutical packaging sector, to be considered not only as a market-oriented product - like all types of packaging - but above all as a communication medium containing all the technical/scientific information that designers are required to translate in order to make them readable and understandable for the widest possible number of users. This translation operation, as we will be able to articulate more in detail later, puts the designers in the condition to acquire, analyze and extract from the totality of the information related the constraints and specificities related to the different pathologies to which the drugs are addressed (Langella et al. 2019), to develop visual systems for the dissemination of knowledge that users must be able to correctly decode.

Technological innovation and the evolution of scientific knowledge, therefore, allows conceiving devices that provide innovative ways of use, offering possible alternatives to conventional methods and techniques. In particular, the area of intervention consisting of orthopedic medical supports, such as braces, orthoses, and prostheses, characterized by a strong need for customization due to the variation both of the anatomical characteristics of people, and the type of trauma or pathology, requires the design of characterize these products with specific solutions, promoting the improvement of therapeutic efficacy.

Thanks to parametric design, the study of projects that optimize the therapeutic conditions, with particular attention to the well-being and quality of life of the patients, it is possible to overcome the critical issues of an artisan approach adopted by companies and healthcare facilities for the creation of therapeutic devices, also in consideration of the diffusion of digital technologies and their introduction into the process.

The numerous implementations that can be pursued thanks to digital tools, environments, and techniques of design and production, allows not only designers and companies in the sector to make use of automatisms that would reduce human error and would allow to increase production capacity, but above all to make orthopedic devices closer to the daily needs of patients, also in terms of access to knowledge.

As highlighted by the state of the art, the development of e-health medical products that can integrate a specific sensor system contributes not only to the creation of strategic databases for the storage and future availability of information useful for the study of the different realities pathologies that assume increasing importance with the increase in the international circulation of citizens and the number of patients but above all to improve the access and use of treatments, contributing to increase the general efficiency and sustainability of the health sector.

An example of what has been stated is the Fastfocus wearable device, which constantly monitors vital parameters such as blood pressure, patient movements, as well as oxygen saturation in the blood with minimal impact on the patient's quality of life because it is worn behind an ear - like a hearing aid. The information collected by the device helps doctors in remote monitoring of patients and also facilitates the triage phase in case of hospitalization.

Finally, it is specified that the outlined issues that see the use of digital technologies as possibilities for making therapeutic devices more efficient are closely linked to numerous international actions, as demonstrated by the Horizon Europe Development Programs - in force since 2021 - and the UN Sustainable Development Goals.

## 4   Data Visualization for the Therapeutic Field

The scenario outlined above has highlighted how the possibility of developing therapeutic products through the tools of digital technologies, allows not only to achieve the creation of innovative artifacts characterized by customization, clinical efficacy, and psychological acceptability, through the use of methods and more performing development and production techniques, but to be able to integrate, thanks to the ever-greater miniaturization of the sensor systems, detection, and measurement tools, which become data generators. Just as Big Data represents the massive set of data that describe the complexity of contemporaneity, coming from different types of sources including devices equipped with detectors and sensors, the data produced by the use of e-health devices can become material translation, of a flow of data related to the medical field which, once displayed, facilitates the acquisition and transfer of data and, therefore, the monitoring of the therapeutic path.

The possibility of translating complex data and information from the so-called hard sciences - and not only - such as physics, mathematics, chemistry and biology (De Vries et al. 1993) into visual form is not a new thing, but according to Cairo (2014), the first diagrammatic visualization experiments, which provided for a process of analysis and synthesis of the contents, could be placed in the eighteenth century (2014), when in particular the use of statistical cartography began to spread as a tool for the dissemination of information from the technical/scientific sector of reference.

The need to represent data visually to communicate complex ideas with precision and efficiency (Tufte 1987), which boasts consolidated roots as evidenced by the institution in 1979 of the Information Design Journal[1], today defines important experimentation field mainly due to two factors: on the one hand, the quantity and complexity of the data available and that users contribute to producing through the use of software, web platforms or digital devices is increasing more and more; on the other contemporary society, known with the neologism Knowledge Society[2], wants more and more access to data, to be not only aware but also proactive concerning emerging facts and issues.

At the same time, it should be borne in mind that the representation operation that scientists used to carry out for the communication and presentation of the results achieved among peers, is no longer sufficient, even compared to the Citizen Science[3] strategy, included in the Horizon Europe development program, that provides for an increase in the level of scientific literacy through the democratization of science.

These considerations cannot be considered extraneous to the research conducted, rather it is necessary to understand how and above all in what forms the representation and visualization of data are linked to the development and design of therapeutic devices.

Starting from the assumption that data is the key element of our time, it is evident how technologies are transforming the times and spaces of health, in particular through the continuous monitoring of people - at home, during free time, and also in the workplace - radically changing the traditional doctor-patient relationship (Collecchia 2018).

From this point of view, it is life itself that becomes a pertinence of medicine, as it can be objectified in medical terms. The new wearable technologies, useful for studying pathological conditions, highlight the importance that many people attribute, in today's

---

[1] The Information Design Journal first placed the visualization of data as a relevant design theme at the center of the cultural debate for the identification of issues relating to fields of opportunity in which design, thanks to the convergence between art and science, could become a strategic vehicle for the diffusion of knowledge.

[2] Society that generates, shares and makes available to all members of society knowledge that can be used to improve the human condition. The knowledge society differs from the information society, in that the latter disseminates only raw data, while the former intends to transform information into resources that allow the company to act effectively. The spread of this form of the company derives, among other things, from the innovation of information technologies - IT.

[3] Citizen science is the involvement of the public in scientific research – whether community-driven research or global investigations. The Citizen Science Association unites expertise from educators, scientists, data managers, and others to power citizen science.

culture, to monitoring their health conditions, reinforcing the idea of a data-driven world (Henke et al. 2016).

The main tools of digital medicine, in addition to the technology of electronic records, online services for consulting diagnostic and specialist reports, and the tools used for doctor-patient interaction, are therefore enriched with wearable devices, consisting of one or more biosensors, inserted on clothing items such as watches, T-shirts, shoes, bands, etc., useful for non-invasive measurement, can detect and measure various biological parameters - such as heart rate, respiratory parameters, oxygen saturation, body temperature, blood pressure, glucose, sweat, brain waves, etc. - and provide information on the user's lifestyle - physical activity, sleep, nutrition, etc. - as well as on specific therapeutic procedures - for example magnetotherapy, diabetes management through skin patches, EEG monitoring for epileptic patients, etc. – (Fig. 1). The collected data are available as raw data which, through the techniques of data analysis and machine learning, can be transformed into visible information, as demonstrated by many commercial devices available today – such as FitBit, Apple Watch, etc. - (Kamišalic et al. 2018).

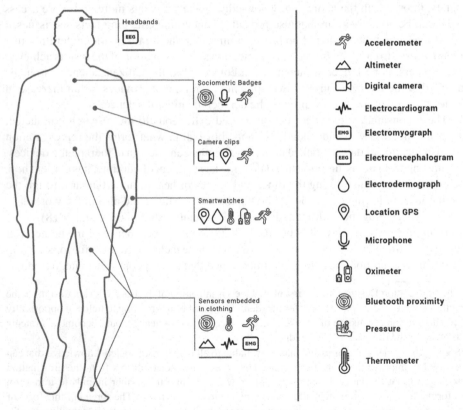

**Fig. 1.** Infographic of kinds and applications of different sensors integrated in wearable devices (Collecchia 2018).

Similar findings are useful to more accurately assess the effectiveness of therapy with the aim of creating a sort of continuous window on the patient's pathological state, not limited in time and space in clinics and hospitals.

What has been said converges in the design of orthopedic therapeutic devices that integrate detection and monitoring sensors of the treatment, as it is not so important to dwell on the type of diagrammatic representation that you want to adopt, as to go to define a model and structure a matrix through which the *income* data, detected by the sensors, can be processed, translated and displayed, to be made legible and decodable through interaction with the user, no longer just a medical specialist, but increasingly more patient.

## 5  A Case of Applied Research

Physical and rehabilitative medicine, also known as physiatrics, is a branch of medicine that deals with the prevention, diagnosis, therapy, and rehabilitation of a disability. This paragraph reports the results of an ongoing research, which aims to respond to the need for therapeutic devices for the rehabilitation of the upper limbs, which present a high level of innovation in design and production methods and techniques, an optimal clinical efficacy and high psychological acceptability.

Physiatrics, as a discipline, plays a role of great importance because it is capable of working on patient autonomy, improving it. In particular, it is possible to observe how the integration of digital technologies, for this discipline, is a strategic tool that allows the development of products that intervene directly on the functional recovery of patients, not only promoting dialogue with doctors but also offering studied devices and customized to specific needs and rehabilitation programs that integrate fundamental daily exercises for faster and more efficient recovery.

The field of the pathology considered is limited to the rehabilitative treatment of diseases such as rhizarthrosis, De Quervine Tendonitis, carpal tunnel, hand atrophy, as well as nerve injury, peripheral neuropathy, polyneuropathy, and other incidental injuries, so to all the kind of pathologies that cause the disability of the upper limbs, and more particularly of the hand, that can be caused by various types of nerve injuries or by accidents, all treated through specific therapies for recovery of functional re-education, to be carried out at the hospital facility or home (Caliendo et al. 2018). Similar treatments can be self-administered by the patient, independently, also if the main criticality deduced from the analysis of the state of the art, highlights the difficulty for the user to use this kind of devices independently, as it is difficult to wear and program it – we specified that the therapeutic systems for the physiatric field are worn by patients for a time-limited, to the administration of a specific treatment to be carried out, usually, daily and often for long periods.

With this in mind, it was decided to respond to these pathologies by designing a therapeutic device that is easy to wear and manage, for the performance of rehabilitation exercises, as well as aesthetically pleasing, to help the patient's rehabilitation, increasing compliance and optimizing the overall period of therapy. To do this, the device, designed for home use, integrates specific mechanical and technological components, both for mechanical and electronic therapeutic techniques currently applied separately, for the rehabilitation of muscle, nerve stimulation, an analgesic therapy (electrostimulation - TENS).

The latter is used in the rehabilitation of the hand, as it allows to improve muscle tone and tropism both following trauma and to speed up the rehabilitation phase. Furthermore, thanks to the TENS mode, it is also possible to use the device for the analgesic treatment for rhizoarthrosis, or rather as a painkiller.

The identification of the most suitable therapy takes place through discussion with the doctor, who examines the case and assigns the use of the device according to the most suitable times and methods. Even the anthropometric data are collected by the doctor who, based on the morphology of the patient's hand, assigns a certain size of the same (S - M - L), in case of special needs there, remains the possibility to further adapt the device and customize it thanks additive manufacturing technology adopted for the realization of the same (Fig. 2 and 3).

**Fig. 2.** Design model: the patient addresses the doctor who carries out the collection of anthropometric data and assigns the most suitable therapy. The data is used to three-dimensionally tailor-made the device, which is then 3D printed. The components necessary for the operation of the device are then added to the printed object. Once completed, the device is ready to be worn by the user and used.

**Fig. 3.** Prototype of the device made by 3D printing. The prototype, in black resin, was created using the Formlabs SLA Form2 printer, chosen for its high definition and the type of materials that can be used.

The electronic heart of the device, located on the part above the wrist, includes a sensor for detecting movements, as well as the system electronics for the correct functioning of electrodes and sensors and an intuitive user interface for switching the device on and off finally, there is a Bluetooth card, which allows the recording of data and the transmission of the latter to the application for therapeutic tracking (Fig. 4). Once the device is worn and switched on, the patient will have to connect to the appropriate application, to carry out the therapeutic exercises assigned by the doctor and synchronize the course of the therapy in parallel, also through visual feedback.

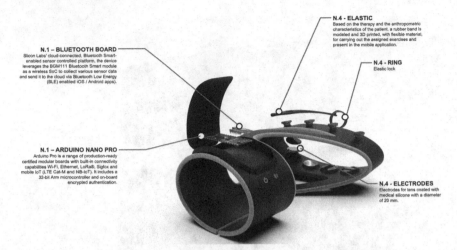

**N.4 - ELASTIC**
Based on the therapy and the anthropometric characteristics of the patient, a rubber band is modeled and 3D printed, with flexible material, for carrying out the assigned exercises and present in the mobile application.

**N.1 – BLUETOOTH BOARD**
Silicon Labs' cloud-connected, Bluetooth Smart-enabled sensor controlled platform, the device leverages the BGM111 Bluetooth Smart module as a wireless SoC to collect various sensor data and send it to the cloud via Bluetooth Low Energy (BLE) enabled iOS / Android apps).

**N.4 - RING**
Elastic lock

**N.1 – ARDUINO NANO PRO**
Arduino Pro is a range of production-ready certified modular boards with built-in connectivity capabilities Wi-Fi, Ethernet, LoRa®, Sigfox and mobile IoT (LTE Cat-M and NB-IoT). It includes a 32-bit Arm microcontroller and on-board encrypted authentication.

**N.4 - ELECTRODES**
Electrodes for tens coated with medical silicone with a diameter of 20 mm.

**Fig. 4.** Datasheet of the electronic components present on the device.

The collected data, through specific computer languages based on MySql (database) and JavaScript (for the conversion of data into code and consequent display), are converted into mappings studied with a dual language: in fact, both a frontend interface is provided, which offers less medical and more emotional feedback to the patient, linked to gratification and to incentivize the user in carrying out the therapy thanks to the achievement of the required results, and a backend interface dedicated to the doctor, more technical and linked to scientific visualization, to allow him to keep trace of the progress and actual performance of the assigned therapy.

Another innovative feature of the device is wearability, as it is designed for easy application and, as previously mentioned, can be worn independently by patients of all ages without difficulty (Fig. 5 and 6).

What has been described leads to the effect of inserting the designed device, in the broader context of e-health medical products, placing the patient not only in the condition of actively interacting with the therapeutic device/system, but also to improve the efficiency of the therapy, facilitate access to the treatment and management of the same, as well as contribute to the diffusion and dissemination of technical/scientific knowledge thanks to the provision of specific visual tools and interfaces.

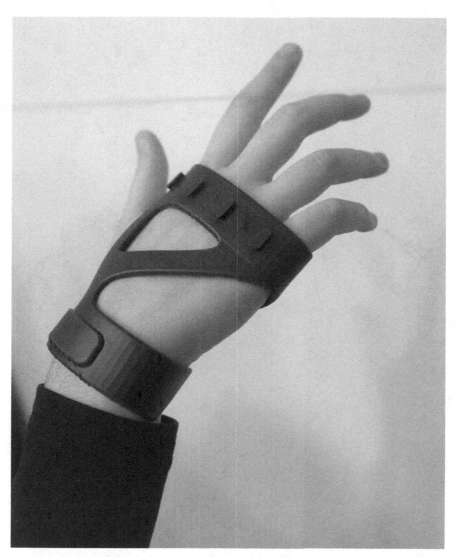

**Fig. 5.**  Prototype of the therapeutic device worn. As you can see from the image, the adherence of the device to the user's hand is perfect, this is due also to the use of digital modeling and advanced prototyping techniques.

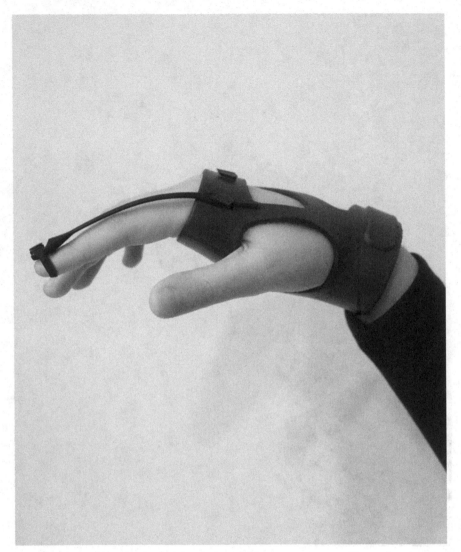

**Fig. 6.** Prototype of the therapeutic device worn. In this image it is possible to see the integration of flexible elements necessary for carrying out the therapy.

**Acknowledgments.** Thanks to the designer Francesco Gravante, whose thesis project "El-Cast", with Supervisor Carla Langella and Referee Gabriele Pontillo, represents the case of applied research. It is specified that this thesis was discussed in December 2019 at the Department of Architecture and Industrial Design – DADI - of the University of Campania "Luigi Vanvitelli".

We would like to thank Fondazione IDIS - Città della Scienza and D.RE.A.M. FabLab for the support in the realization of the prototype.

# References

Sabine, B., Dietrich, P.: Computational simulation as an innovative approach in personalized medicine. Innovations in Spinal Deformities and Postural Disorders (2017)

Stoll, M.: Ridimensionamento adattivo. Il suo ruolo nella trasmissione visiva delle informazioni. Progetto Grafico **25**, 104–115 (2014)

Ito, J.: Design and science. J. Design Sci. **1**, 1–9 (2016). https://doi.org/10.21428/f4c68887

Langella, C.: Design & Scienza. LIStLab. (2019)

Olson, G.B.: Designing a new material world. Science **288**(5468), 993–998 (2000)

Chan, J.K.: Design ethics: reflecting on the ethical dimensions of technology, sustainability, and responsibility in the anthropocene. Des. Stud. **54**, 184–200 (2018)

Katz, D.E., Durrani, A.A.: Factors that influence outcome in bracing large curves in patients with adolescent idiopathic scoliosis. Spine **26**(21), 2354–2361 (2001)

Landauer, F., Wimmer, C., Behensky, H.: Estimating the final outcome of brace treatment for idiopathic thoracic scoliosis at 6-month follow-up. Pediatric Rehabil. **6**(3–4), 201–207 (2003)

Sifert, J., Selle, A., Flieger, C., Günther, K.P.: Compliance as a prognostic factor in the treatment of idiopathic scoliosis. Der Orthopade **38**(2), 151–158 (2009)

Rivett, L., Rothberg, A., Stewart, A., Berkowitz, R.: The relationship between quality of life and compliance to a brace protocol in adolescents with idiopathic scoliosis: a comparative study. BMC Musculoskelet. Disord. **10**(1), 5 (2009)

MacLean WE et al. (1989)

De Vries, M.J., Cross, N., Grant, D.P. (eds.).: Design Methodology and Relationships with Science. Kluwer Academic Publishers, Dordrecht (1993)

Cairo, A.: Dati visuali. Brevi note per una storia dei grafici quantitativi. In: Colin, G., Troiano A.: Le mappe del sapere. Rizzoli, Milano (2014)

Tufte, E.: The Visual Display of Quantitative Information. Graphics Press, Cheshire (1987)

Collecchia, G.: La medicina digitale: l'impero dei sensori. Informazioni sui farmaci **3** (2018). https://www.informazionisuifarmaci.it/la-medicina-digitale-limpero-dei-sensori

Henke, N., et al.: The Age of Analytics: competing in a data-driven world. McKinsey Global Institute (2016). https://www.mckinsey.com

Kamišalic, A., Fister, I., Turkanovic, M., Karakatic, S.: Sensors and functionalities of non-invasive wrist-wearable devices: a review. Sensors **18**, 1714 (2018)

Caliendo, C., Langella, C., Santulli, C.: Hand orthosis designed and produced in DIY biocomposites from agrowaste. Design Health **2**(2), 211–235 (2018)

# Design of an Innovative Integrated System
# for Upper Limb Prosthesis

Paolo Perego[1], Roberto Sironi[1]([⊠]), Emanuele Gruppioni[2], Angelo Davalli[2],
Simone Pittaccio[3], Jacopo Romanò[3], Lorenzo Garavaglia[3], and Giuseppe Andreoni[1]

[1] Dipartimento di Design, Politecnico di Milano, via Durando 38/a, 20158 Milan, Italy
roberto.sironi@polimi.it
[2] Centro Protesi INAIL, via Rabuina 14, 40054 Vigorso di Budrio, BO, Italy
[3] CNR ICMATE, Via Gaetano Previati 1E, 23900 Lecco, Italy

**Abstract.** Nowadays the prosthetic system can be configured as a multifactorial
set that includes reciprocal relationships between the stump, the socket, the prosthesis and the tridigital/robotic hand. This system presents some critical issues that
can be addressed by improving the integration between the parts and redesigning
some components through innovative design-driven solutions. The paper describes
the design of a sensorized liner for upper limb prostheses according to the User
Centered Design methodology, focusing on the socket - which is conceived as
an integrated system composed by Hypermat (the external rigid meta-structure)
and the sensorized liner. The system was designed on the basis of the results that
emerged in the focus group which involved amputee users, technologists and a
heterogeneous set of design figures.

The project requirements on which the liner development and its integration
with the Hypermat metastructure were based were defined. The paper describes
the design of the sensorized liner taking into consideration the choice of materials,
the application of myoelectric textile sensors and pressure sensors, the connector design for the connection between sensors and circuitry, the assembly and
production methods.

**Keywords:** Sensorized liner · Smart textile · Upper limb prosthesis · Design for
healthcare · EMG sensors · Pressure sensors

## 1 Introduction

People who underwent an upper limb amputation - due to occupational accidents, trau-
matological phenomena, diseases or musculoskeletal malformations need an adequate
prosthesis that can restore autonomy and at the same time encourage work and social
reintegration:

Upper limb prostheses can be classified as passive - those that don't have an actuator
that activates the robotic hand - or on contrast active, those activated by body energy
(kinematic) and/or extracorporeal energy (with myoelectric or electronic control).

P. Perego et al. (Eds.): ICWH 2020, LNICST 376, pp. 154–160, 2021.
https://doi.org/10.1007/978-3-030-76066-3_12

Upper limb prosthetic systems should be developed according to specific requirements in terms of electromechanical functions combined with aspects of aesthetics for acceptability and comfort. The main elements to consider in the design process are:

- the design of the system scalable on anthropometrics
- morphological and functional adaptation based onto anthropometry of the residual limb
- mechanical properties for supporting the motor of the hand and body integration
- usability and wearability for comfort and acceptance
- skin biocompatibility
- low weight
- aesthetic acceptability
- biosignals detection and processing for the actuation of electromechanical and/or robotic elements

Although the development of prostheses evolved a lot in recent decades, combining the manual skills of orthopedic technicians with technological know-how in terms of materials and sensors, some critical issues remains and must be analyzed and tackled while designing the prosthesis. From researches with users, the problems concern in particular the relationship between stump, socket and prosthesis are retrieved from literature and here below summarized:

- the perception in terms of stability of the stump-socket interface
- pressure points in specific areas that cause ulcers and skin irritation
- low breathability of the socket
- difficulties in the positioning of electromyographic electrodes
- the maintenance of necessary but comfortable friction forces
- the lack of customizable aesthetic and functional prosthetic cover

## 1.1 The Project

The aim of the Maps project is to improve the prostheses through the design of an integrated system based on innovative multifunctional materials and developed according to the User Centered Design (UCD) methodology.

A meta-structure has been designed, called Hypermat (Fig. 1), that is configurable according to the individual anatomical shapes needs of the user with a mapping of the distribution of the surface in relation to the functional areas of the prosthesis. The Hypermat was designed as an integrative solution between prosthesis and socket, which is conceived as a combination between the meta-structure that performs mechanical function and a sensorized textile liner for the detection of bio-signals (Fig. 2).

Innovative materials have been developed to integrate the ergonomic functional characteristics of Hypermat: phase shift materials (PCM) and graphene-based multilayers for better thermal behavior and piezoresistive materials inserted in the liner for the monitoring of pressure points.

This paper describes the methodology and development of the sensorized liner and its integration with Hypermat.

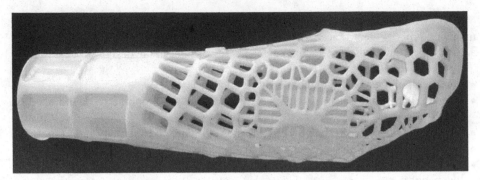

**Fig. 1.** The Hypermat meta-structure, designed by CNR ICMATE.

## 2  Materials and Methods

### 2.1  User Research

The improvement of the quality of life of the patient with amputation of the upper limb is the primary aim in the design of the liner and its respective integration with Hypermat.

The entire design process was based on the UCD method, in which the user is the central point of the design process. According to this methodology "The designer must understand the users, their cognitive behavior, attitudes and the characteristics of their work task" (Gulliksen and Goransson 2001), developing through an active and collaborative participation of the user in the different design phases.

Focus Group was chosen for the User analysis, and it carried out at the Centro Protesi INAIL in Vigorso di Budrio (Italy).

The focus group was attended by six patients with radial and trans-radial upper limb amputation with different types of prostheses, both active and passive, and the simultaneous presence of seven actors including technologists, bioengineers, designers and materials experts.

Participants were asked to describe the activities they carry out in their daily routine, considering awakening, personal hygiene activities, meals, work and study, sports and leisure, with the aim of understanding and evaluating how they use the prosthesis in these activities.

The results of the Focus Group highlighted a series of user's needs which can be summarized here:

- Excessive system's weight
- Problems related to the stump/socket interface in terms of perception of stability
- Difficulty in dressing/undressing clothes, in particular as regards friction between the prosthesis and clothes (t-shirt, shirt)
- Difficulty in cleaning and hygienisation of parts
- Skin irritation due to poor breathability and local points pressure
- Overheating of the electronic parts during the summer with consequent malfunctioning
- High cost for replacing EMG sensors in case of failure
- Difficulty in wearing the prosthesis

## 2.2   Requirements Definition

Based on the results emerging from the focus group, the project team has defined the following design requirements for the development of an innovative prosthesis socket integrated with the Hypermat; it should be:

- Integrable with pressure sensors for the monitoring of pressure points
- Morphologically fitted to the volumetric daily variations of the stump
- Increase the wearability in dressing/undressing clothes and of the prosthesis itself
- Washable
- Economically sustainable in terms of replacement for breakdown or malfunctioning
- Reproducible for easy substitution
- Integrable with the electronic components of the robotic hand
- Aesthetically fine and customizable

## 2.3   Project Developments

Refers to the design requirements, a sensorized liner intended as an interface between the meta-structure and the stump was designed (Fig. 2). The liner - developed in fourway stretch fabric - supports myoelectric sensors and two pressure sensors. These sensors embedded in the liner are made in conductive fabric based on silver yarn to detect the myoelectric signal, and in sintered TPU loaded with graphene to detect the pressures.

The myoelectric ones are made by laser cutting the silver-based 3D fabric and embedding them within the liner through thermo-adhesivation process, meanwhile the pressure ones are fabricated through an innovative sintering process developed by CNR IPCB.

The realization of the sensorized fabric liner allows to produce the system with lower costs than the production method currently in use, since the sensors can be reproduced at the INAIL Centro Protesi's production department. In addition to the EMG sensors, two pressure sensors are embedded on the liner, which are placed in two specific points that are identified like the most stressed area in terms of daily volumetric variation of the stump.

In addition, the textile sensorized liner can be washed to allow a better hygienisation of the system.

The myoelectric sensors, made in 3D fabric, were tested through 50 manual washes, reporting a negligible loss of conductivity. The pressure sensors are instead embedded in the liner through a double thermo-adhesive protective film that makes them waterproof.

In the lower part of the liner - near the apical area of the stump - there is a connector that carries the EMG and pressure signals to the electronic unit for the movement of the robotic hand.

The liner required the implementation of specific materials and technologies in the development process. EuroJersey's Sensitive Bold fabric was implemented for the textile support, which answer the requirements of elasticity, breathability, mechanical strength and biocompatibility.

From the production point of view, it was decided to develop the liner through a manufacturing process that involves the use of laser cutting, additive and thermoadhesive printing technologies.

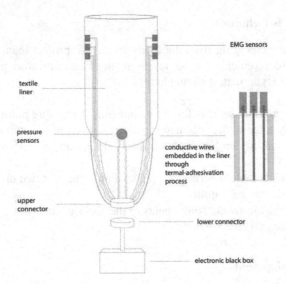

**Fig. 2.** Drawing of the liner and its components.

The choice was based on the design decision to use the same tools and production processes both in the prototyping phase and in anticipation of the subsequent production phase, starting from two-dimensional mathematical models easily scalable according to the different anthropometries of the patients. This solution involved the implementation of a thermo-adhesive system based on double-sided elastic glue to allow stable bonding and waterproofing of the parts.

The EMG sensors have been made of conductive fabric based on silver yarn, laser cut and applied to the textile structure through thermo-adhesive. The myoelectric signal is carried by the sensors to the terminal base of the liner by conductive filaments that are inserted inside metal probes. These probes, three for each of the two EMG sensors, are mechanically inserted and welded inside a male connector, made of polymeric material, on which a connection plate is inserted. The male connector is inserted in the female connector through a system of magnets which allows to stabilize the contact between the parts (Fig. 3).

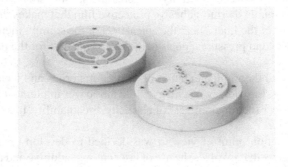

**Fig. 3.** The male-female connector to carry the signals to the electronic device

The connector plate has been designed to house 6 connections for the electromyographic signals and 4 connections for the signals deriving from the two pressure sensors. These one have embedded in the liner trough by thermo-adhesive and also they have a connective structure based on metallic wires and probes the same one used for EMG sensors. The sensorized liner was completed with the electronic board which allows to detect the signals from the pressure and EMG sensors. The electronic system was equipped with two OY Motion Gravity digital boards for acquisition, processing and transmission of EMG signals, a custom made board for the acquisition of pressure sensors' signals and 500 mA battery (Fig. 4).

**Fig. 4.** The final prototype, ready for the testing.

## 3   Conclusions and Future Developments

The development of a sensorized upper limb liner integrated with Hypermat allows the replacement of the reservoir currently used in orthopedic prosthetic departments with a scalable solution based on patient anthropometrics and economically sustainable. The proposed solution also allows the monitoring of point pressures on the stump on two different skin areas of the stump and improves the hygienisation of the socket system thanks to the breathability and washability of the fabric. The next steps will focus on the improvement of different system components such as: the development of semi-finished composites made with single-sided adhesive and metal fibers arranged sinusoid to ensure more stable and flexible connections between the sensors and the connector and the realization ad hoc of metal probes inside the connector itself. Positive preliminary comfort test was done with users. No group comparison because of unicity of the prosthesis. In a subsequent phase, extensive of usability tests are planned with a panel of users of the INAIL Prosthesis Center for the quantitative assessments of the prototype.

**Acknowledgement.** This study was supported by an INAIL Research Grant CUP E52F16003040005. The authors want to thanks all to the subjects who participated in the experimental sessions.

# References

1. Luma Institute: Innovating for People Handbook of Human-Centered Design Methods (2012)
2. Andreoni, G., Perego, P., Frumento, E. (eds.): M_Health Current and Future Applications. Springer, Cham (2019). https://doi.org/10.1007/978-3-030-02182-5
3. Andreoni, G., Massimo, B., Barbara, C.: Emerging issues in healthcare. In: Developing Biomedical Devices, pp. 3–14. Springer, Cham (2014)
4. Andreoni, G., Standoli, C.E., Perego, P.: Defining requirements and related methods for designing sensorized garments. Sensors **16**(6), 769 (2016)
5. Biddiss, E., Beaton, D., Chau, T.: Consumer design priorities for upper limb prosthetics. Disabil. Rehabil. Assist. Technol. **2**(6), 346–357 (2007)
6. Cordella, F., et al.: Literature review on needs of upper limb prosthesis users. Front. Neurosci. **10**, 209 (2016)
7. Antfolk, C., et al.: Sensory feedback in upper limb prosthetics. Expert Rev. Med. Devices **10**(1), 45–54 (2013)
8. Farina, D., Amsüss, S.: Reflections on the present and future of upper limb prostheses. Expert Rev. Med. Devices **13**(4), 321–324 (2016)
9. Leone, F., et al.: Simultaneous sEMG classification of wrist/hand gestures and forces. Front. Neurorobotics **13**, 42 (2019)

# Participant Modeling: The Use of a Guided Master in the Modern World of Virtual Reality Exposure Therapy Targeting Fear of Heights

Pamela Caravas[1](✉), Jacob Kritikos[2], Giorgos Alevizopoulos[3,4], and Dimitris Koutsouris[5]

[1] Member of Institute of Coaching, McLean Hospital, Harvard Medical School Affiliate, Boston, MA, USA
pamela@coachingevolution.org

[2] Department of Bioengineering, Imperial College London, South Kensington Campus, London, UK
jacob.kritikos20@imperial.ac.uk

[3] Head of Psychiatry Department of the General and Oncological Hospital, 14564 Athens, Greece
galev@nurs.uoa.gr

[4] National Kapodistrian University of Athens, 15784 Athens, Greece

[5] Head of Biomedical Engineering Laboratory, School of Electrical and Computer Engineering, National Technical University of Athens, 15780 Athens, Greece
dkoutsou@biomed.ntua.gr

**Abstract.** With the percentage of mental health disorders on the rise and the cost for their treatment reaching astounding proportions, research in their treatment has also become quite extensive. Individuals suffering from the effects of their disorder constituting them incapable at various levels to lead a normal life, the need for a more effective treatment has been well established. We have focused on anxiety disorders specifically, which have mainly fear as their common denominator, and using this we decided to look into the role of the clinician in live ET sessions so as to examine whether this role can be replicated in a VRET simulation with similar or better outcomes for the patient, i.e. a more effective treatment. Our hypothesis was tested in an outpatient setting with patients being separated into two groups. We examined whether the presence of a virtual guided master using participant modeling in a virtual environment was as effective or more effective than the Standard ET method. Our VR system is based on the Full Body Immersive Virtual Reality System with Motion Recognition Camera created by Jacob Kritikos. The outcomes were gathered via the Session Rating Scale by Miller which led to the conclusion that participant modeling within a VRET approach can lead to a better treatment quality.

**Keywords:** Virtual reality · Cognitive behavioral therapy · Exposure therapy · Anxiety disorders · Specific phobias · Acrophobia · Motion tracking sensor · Motion recognition camera

© ICST Institute for Computer Sciences, Social Informatics and Telecommunications Engineering 2021
Published by Springer Nature Switzerland AG 2021. All Rights Reserved
P. Perego et al. (Eds.): ICWH 2020, LNICST 376, pp. 161–174, 2021.
https://doi.org/10.1007/978-3-030-76066-3_13

# 1  Introduction

Virtual Reality (VR) is still not ubiquitous in our daily lives, yet it seems to be so in the world of gaming and medicine. VR and its technological evolution, known as augmented reality (AR), have replaced Bandura's videotaping and adapted his theory of "guided participant modeling", in which skills during a session to treat fear and phobias are modelled by clinicians or coaches, discussed as part of the CBT session, and then practiced [1]. Videotaping was widely used in the past as a means of feedback after practice along with the modeling aspect. What was also the case in the past in therapy sessions was focusing on affective and cognitive as well as behavioral aspects of performance.

The emerging technologies of VR and AR have certainly replaced videotaping, as also the presence of actual people in a room. They are shaping a new world affecting the socioeconomic domains exerting a considerable impact observed in the terms of financial expenditure and time. According to Rotolo et al., such technology is characterized by novelty, it is fast growing, it has impact in socioeconomics, it is defined by its impact and uncertainty [2]. VR falls in this domain even today.

Classical theories of treating phobias suggest that there are a number of reasons why people avoid seeking treatment leading to social and employment issues and relapses following initial attempts which, overall, cost the US health system $193.2 billion in lost earnings per year [3]. The hesitation to do so seems to be an established fact despite the growing number of effective interventions [4, 5]. Phobic individuals view their anxiety disorder as untreatable. A great number are not aware of available treatments and interventions. Also, there is approximately 25% of phobic patients who refuse to seek treatment as it involves confrontation with the phobic stimulus, therefore avoid exposure-based treatments, i.e., Exposure Therapy [5].

In the past, treatment of fears and phobias were characterized by the widespread belief that anxiety and fear can only be treated through verbal interpretive means, essentially making CBT the most prominent form. More recently, phobic individuals may choose among cognitive therapy, systematic desensitisation, modeling, imaginal or virtual reality exposure, and direct in vivo exposure [5, 6]. In this paper, and despite the doubt Bandura et al. have voiced as regards direct treatment approaches, we are examining the widely used Exposure Therapy (ET), which is also a cognitive behavioral technique [4, 7].

The reason we used Exposure Therapy as our preferred mode of treatment is its dictionary definition by the American Psychological Association: "*it works by habituation [...], disconfirming fearful predictions; and increasing feelings of self-efficacy and mastery*" [8]. In therapy, as well as in coaching, the element of self-efficacy and personal mastery hold a prominent position when it comes to developing skills and the right mentality for effective reaction to a fearful stimulus. This can be leveraged by repeated exposure that leads to eliminating anxiety over time [9, 10]. As mentioned earlier, an estimated 25% of phobic individuals avoid treatments and interventions for fear of directly confronting their phobia. ET assists in the right direction by creating a mindset that modifies the current perception of the phobia and the way it might "harm" those individuals [11].

Considering the socioeconomic issues caused by phobic individuals who have avoided the direct confrontation approach, VR has also come to assist the medical field in one more way: it offers the safety and security needed by individuals to pursue, become engaged in and complete their treatment. The combination of a most effective, yet avoided, exposure-based treatment and the emerging technology of VR has led to Virtual Reality Exposure Therapy (VRET) as being one of the most common in the past years. VRET allows for a fully immersive experience, rather similar to real life, that evokes all emotions the individual receiving the treatment would have in the physical world [12–20]. When comparing virtual reality with *in vivo* exposure, it has become clear that technology provides a greater number of benefits, including the actual intervention a clinician can offer when being "present" during a VR-based session with direct coaching on daily circumstances that affect the patient's quality of life [21].

The focus of this paper has also been the safety that VR simulated environments provide the phobic individuals, while establishing their willingness to engage in an exposure-based treatment and an open mindset that will allow them to test out new reactions as modeled by their clinician or coach. Using the principle of far transfer of knowledge, any knowledge acquired in the virtual environment can be adopted easier in the physical world [22]. Bandura, Blanchard and Ritter's beliefs are also satisfied in the sense that treatment approaches that are based on socio-learning principles have a higher likelihood of being effective in creating generalized and enduring psychological changes [4].

The most important feature that has been taken to be critical for distinguishing between CBT, Standard ET and VRET theories of safety and effectiveness is that of the guided master in the guided participant modeling element that was designed by one of our authors, Jacob Kritikos. Film modeling, peer-modeling and self-modeling have been used effectively as a treatment intervention for adults with fears [23, 27]. While designing the apparatus and systems used, the aim was to integrate the concept of the virtual presence of another individual acting as the clinician, guiding and demonstrating non-fearful behavior, thus helping the adult handle the feared stimulus. Anxiety has been seen to be reduced in the phobic individual, physiological arousal and negative thoughts minimized, and core skills are acquired that may then be transferrable in real life [28].

The purpose of this paper was to compare VRET and Standard ET in addition to CBT and establish that, in ET, the presence of the therapist in the virtual environment could be a factor that affects trust, thus increasing the sense of safety in the phobic individual, that would make VRET an effective method of treatment. Our research aimed to suggest that the presence of the clinician is essential either for providing instructions and coaching or to ensure that the participant feels safe and willing prior to engaging in the simulation [29]. Using Rosenthal and Bandura's socio-learning principles, i.e. requesting from participants to actively model behavior after they have received clear instructions, seen the non-fearful behavior by the clinician and fully comprehended the benefits of this behavior, we expect to show that the presence of the therapist leads to a reduction in ineffective reactions and increased self-efficacy [30, 31].

It is currently acknowledged that the therapist's presence and guidance throughout the ET yields higher success rates [17, 32–35]. Although we understand that the combination of CBT or Standard ET with VR and guided mastery requires further investigation, the value of the participant modeling approach has already become the focus of the scientific community for the benefits it yields.

Using technology and the system proposed by one of our authors [16, 35], we make use of the classical Bandura theory of guided participant modeling in a raw form, to the extent the simulation properties currently allow us. The design of the system helps investigate whether VRET with a virtual clinician present in the VR environment facilitates knowledge transfer, thus improving practical application in the physical world, increasing the levels of self-efficacy and confidence and, consequently, establishing the effectiveness of the technology-based intervention [28, 30, 36]. Currently, we propose that the presence of a clinician in the VR environment be added to the VRET approach as a guided master (Fig. 1) as we presume that the virtual clinician may increase the level of safety, comfort and willingness to handle fears and phobias, and, more specifically, acrophobia, which is the focal point of the present paper.

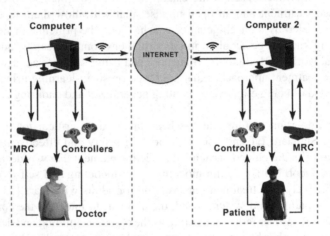

**Fig. 1.** System flow of the proposed system.

## 2  System Description

### 2.1  Hardware

[a] Two Desktop Computers with the following specifications: Graphics Card: NVIDIA GeForce GTX 1070, CPU: AMD Ryzen 7 2700X, RAM: 16 GB G.Skill TridentZ DDR4, Video Output: HDMI 1.3, USB Ports: 3x USB 3.0 and 1x USB 2.0. [b] Two Oculus Rift Virtual Reality Headsets with their Touch Controllers, one for each hand. [c] Two Astra Motion Recognition Cameras (MRC) designed by Orbbec, one for each Computer. The MRCs are connected to the Computers with a USB 2.0 cable. The motion tracking accuracy has an error range of $\pm$ 1–3 mm from a 1 m distance, whereas at a 3 m distance, it is estimated at approximately $\pm12.7$ mm. The optimized maximum range is about 6 m. In detail, Astra consists of 2 cameras: a Depth Camera, image size 640 * 480 (VGA) @ 30FPS and an RGB Camera, image size 1280 * 720 @ 30FPS (UVC Support), which have 60° horiz × 49.5° vert. (73° diagonal) field of view.

## 2.2 Software

The software used is the following [a] Windows 10 Operating System with the drivers for the Orbbec Astra MRC and Oculus Rift installed. [b] Unity 3D, which is used as the basic program for creating the virtual environment. All the hardware pieces (i.e. sensors, controllers, trackers, headset, camera etc.) are controlled by Unity 3D [c] Blender 3D Computer Graphics Software is used for creating 3D objects, animated visual effects, UV Mapping and materials integrated in Unity 3D; [d] Adobe Photoshop is used for creating images for the materials integrated in Blender; [e] OVRPlugin for the operation of the Oculus Rift equipment in Unity 3D; [f] Nuitrack SDK as the motion recognition middleware between the developed software and the MRC.

## 2.3 Body Recognition

The Orbbec Persee MRC can recognize 19 joints of the human body (Fig. 2). Each joint is essentially a point in 3D space represented by 3 coordinates: x, y, and z, where the y-axis is the height axis and the x-z plain is the floor on which the user moves. This topology can be seen in (Fig. 3). The MRC is placed across the user on the -z axis. Therefore, the user can walk on the x-z plain, constantly remaining within the tracking field of the MRC while still facing it.

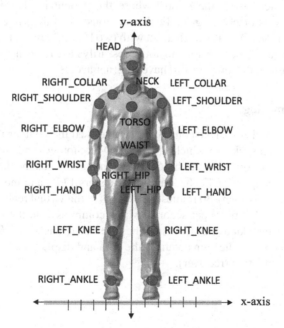

**Fig. 2.** The joints used to track the body.

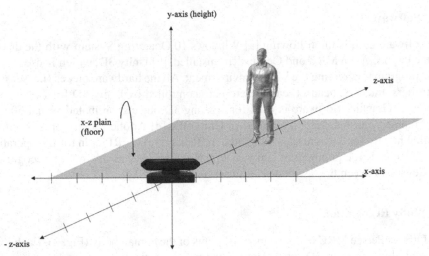

**Fig. 3.** Representation of the MRC recognition topology. The MRC is the reference point at $(0, 0, 0)$ and can recognize at a range of $(x, y, z > 0)$.

### 2.4 System Setup

We have two physical areas, the Area-P where the patient is placed, and the Area-D where the doctor is placed (Fig. 1). Each area consists of the same equipment: one Desktop Computer, one Oculus Rift Headset with two Hand Controllers, and one Motion Recognition Camera. Those two areas do not necessarily have to be in the same premises, but it is required for both Computers to have internet access.

### 2.5 Data Transmitting

In order for Area-P and Area-D to communicate, we used the UDP protocol. The Area-P Computer creates a socket in which, the Area-D Computer sends data. The Area-D Computer creates a socket in which the Area-P Computer sends the data; thereby, both Computers can exchange data. Each Computer transfers 17 data points of 4 bytes every frame. Consequently, for every 30 frames, i.e. the fps of the virtual reality simulation, we have to transmit 2.04 kilobytes per second, which complies with the HiveMQ transfer limits. A C# script embedded in Unity dispatches the data (transmitter). Then, a C# script embedded in the Unity application acquires the data and displays each other's avatar in the same virtual simulation (receiver).

## 3 Method

To overcome the disadvantages of exposure-based treatment that may deter phobic adults from engaging in an effective intervention, we investigated the value of a virtual clinician's presence in the Virtual Reality simulation as part of the VRET approach. We collected data from a total of 12 participants (7 men and 5 women) who were recruited after being diagnosed with acrophobia. These were randomly distributed into two groups,

**Fig. 4.** Virtual reality environment. The blue skeleton is the patient and the orange is the doctor.

[A] and [B]. All participants had to perform the same tasks assigned to them once they entered the VR room. Both groups were given the same instructions prior to the session. The session lasted approximately 10 min. The assigned tasks are described as follows: Each participant proceeds to Area-P in the actual room and puts on the Oculus Rift Virtual Reality Headset the moment they feel ready to engage in the session. Prior to this, they have consulted with their clinician or coach and have discussed the key benefits of the sessions, that is, to feel safe and have reduced anxiety afterwards as regards their phobia. The participant, then, enters the virtual environment, specifically designed to induce acrophobia. The environment is an apartment room located on the 5$^{th}$ floor of a building with an open balcony door (Fig. 4). Each participant is told that a "skeleton" figure is a reflection of their body and any move they make, consciously or subconsciously, in the real, physical world, they will see taking place as they move around the virtual environment.

The participants in both groups are instructed, during their session, to complete three consecutive tasks. They are not aware of these tasks prior to the session. The first task is to move towards the balcony, exit the open doors and step out on the balcony. They, then, need to place their hands (the Controllers) on the front railing of the balcony and remain in this state for a number of minutes. Following this, they are requested to lean forward and catch a dangling object which is at a significant distance from the railing. The final task is to return inside the apartment after they have caught the dangling object. The session is considered complete. The participants remove the Headset and the Controllers allowing them to return to the real world. A demonstration video is available here: vimeo.com/486699554.

Group-A had an additional "skeleton" figure representing the clinician. At this stage we did not add the clinician modeling the non-fearful behavior as the focus was on investigating the impact of the mere presence of a clinician in the room. Group-B had to perform the tasks with no other figure in the virtual environment. The phobic participants in Group-A were informed of the clinician being present the moment they saw his figure in the VR environment. The particular trial was approved by the Ethics Committee of the National Technical University with protocol number #9824.

## 4 Data Analysis

In order to evaluate the presence of the clinician in the VR simulation, we used Dr. Scott D. Miller's questionnaire (Appendix), founder of the 'International Center for Clinical Excellence', an international community of clinicians, researchers, and educators working together, in order to promote excellence in behavioral health services. Over the past few years, Scott D. Miller has created numerous rating questionnaires, which aim to provide psychiatrists with solid information on the quality of their sessions from the patient's perspective. We decided to include this particular questionnaire in our study, as opposed to other rating questionnaires, due to the fact that we considered it the most fitting for our experiment; more specifically, the questionnaire focuses on the level as well as the quality of interaction between the patient and the therapist within the VR environment throughout the course of the session, the extent to which the patient's anxiety and phobia was addressed in the VR setting with the interactive assistance of the psychiatrist, and whether the presence of the therapist in the VR environment was beneficial and constructive for the patient.

**Table 1.** The answers of the questions from Group A.

| Participant no. | Q1 | Q2 | Q3 | Q4 |
|---|---|---|---|---|
| 1 | 8 | 7 | 9 | 8 |
| 2 | 8 | 6 | 8 | 8 |
| 3 | 7 | 6 | 7 | 7 |
| 4 | 10 | 9 | 7 | 9 |
| 5 | 9 | 6 | 8 | 8 |
| 6 | 7 | 8 | 8 | 7 |

**Table 2.** The answers of the questions from Group B.

| Participant no. | Q1 | Q2 | Q3 | Q4 |
|---|---|---|---|---|
| 1 | 5 | 6 | 6 | 6 |
| 2 | 8 | 7 | 8 | 7 |
| 3 | 7 | 7 | 6 | 8 |
| 4 | 5 | 5 | 7 | 6 |
| 5 | 6 | 8 | 8 | 7 |
| 6 | 4 | 6 | 7 | 5 |

According to the answers of each participant (Table 1 and 2) the Q1 from Group A has Mean $= 8.17$, SD $= 1.116$ and from Group B has Mean $= 5.83$, SD $= 1.47$. The Q2 from Group A has Mean $= 7$, SD $= 1.26$ and from Group B has Mean $= 6.5$, SD $= 1.04$. The Q3 from Group A has Mean $= 8$, SD $= 0.89$ and from Group B has Mean $= 7.5$, SD $= 0.89$. The Q4 from Group A has Mean $= 7.83$, SD $= 0.75$ and from Group B has Mean $= 6.5$, SD $= 1.04$.

An independent sample t-test was conducted for each question. The alpha level is a $= .05$ and the degrees of freedom are df $= 11$. Therefore, according to the Table of Student t-Distribution, the critical value is cv $= \pm 2.20$. Running the t-test concerning Q1 question, the value is $t(11) = 3.04$, p $= .012$. So, the obtained t-value exceeds the critical value. Subsequently, the t-test is significant, and the two samples are -statistically-significantly different. In conclusion, participants from Group-A feel more heard and understood than the participants from Group-B. Running the t-test concerning Q2 question, the value is $t(11) = .745$, p $= .473$. So, the obtained t-value does not exceed the critical value. Subsequently, the t-test is not significant, and the two samples are not -statistically- significantly different. In conclusion, participants from both groups worked on the same degree of anxiety issues. Running the t-test concerning Q3 question, the value is $t(11) = 1.93$, p $= .082$. So, the obtained t-value does not exceed the critical value. Subsequently, the t-test is not significant, and the two samples are not -statistically- significantly different. In conclusion, participants from both groups understood approximately in the same way the virtual reality simulation. Finally, running the t-test concerning Q4 question, the value is $t(11) = 2.53$, $p = .032$. So, the obtained t-value marginally exceeds the critical value. Subsequently, the t-test is marginally significant, and the two samples are marginally statistically significantly different. In conclusion, participants from Group-A felt better about the overall experience in comparison with Group-B.

## 5  Discussion

The hypothesis that the presence of the therapist in the VR simulation assists patients in confronting their phobia to a greater extent has been confirmed by the data gathered from the participants' results, as these were demonstrated in the responses given to the questionnaire they completed as well as the data analysis we conducted. The questionnaire is the main source of data as it focused on emotions and thoughts on the patient's end following the VRET sessions with the presence of a VR clinician within the simulation.

Question 1 concerns the extent to which the participant felt heard and understood throughout the VR simulation. In this question, we observed a significant difference between the answers of the two groups; this was primarily due to the fact that participants in Group-A were guided by a professional therapist, whereas, in Group-B, participants had to execute the entire exercise on their own, simply by following the oral instructions given by the therapist. That means that participants in Group-A felt the presence of the therapist in a more intense manner, since they could not only hear, but also see the psychiatrist providing them with guidance to successfully complete the task.

On the other hand, question 2, which concerns the extent to which the patient's anxiety was dealt with during the session, did not present big variations between the two groups. More specifically, both groups felt that their anxiety was confronted almost equally during the simulation, with or without the presence of the clinician.

In question 3, which refers to how much the system and the process of the session made sense to the participant, we observed a difference between the two groups; however, the difference was narrow, since neither group showed difficulty in understanding the way our VR system works.

Finally, in question 4, we observed a big difference between the two groups yet again, since the question concerns the overall rating of the session. In particular, Group-A participants felt that the presence of the therapist in the VR simulation assisted them more in confronting their phobia compared to Group-B participants, who had to execute the task only by receiving oral instructions.

Moreover, it is important to point out that, the MRC tracks patients' movements, places their physical body within the virtual environment and gives them the impression that they are moving and fully interacting with that environment, as they would in the real world. This allows patients to practice tasks whilst in the virtual environment, since it can recognize the entire body and movements of its limbs. Another interesting aspect of our study was that MRCs offer a remarkable feature: the tracking of the patient's physical movements is not only useful for placing their body in the virtual environment, but also for dispatching the information obtained by their movements in real time. Measurements of the patient's movements as they executed the exercises can help draw further conclusions about the patient's performance, i.e. whether the phobic patient completed the task effortlessly or not.

One primary limitation to our study was the fact that our experiment was short in duration and consisted of only some simple tasks. Thus, we presume that the addition of more tasks could increase the feeling of the clinician's presence in the VR room even for patients who were slightly apprehensive and uncomfortable with the feel of someone else "being around" in the VR room, considering that they would gradually get accustomed to the simulation and subsequently enhance their performance.

## 6 Conclusion

By analyzing the results of our study, we can deduce that there was an undeniable difference between the two groups concerning their performance quality within the VR simulation. Group-A, which was offered the assistance of a professional clinician in order to complete the exercise, presented a higher quality performance compared to Group-B, since the virtual presence of the clinician offered them a greater sense of safety and understanding of the procedure. Additionally, according to the data analysis mentioned above, we can deduce that participants in Group-A evidently found their session much more efficient and beneficial, than those in Group-B; more specifically, participants in Group-A stated they felt much more heard and understood, they comprehended the treatment process with consummate ease, and, finally, they confronted their phobia in a more constructive and effective way. Therefore, we conclude that the clinician's presence within the VR environment can assist patients in confronting their fears as well as successfully executing the tasks assigned to a greater extent.

## Appendix

**Q1:** On a scale of 0–10, to what degree did you feel heard and understood today during the Virtual Reality simulation, 10 being completely and 0 being not at all?

If the client gives you two numbers, you should ask, "which number would you like me to put?" or, "is it closer to X or Y?"

If the client gives one number for heard and another for understood, then go with the lowest score.

**Q2:** On a scale of 0–10, to what degree did we work on the anxiety issues that you wanted to work on through the Virtual Reality simulation today, 10 being completely and 0 being not at all?

If the client asks for clarification, you should ask, "did we talk about what you wanted to talk about or address? How well on a scale from 0–10?"

If the client gives you two numbers, you should ask, "which number would you like me to put?" or, "is it closer to X or Y?"

**Q3:** On a scale of 0–10, how well did the Virtual Reality simulation make sense and fit for you?

If the client gives you two numbers, you should ask, "which number would you like me to put?" or, "is it closer to X or Y?"

If the client gives one number for make sense and then offers another number for fit, then go with the lowest score.

**Q4:** So, given your answers on the Virtual Reality simulation, how would you rate how things were in today's session overall, with 10 meaning that the session was right for you and 0 meaning that something important that was missing from the visit?

If the client gives you two numbers, you should ask, "which number would you like me to put?" or, "is it closer to X or Y?".

# References

1. Greco, A., Valenza, G., Scilingo, E.P.: Advances in electrodermal activity processing with applications for mental health: From heuristic methods to convex optimization (2016)
2. Rotolo, D., Hicks, D., Martin, B.R.: What is an emerging technology? Res. Policy **44**, 1827–1843 (2015)
3. Insel, T.R.: Assessing the economic costs of serious mental illness. Am. J. Psychiatry **165**(6), 663–665 (2008)
4. Bandura, A., Blanchard, E.B., Ritter, B.: Relative efficacy of desensitization and modeling approaches for inducing behavioral, affective, and attitudinal changes. J. Pers. Soc. Psychol. **13**, 173 (1969)
5. Wolitzky-Taylor, K.B., Horowitz, J.D., Powers, M.B., Telch, M.J.: Psychological approaches in the treatment of specific phobias: a meta-analysis. Clin. Psychol. Rev. **28**, 1021–1037 (2008)
6. Wells, A., Papageorgiou, C.: Brief cognitive therapy for social phobia: a case series. Behav. Res. Ther. **39**, 713–720 (2001)
7. Gromer, D., et al.: Height simulation in a virtual reality CAVE system: validity of fear responses and effects of an immersion manipulation. Front. Hum. Neurosci. **12**, 372 (2018)
8. Craske, M.G., Treanor, M., Conway, C.C., Zbozinek, T., Vervliet, B.: Maximizing exposure therapy: an inhibitory learning approach. Behav. Res. Ther. **58**, 10–23 (2014)
9. Baker, A., Mystkowski, J., Culver, N., Yi, R., Mortazavi, A., Craske, M.G.: Does habituation matter? Emotional processing theory and exposure therapy for acrophobia. Behav. Res. Ther. **48**, 1139–1143 (2010)
10. Herrmann, M.J., et al.: Medial prefrontal cortex stimulation accelerates therapy response of exposure therapy in acrophobia. Brain Stimul. **10**, 291–297 (2017)
11. Cohen, D.C.: Comparison of self-report and overt-behavioral procedures for assessing acrophobia. Behav. Ther. **8**, 17–23 (1977)
12. Krijn, M., Emmelkamp, P.M.G., Biemond, R., De Wilde De Ligny, C., Schuemie, M.J., Van Der Mast, C.A.P.G.: Treatment of acrophobia in virtual reality: the role of immersion and presence. Behav. Res. Ther. **42**, 229–239 (2004)
13. Müller, M., et al.: Height simulation in a virtual reality CAVE system: validity of fear responses and effects of an immersion manipulation. Front. Hum. Neurosci. **12**, 372 (2018)
14. Emmelkamp, P.M.G., Bruynzeel, M., Drost, L., van der Mast, C.A.P.G.: Virtual reality treatment in acrophobia: a comparison with exposure in vivo. CyberPsychol. Behav. **4**, 335–339 (2002)
15. Carlin, A.S., Hoffman, H.G., Weghorst, S.: Virtual reality and tactile augmentation in the treatment of spider phobia: a case report. Behav. Res. Ther. **35**, 153–158 (1997)

16. Kritikos, J., et al.: Comparison between full body motion recognition camera interaction and hand controllers interaction used in virtual reality exposure therapy for acrophobia. Sensors (Switzerland), vol. 20, no. 5 (2020)
17. Kritikos, J., Poulopoulou, S., Zoitaki, C., Douloudi, M., Koutsouris, D.: Full body immersive virtual reality system with motion recognition camera targeting the treatment of spider phobia. In: Cipresso, P., Serino, S., Villani, D. (eds.) MindCare 2019. LNICST, vol. 288, pp. 216–230. Springer, Cham (2019). https://doi.org/10.1007/978-3-030-25872-6_18
18. Kritikos, J., Caravas, P., Tzannetos, G., Douloudi, M., Koutsouris, D.: Emotional stimulation during motor exercise: an integration to the holistic rehabilitation framework. In: Proceedings of the Annual International Conference of the IEEE Engineering in Medicine and Biology Society, EMBS (2019)
19. Kritikos, J., Mehmeti, A., Nikolaou, G., Koutsouris, D.: Fully portable low-cost motion capture system with real-time feedback for rehabilitation treatment. In: International Conference on Virtual Rehabilitation, ICVR, vol. 2019 (2019)
20. Kritikos, J., Tzannetos, G., Zoitaki, C., Poulopoulou, S., Koutsouris, P.D.: Anxiety detection from Electrodermal Activity Sensor with movement interaction during Virtual Reality Simulation. In: International IEEE/EMBS Conference on Neural Engineering, NER (2019)
21. Coelho, C.M., Waters, A.M., Hine, T.J., Wallis, G.: The use of virtual reality in acrophobia research and treatment. J. Anxiety Disord. **23**, 563–574 (2009)
22. Freeman, D., et al.: Automated psychological therapy using immersive virtual reality for treatment of fear of heights: a single-blind, parallel-group, randomised controlled trial. The Lancet Psychiatry **5**, 625–632 (2018)
23. Bandura, A., Grusec, J.E., Menlove, F.L.: Vicarious extinction of avoidance behavior. J. Pers. Soc. Psychol. **5**, 16 (1967)
24. Bandura, A., Menlove, F.L.: Factors determining vicarious extinction of avoidance behavior through symbolic modeling. J. Pers. Soc. Psychol. **8**, 99 1968
25. Ladouceur, R.: Participant modeling with or without cognitive treatment for phobias. J. Consult. Clin. Psychol. **51**, 942 (1983)
26. Meichenbaum, D.H., Examination of model characteristics in reducing avoidance behavior. J. Pers. Soc. Psychol. **17**, 298 (1971)
27. Melamed, B.G., et al.: Effects of film modeling on the reduction of anxiety-related behaviors in individuals varying in level of previous experience in the stress situation. J. Consult. Clin. Psychol. **46**, 1397 (1978)
28. Milosevic, I., Radomsky, A.S.: Safety behaviour does not necessarily interfere with exposure therapy. Behav. Res. Ther. **46**, 1111–1118 (2008)
29. Gilroy, L.J., Kirkby, K.C., Daniels, B.A., Menzies, R.G., Montgomery, I.M.: Controlled comparison of computer-aided vicarious exposure versus live exposure in the treatment of spider phobia. Behav. Ther. **31**, 733–744 (2000)
30. Klingman, A., Malamed, B.G., Cuthberg, M.I., Hermecz, D.A.: Effects of participant modeling on information acquisition and skill utilization. J. Consult. Clin. Psychol. **52**, 414 (1984)
31. Müller, B.H., Kull, S., Wilhelm, F.H., Michael, T.: One-session computer-based exposure treatment for spider-fearful individuals - Efficacy of a minimal self-help intervention in a randomised controlled trial. J. Behav. Ther. Exp. Psychiatry **42**, 179–184 (2011)
32. Williams, S.L., Zane, G.: Guided mastery and stimulus exposure treatments for severe performance anxiety in agoraphobics. Behav. Res. Ther. **27**, 232–245 (1989)
33. Hoffart, A., Sexton, H., Hedley, L.M., Martinsen, E.W.: Mechanisms of change in cognitive therapy for panic disorder with agoraphobia. J. Behav. Ther. Exp. Psychiatry **39**, 292 (2008)
34. Hoffart, A.: Cognitive and guided mastery therapy of agoraphobia: long-term outcome and mechanisms of change. Cognit. Ther. Res. **22**, 195 (1998)

35. Kritikos, J., Alevizopoulos, G., Koutsouris, D.: Personalized virtual reality human-computer interaction for psychiatric and neurological illnesses: a dynamically adaptive virtual reality environment that changes according to real-time feedback from electrophysiological signal responses. Front. Hum. Neurosci. (2021)
36. Bandura, A., Jeffery, R.W., Wright, C.L.: Efficacy of participant modeling as a function of response induction aids. J. Abnorm. Psychol. **83**, 56 (1974)

# Wearable Applications

# Automatic Assessment of Clinical Frailty
# of Parkinson's Disease Subjects

Marcello C. Fusca[1] (iD), Emanuela Riva[2], Paolo Perego[1] (iD), Francesca Omini[3],
Emanuele Conte[2], Marco Impallomeni[2], Stefania Rosaspina[2], Antonio Grillo[2],
Suardi Teresa[2], Stefano Fabbrini[2], and Giuseppe Andreoni[1,4(✉)] (iD)

[1] Design Department, TeDH-SensibiLab, Politecnico di Milano, Milan, Italy
giuseppe.andreoni@polimi.it
[2] A.S.P. "Golgi-Redaelli", Milan, Italy
[3] Università degli Studi di Milano-Bicocca, Scuola di Specialità in Medicina Fisica e
Riabilitativa, Milan, Italy
[4] CNR, Institute of Molecular Bioimaging and Physiology - IBFM, Segrate (Milan), Italy

**Abstract.** A wearable actigraph was applied in the functional assessment of subject affected by Parkinson Disease in Day Hospital setting. 24 Parkinson Disease
patients participated in this study. A set of standard functional tests (6-Minutes
Walking Test, Timed-Up-and-Go test, 10-m and 50-m) were administered to collect data of functioning and physiatrist assigned the score according to the Clinical
Frailty Scale. An automatic evaluation of this frailty score is proposed using data
from 6-Minutes Walking Test and Timed-Up-and-Go test. The coherence of this
automated classification method based on a basic summative linear equation of the
2 functional scores, is 66,7% with respect to the score assigned by skilled physiatrists. The inclusion of the other data is expected to improve reliability and the
possibility to have an automatic identification of the frailty level through quantitative data could open the possibility to have a more detailed assessment and even
continuous and domiciliary follow ups. Our goal is to have a predictive tool for
the patient's state of frailty.

**Keywords:** Clinical frailty scale · Wearable · Actigraphy · Parkinson's disease ·
Functional assessment

## 1 Introduction

Parkinson's disease (PD) is a neurodegenerative disease of the central nervous system
(CNS) with reduced levels of dopamine due to the degeneration of neurons in the *sub-
stantia nigra* area. It is characterized by a progressive and chronic disorder, mainly
concerning the control of movements and balance [1]. PD is characterized clinically by
precise distinctive signs:

P. Perego et al. (Eds.): ICWH 2020, LNICST 376, pp. 177–187, 2021.
https://doi.org/10.1007/978-3-030-76066-3_14

- involuntary tremors at rest of some parts of the body (e.g. one hand, one foot)
- muscle stiffness (linked to an involuntary increase in muscle tone) which makes a series of movements, such as getting up from an armchair, difficult or impossible. It can affect the limbs, but also the neck or trunk
- *bradykinesia*, i.e. progressive and important slowing of movements
- *akinesia*, i.e. the difficulty in starting a movement (e.g. starting to walk)
- postural instability with loss of balance (in the late stages of the disease).

Often this disease is associated with the elderly population. Fragility is also related to being elderly. In a frail elderly person, the onset of PD creates an exacerbation of his vulnerability to the various internal and external stimuli to which the subject tries to balance. All these factors strongly affect the ability to stand of the subjects so that falls are one of the most frequent complications in people with PD and are the main cause of morbidity and hospitalization [2]. The prevalence of falls ranges from 11% to 68% in subjects with PD. The development of measures that discriminate "fallers" from "non fallers" in people with PD will allow to steer interventions to prevent the risk of falls.

The state of frailty of the subject is assessed by physiatrists by assigning a proper score or level according to the Clinical Frailty Scale (CFS) [3, 4]: 1 = Very Fit, 2 = Well, 3 = Managing Well, 4 = Vulnerable, 5 = Mildly Frail, 6 = Moderately Frail, 7 = Severely Frail, 8 = Very Severely Frail, 9 = Terminally Ill. The CFS was a signi-ficant predictor of inpatient mortality in idiopathic Parkinson's disease patients admitted to the acute hospital and it may be useful as a marker of risk in this vulnerable population [15]. For every subject, the revision of this index is not frequent because it is related to follow-up visits. Indeed, its continuous update could be relevant for PD patient monitoring. The possibility of monitoring the patient both in hospital and at home opens up the ability to better treat the person by continuously adapting the interventions necessary to safeguard his quality of life. An even priority mission is the possibility to define a personalized therapy program, that is crucial since the early beginning of the pathology so to have a stable functioning and high quality of life. Despite lack of training for medical staff, increasing frailty was correlated with functional decline and mortality supporting the validity of the CFS as a frailty screening tool for clinicians [16].

The recent introduction of wearables systems for monitoring subject's parameters including gait performance and variables and physiological signals offers a unique opportunity to help clinician in assessing the conditions of the patients and tune the therapy accordingly [5]. Automatic evaluation of PD symptoms using wearable sensors has been proposed. This quantitative approach may improve patient-doctor interaction, influence therapeutic decisions, and ultimately ameliorate patients' global health status [19]. The wearable sensor-based gait analysis reaches clinical applicability providing a high-biomechanical resolution for gait impairment in PD [21]. In our previous work [6, 7], a Wearable Actigraph (WA) was developed and validated [8] for collecting biome-chanical parameters of human gait even during the execution of specific functional tests:

6-Minutes Walking Test (6MWT), Timed-Up-and-Go test (TUG), 10-m and 50-m test. This new wearable device for functional evaluation provides a set of parameters that integrate the standard clinical outcome of each test for evaluating the global motor functioning of subjects. When considering an elderly person, his state of health can be more or less compromised depending on the particular state in which he is found after personal life experiences. The biological subsystems that make up the organism have complex correlations that only an expert doctor can evaluate deeply and correctly. The geriatrician who must evaluate the health status of an elderly person is faced with a particularly complex clinical picture because each of these biological systems can be more or less compromised by disease and age and consequently also the relative interaction dynamics of biological systems are more complex to interpret. The frailty of the elderly is a particularly complex and highly dynamic state of equilibrium in the sense that small perturbations can induce large and drastic changes in his health. These dynamics if neglected, can also lead to the death of the elderly. When the fragile situation is acute, death may be inevitable in the three months following its appearance. Among the various tools that the physiatrist has available to assess the patient's frailty, there is the CFS. The complexity and variability of compromise of biological systems requires an expert physician and the patient's evaluation becomes subjective. Quantitative tools can help.

We will focus on the global functional outcome of walking test and the clinical frailty scale classification of the PD patient. The goal of the study here described is the possibility to develop a method and an algorithm for an automatic classification system of the frailty level of PD patients based on the recorded biomechanical outcomes in standard functional tests using 6MWT and TUG test. If this is possible, it means that we can use functional tests as a personalized database to have a predictive tool for the patient's state of fragility. Although for what has been said, the state of frailty of the elderly subject described as CFS can be correctly and specifically assessed by a geriatrician, we propose the use of wearable technologies such as WA to help the geriatrician in a pre-triage by applying a two-steps approach. In the first phase, WA can be used as source of data to score the patient's state of fragility according to predicted CFS by the proposed algorithm. In the second phase, the physiatrist evaluates the patient's state of fragility according to his expert clinical judgement using CFS. This means that beyond the precision of the proposed method (that is, even if good percentages of correct evaluation are demonstrated), it can be seen as an "inexperienced geriatric practitioner". However, it has its own importance in the management of the clinical entry or follow-up routine both in the hospital and at home because the healthy status of a PD subject is not the same within and across days. In fact, the system in phase 1 can be seen as a monitoring of the patient's state of frailty which can generate an alarm to activate actions in a short time. This allows to anticipate an evaluation of the patient by the physiatrist which otherwise would have only taken place in subsequent times depending on the programming carried out in the previous visit and without any information on the evolution of the fragile condition over time.

## 2 Materials and Methods

### 2.1 Subjects

As study population, a court of 24 subjects (19 males and 5 females), aged between 68 and 91 years with a PD diagnosis, was recruited at the geriatric institute *Azienda Servizi alla Persona "Piero Redaelli"* in Milan (Italy). All subjects were able to walk alone. The use of walking aids was permitted. The following Table 1 describes the characteristics of the participants to the study. The execution of the tests was limited to those already programmed by the attending physiatrist for the patient. We have limited ourselves only to adding a non-invasive tool for recording the data of interest. Before performing the functional tests, the subject was received in a study by his physiatrist where he was explained how the tests would be performed, with what tools, what they entailed for him and for what purpose. The subject was also introduced to the operators who would perform the tests (some of these were already known to patients). Having received complete information, the subject could decide whether to sign the individual informed consent. All the enlisted subjects chose to participate in the project and signed the individual informed consent. All subjects were able to complete the protocols of test setup.

### 2.2 Anthropometric Measures and Data Collection

The personal data, age, height and weight are recorded. Anthropometric measures of the lower limbs were measured for each subject as input for biomechanical model. Shoes are included for anthropometric measurement on the initial setup. Anthropometric segments are measured while the subject is standing: lower limb (ground-greater trochanter), ground- malleolus, lateral condyle-greater trochanter, malleolus- lateral condyle, and fifth metatarsal-malleolus. The width of the foot, length of the foot, and outer distance between the feet are acquired to the ground when the subject is resting in natural balance. The physiatrist assesses the subject's state of fragility using the score of CFS. All data are recorded by hand of physiatrist on paper forms defined by protocol.

### 2.3 System for Data Collection and Protocol Setup

Patients should not perform tests other than those already scheduled. Data were collected while performing the standard programmed clinical assessment during the routine Day Hospital activity and periodical follow up. Each subject must perform four functional walking tests (10-m, 50-m, TUG and 6MWT). All data are recorded by hand of physiatrist on paper forms defined by protocol. The sequence of tests and the pause between tests were chosen to take account of the patient's fatigue and fragility. The functional walking tests were executed in a large corridor of Hospital. Any approaches with other people (both staff and otherwise) were managed in time by the operators asking to clear the passage. A linear path of 10 meters was used for the 10-m test. A linear path of 25 m was used for 50-m test with one turn back around a visible corner. A linear path of 3 m with a corner for turn back and a rigid chair with four legs without wheels and armrests was used for TUG. A linear path of 30 m with two corner for turn back was used for

**Table 1.** Subjects sample and characteristics.

| ID No. | Age (yrs) | Gender | Weight (Kg) | BMI | Stature (cm) | Walking aid |
|---|---|---|---|---|---|---|
| GRP001 | 80 | M | 66 | 28,2 | 153 | None |
| GRP002 | 77 | M | 79 | 26,4 | 173 | None |
| GRP003 | 82 | M | 72 | 24,1 | 173 | Stick |
| GRP004 | 83 | M | 96 | 32,1 | 173 | None |
| GRP005 | 91 | M | 82 | 32,0 | 160 | Stick |
| GRP006 | 81 | M | 70 | 22,9 | 175 | None |
| GRP007 | 81 | M | 84 | 29,8 | 168 | Walker |
| GRP008 | 68 | M | 65 | 23,6 | 166 | None |
| GRP009 | 81 | M | 80 | 24,7 | 180 | None |
| GRP010 | 78 | M | 82 | 32,4 | 159 | Walker |
| GRP011 | 77 | F | 69 | 29,1 | 154 | Quadripod |
| GRP012 | 69 | M | 56 | 21,3 | 162 | Stick |
| GRP013 | 78 | M | 49 | 17,8 | 166 | Quadripod |
| GRP014 | 82 | F | 78 | 27,3 | 169 | None |
| GRP015 | 88 | F | 75,5 | 24,7 | 175 | None |
| GRP016 | 79 | M | 82 | 28,4 | 170 | Stick |
| GRP017 | 81 | M | 70 | 22,9 | 175 | None |
| GRP018 | 75 | M | 83 | 27,1 | 175 | Stick |
| GRP019 | 78 | F | 60 | 28,5 | 145 | None |
| GRP020 | 84 | M | 79 | 24,4 | 180 | None |
| GRP021 | 83 | F | 50 | 21,9 | 151 | None |
| GRP022 | 74 | M | 75 | 27,9 | 164 | None |
| GRP023 | 85 | M | 76 | 26,6 | 169 | None |
| GRP024 | 84 | M | 54 | 18,7 | 170 | None |
| *Average* | *80,0* | | *72,2* | *25,9* | *166,9* | |
| *Std* | *5,2* | | *11,8* | *3,9* | *9,3* | |

6MWT. Along the way of corridor there are signs to define the starting point of the test, the points of turn-back around which to reverse the walking path and the measure of the distance traveled for an easy manual measurement according to the standard protocol. A stopwatch was used for manual measures of time. The subjects walked with their shoes and eventually with their walking aids. The beats per minute (bpm) were registered by oximeter at rest and after the 6MWT was executed. During the tests, measurements were made both automatically by the IMU system (it was turned on and off before and after each test) and manually by a skilled operator registering on a paper report the traveled distance, the number of steps and the time of walking. The step's length and gait speed were self-selected with the only initial request to walk as fast as possible according to protocol.

Before the subject began the test, he stood still and motionless for 10 s to record the acceleration baseline. At the end of the test a 10-s time of motionless was asked before concluding the data recording. In all tests, this baseline was used during data processing for offset compensation with respect to the action of gravity on IMU output. All tests were executed after a proper recovery period in-between two trials. 3D accelerations of the center of mass (COM) were recorded by a small WA whose main elements are: a 3D IMU, microprocessor for basic data preprocessing, Bluetooth data transmission and memory module supporting a microSD card for the logging of data up to 1 week, a LiPo rechargeable battery. The microSD can be removed. Tri-axial accelerations of the pelvis were collected at a sampling frequency of 64 Hz. The WA can store several consecutive tests in different files and subsequently download them in bulk. The data was downloaded at the end of the tests performed by each subject and the device was reset. Four raw data files (one for each test) were generated for each patient. Every file's name was renamed putting in the format label the execution date, the subject identifier and the type of test. A dedicated software developed in Matlab executed off-line data processing using the biomechanical model and the method presented in [6–8]. Post processing of raw data produced by IMU system in all tests used raw data and manual data from 50-m test to define input parameters so to adapt the biomechanical model to the subject.When the subject is moving, in order to measure the acceleration of his COM, the IMU must be placed near the COM itself. The experimental protocol uses a single IMU for the maximum simplification of the procedure and equipment. IMU with a triaxial accelerometer is placed on the back of the subjects on the pelvis and precisely next to the second sacral vertebra. An elastic belt with a pocket firmly fixes the device to the body. This is done to avoid artifacts in raw data originating from movements of the device with respect to the COM. Concerning the biomechanical approach, the wearable IMU-based system for kinematic gait analysis implements the pendulum and harmonic oscillator models [11–13] with an original approach [6–8]. The biomechanical model introduces simplifies the human anatomical structure into a rigid body with the joints which are connected to the bars that represent the legs. Also, the legs are considered as a rigid body hinged on an axis passing through the COM. The swinging movement of the legs in the execution of the steps is assumed to be an oscillation of an equivalent pendulum, and the natural balance is obtained with the legs aligned along the vertical during standing. The COM is a single point where it can be assumed that the whole mass of the body is concentrated. When a subject is at rest in a standing posture, his/her COM position is about 10 cm lower than the navel, in the sagittal plane and in correspondence of the anterior superior iliac crests (the top of the hipbones). The external forces acting on subject's body are equivalent to the same forces acting on the COM. When the subject is stepping, COM descends from its highest point to the lowest one. In the vertical and mediolateral planes, the COM moves along an oscillating path following a quasi-sinusoidal pattern [9, 10]. The trajectory of COM during walking in the sagittal plane can be assumed to have a sinusoidal pattern is the step length. The use of a harmonic oscillator model allows for exploring the human locomotion and analyzing the correlation between the cycle of COM positions and the cycle of walking. Each step (either left or right) is carried out following this pattern. The cycle is repeated at every step with its characteristics, (i.e., the pattern is very similar but not exactly the same). The use of a harmonic oscillator model allows us to define a correlation between the cycle of COM positions and the step cycle during walking. One harmonic oscillator is associated with each step cycle; thus, we look at the walking as a set of oscillators describing human kinematics. The oscillation period defines gait frequency and cadence. Spatial-temporal measures during walking can be evaluated.

## 3  Results and Discussion

### 3.1  Automatic Classification of Functioning in PD Court

One goal of the study is to use the functional tests to produce a simple but efficient score to provide an overall assessment of the PD patient according to the international scale used in clinical practice for CFS. We propose a simple frailty classification algorithm based on the sum of the scores from 6MWT and TUG. The interpretation of the outcome produced by 6MWT uses normalcy thresholds presented in Table 2 and the score patient classification of Table 3. The interpretation of the TUG result is described in Table 4.

**Table 2.**  Normalcy Thresholds (T) of 6-MWT (i.e. walked distance in meters) for different healthy populations in age and sex (M/F).

| Age range (yrs) | 60–64 | 65–69 | 70–74 | 75–79 | 80–84 | 85–89 |
|---|---|---|---|---|---|---|
| M distance (m) | 558 | 512 | 498 | 430 | 407 | 347 |
| F distance (m) | 498 | 457 | 439 | 393 | 352 | 311 |

**Table 3.**  6MWT outcome evaluation. T = threshold of Table 2. M = outcome measured during the test

| 6MWT score | > T | < T | 100*|M-T|/T > T*0,20 and M < T | <300 m |
|---|---|---|---|---|
| Patient cslassification | Normal | Frail | Assistance needed | Very frail |

**Table 4.**  TUG Normalcy thresholds (time in s).

| TUG score (time, s) | 0–10 s | 10, 1–20 s | 20, 1–30 s | >30 s |
|---|---|---|---|---|
| Patient classification | Normal | Frail | Assistance needed | High risk of falling |

The proposed frailty classification algorithm operates using the 6MWT and TUG outcome scores as defined in Table 3 and Table 4, with a first hypothesis of equivalent weight in the classification, and they are the input for the rules in (1) and Table 5. The

**Table 5.** Algorithm for patient frailty classification. The sum of 6MWT and TUG scores produces the assigned automatic classification.

| 6MWT score | TUG score | Automatic computation of clinical frailty scale |
|---|---|---|
| 2 | 0 | 2 - Well |
| 2 | 1 | 3 - Managing well |
| 2 | 1 | 3 - Managing well |
| 2 | 2 | 4 - Vulnerable |
| 3 | 0 | 3 - Managing well |
| 3 | 0 | 3 - Managing well |
| 3 | 1 | 4 - Vulnerable |
| 3 | 2 | 5 - Mildly frail |
| 4 | − 1 | 3 - Managing well |
| 4 | 0 | 4 - Vulnerable |
| 4 | 1 | 5 - Mildly frail |
| 4 | 2 | 6 - Moderately frail |
| 4 | 0 | 4 - Vulnerable |
| 4 | 0 | 4 - Vulnerable |
| 4 | 1 | 5 - Mildly frail |
| 4 | 2 | 6 - Moderately frail |

Frailty classification algorithm used is a linear not-weighted sum of the scores reported in Table 5 for the 2 functional tests. Its formula produces the FS (Frailty Score) index as reported in (1):

$$FS = 6MWT + TUG \tag{1}$$

The proposed index was computed and compared with the PD patient classification given by an expert physiatrist. The corresponding coherence is 16 out of 24 corresponding to an overall reliability of 66,7% (Table 6).

Some small evaluation differences between the expert physiatrist and the automatic algorithm, could be related to some other variable to be investigated as the expert physiatrist evaluates the patient in its entirety. We consider the result to be good and promising.

This is just a preliminary method and but it shows interesting and promising outcomes:

1) This study indicates the possibility to have a methodology based on an automated procedure for functional tests executions, analysis and classification, with the computation of the frailty score as with good reliability with respect to the assessment assigned by skilled physiatrists;

**Table 6.** Automatic algorithm for patient classification: comparison with the standard classification assigned by an expert physiatrist and coherence verification (Yes = 1, No = 0).

| ID No. | Clinical frailty scale - Physiatrist | 6-MWT score | TUG score | Frailty classification algorithm | Coherence (Y = 1, N = 0) |
|---|---|---|---|---|---|
| GRP001 | 3 - Managing well | 383,94 | 10,63 | 3 - Managing well | 1 |
| GRP002 | 4 - Vulnerable | 217,49 | 17,86 | 4 - Vulnerable | 1 |
| GRP003 | 4 - Vulnerable | 259,25 | 18,98 | 4 - Vulnerable | 1 |
| GRP004 | 4 - Vulnerable | 336,25 | 13,84 | 3 - Managing well | 0 |
| GRP005 | 4 - Vulnerable | 278,51 | 13,91 | 4 - Vulnerable | 1 |
| GRP006 | 4 - Vulnerable | 285,28 | 22,92 | 5 - Mildly frail | 0 |
| GRP007 | 5 - Mildly frail | 212,32 | 21,63 | 5 - Mildly frail | 1 |
| GRP008 | 4 - Vulnerable | 521,21 | 9,23 | 2 - Well | 0 |
| GRP009 | 3 - Managing well | 409,28 | 12,05 | 3 - Managing well | 1 |
| GRP010 | 6 - Moderately frail | 234,86 | 33,25 | 6 - Moderately frail | 1 |
| GRP011 | 4 - Vulnerable | 259,86 | 19,28 | 5 - Mildly frail | 0 |
| GRP012 | 5 - Mildly frail | 308,03 | 17,63 | 5 - Mildly frail | 1 |
| GRP013 | 6 - Moderately frail | 179,33 | 23,45 | 5 - Mildly frail | 0 |
| GRP014 | 3 - Managing well | 406,10 | 11,69 | 3 - Managing well | 1 |
| GRP015 | 3 - Managing well | 375,15 | 13,95 | 3 - Managing well | 1 |
| GRP016 | 4 – Vulnerable | 282,03 | 12,16 | 4 - Vulnerable | 1 |
| GRP017 | 3 - Managing well | 381,63 | 12,23 | 3 - Managing well | 1 |
| GRP018 | 3 - Managing well | 408,39 | 13,94 | 3 - Managing well | 1 |
| GRP019 | 2 – Well | 341,51 | 15,59 | 3 - Managing well | 0 |
| GRP020 | 2 – Well | 346,27 | 11,83 | 3 - Managing well | 0 |
| GRP021 | 5 - Mildly frail | 204,53 | 24,97 | 5 - Mildly frail | 1 |
| GRP022 | 4 - Vulnerable | 342,42 | 14,11 | 4 - Vulnerable | 1 |
| GRP023 | 2 - Well | 378,86 | 16,92 | 3 - Managing well | 0 |
| GRP024 | 2 - Well | 437,16 | 8,8 | 2 - Well | 1 |
| | | | | *Total coherence* | 16/24 |
| | | | | *Reliability %* | 66,7% |

2)  The hospital use of this technology and related methodology offer new insights of the simple functional score, so to have a more detailed description of the progression of the PD and its influence on the ability of the subjects;
3)  The study applies easy-to-use wearable sensors to offer a domiciliary solution to carry-out standardized tests for periodic and continuous follow-ups, that are so important in the management of the pathology.

The applied classification model is very basic and future work is dedicated to the evaluation of the other tests that were proposed to the PD subjects (10-m and 50-m) and to the development of a set of weighting coefficients to increase the reliability of the classification. Searching for a reliability of the system better than 66.7% we need to consider that our algorithm works on the basis of motor symptoms but the physiatrist diagnoses the pathology using also many co-factors that are non-motor manifestations such as olfactory disturbances, autonomic dysfunction, sleep fragmentation, depression, bladder disturbances, gastrointestinal symptoms, and dementia (17,18). The clinical scale is subjective with high inter-rater variability evaluation over physiatrists and time. The algorithm proposed can help to have a controlled variability over the clinical evaluation frailty scale.

The weights used in the construction of the evaluation scale of the two gait tests could be further optimized, for example through machine learning [20]. Deep learning techniques offer a high potential to autonomously detect motor states of patients with PD [22]. This should be done using a larger number of observed cases. The evaluation could be explored also using repeated assessment in protocol setup. About TUG test, the system produces also fraction time of execution (time of sit to stand, time of walking and time of stand to sit). We are exploring if the use of these fraction times gives a better result in CFS prediction [23].

## 4  Conclusions

The wearable actigraphy system is able to allow for the evaluation of the clinical frailty status of subjects both to clinical operators and familiar caregivers. The first results with simplest summative linear method is has a reliability of 66,7%. The usability assessment is still under evaluation but the two users (therapists and patients) have demonstrated high compliance and easiness of use.

A larger court is under recruitment for hospital evaluation so to improve the dataset; this greater number of subjects analyzed will allow to better define the algorithm and its reliability.

The same tests could be performed by the patient at home. This will be the second exploitation direction. We will soon make available a semi-commercial solution based on a COTS (commercial-off-the-shelf) device properly programmed to expand the research with the domiciliary follow-ups. If the data transmission and their analysis led to evidence of a regularity or variation in the classification of fragility, there could be continuous monitoring of the patient which could prevent risk situations or require an urgent clinical re-assessment before the three-monthly scheduled check.

## References

1. DeMaagd, G., Philip, A.: Parkinson's disease and its management: part 1: disease entity, risk factors, pathophysiology, clinical presentation, and diagnosis. P & T: a peer-reviewed J. formulary Manage. **40**(8), 504–532 (2015)
2. Allen, N.E., Schwarzel, A.K., Canning, C.G.: Recurrent falls in Parkinson's disease: a systematic review. Parkinson's disease, 906274 (2013). https://doi.org/10.1155/2013/906274
3. Canadian Study on Health & Aging (2008)
4. Rockwood, K., et al.: A global clinical measure of fitness and frailty in elderly people. CMAJ **173**, 489–495 (2005)
5. Dias, D., Paulo Silva Cunha, J.: Wearable health devices-vital sign monitoring, systems and technologies. Sensors (Basel, Switzerland) **18**(8), 2414 (2018). https://doi.org/10.3390/s18082414

6. Fusca, M., Perego, P., Andreoni, G.: Method for wearable kinematic gait analysis using a harmonic oscillator applied to the Center Of Mass. J. Sensor **2018**, 14 p. (2018). https://doi.org/10.1155/2018/4548396. Article ID 4548396

7. Fusca, M., Perego, P. and Andreoni, G.: A novel kinematic model for wearable gait analysis. In: eTELEMED 2017: The Ninth International Conference on eHealth, Telemedicine, and Social Medicine, March 19–23 2017 Nice, France, IARIA, 2017, pp. 123-128 (2017). ISBN: 978-1-61208-540-1

8. Fusca, M., Negrini, F., Perego, P., Magoni, L., Molteni, F., Andreoni, G.: Validation of a wearable IMU system for gait analysis: protocol and application to a new system. Appl. Sci. **8**(7), 1167 (2018). https://doi.org/10.3390/app8071167

9. Orendurff, M.S., Segal, A.D., Klute, G.K., Berge, J.S., Rohr, E.S., Kadel, N.J.: The effect of walking speed on center of mass displacement. J. Rehabil. Res. & Develop. **41**(6), 829–834 (2004)

10. Jurcevic Lulic, T., Muftic, O.: Trajectory of the human body mass centre during walking at different speed. In: DS 30: Proceedings of DESIGN 2002, the 7th International Design Conference, Dubrovnik (2002)

11. Holt, K.G., Hamill, J., Andres, R.O.: The force-driven harmonic oscillator as a model for human locomotion. Hum. Mov. Sci. **9**, 55–68 (1990)

12. Moe-Nilssen, R., Helbostad, J.L.: Estimation of gait cycle characteristics by trunk accelerometry. J. Biomech. **37**, 121–126 (2004)

13. Zijlstra, W., Hof, A.L.: Assessment of spatio-temporal gait parameters from trunk accelerations during human walking. Gait Posture **18**, 1–10 (2003)

14. Evans, S.J., Sayers, M., Mitnitski, A., Rockwood, K.: The risk of adverse outcomes in hospitalized older patients in relation to a frailty index based on a comprehensive geriatric assessment. Age Ageing **43**(1), 127–132 (2014). https://doi.org/10.1093/ageing/aft156

15. Torsney, K.M., Romero-Ortuno, R.: The clinical frailty scale predicts inpatient mortality in older hospitalised patients with idiopathic Parkinson's disease. J. R. Coll. Physicians Edinb. **48**, 103–107 (2018). https://doi.org/10.4997/jrcpe.2018.201

16. Gregorevic, K.J., Hubbard, R.E., Katz, B., et al.: The clinical frailty scale predicts functional decline and mortality when used by junior medical staff: a prospective cohort study. BMC Geriatr. **16**, 117 (2016). https://doi.org/10.1186/s12877-016-0292-4

17. Rovini, E., Maremmani, C., Cavallo, F.: How wearable sensors can support Parkinson's disease diagnosis and treatment: a systematic review. Front. Neurosci. **11**, 555 (2017). https://doi.org/10.3389/fnins.2017.00555

18. Wolters, E.C.: Variability in the clinical expression of Parkinson's disease. J. Neurol. Sci. **266**, 197–203 (2008). https://doi.org/10.1016/j.jns.2007.08.016

19. Maetzler, W., Domingos, J., Srulijes, K., Ferreira, J.J., Bloem, B.R.: Quantitative wearable sensors for objective assessment of Parkinson's disease. Mov. Disord. **28**(12), 1628–1637 (2013). https://doi.org/10.1002/mds.25628. Epub 2013 Sep 12 PMID: 24030855

20. Lonini, L., Dai, A., Shawen, N., et al.: Wearable sensors for Parkinson's disease: which data are worth collecting for training symptom detection models. npj Digit. Med. **1**, 64 (2018). https://doi.org/10.1038/s41746-018-0071-z

21. Schlachetzki, J.C.M., et al.: Wearable sensors objectively measure gait parameters in Parkinson's disease. Plos One **11** (2017). https://doi.org/10.1371/journal.pone.0183989

22. Goschenhofer, J., Pfister, F., Yuksel, K., Bischl, B., Fietzek, U., Thomas, J.: Wearable-based Parkinson's disease severity monitoring using deep learning. ArXiv abs/1904.10829 (2019)

23. Weiss, A., et al.: Can an accelerometer enhance the utility of the timed up & go test when evaluating patients with Parkinson's disease? Med. Eng. Phys. **32**(2), 119–125 (2010). https://doi.org/10.1016/j.medengphy.2009.10.015. Epub 2009 Nov 25 PMID: 19942472

# Development of a Wearable Sensors System to Monitor Foot-Transmitted Vibration

Pietro Marzaroli[1], Alex P. Moorhead[1]([⊠]), Marco Tarabini[1], Manuela Galli[2], Filippo Goi[3], and Roberto Caimi[4]

[1] Department of Mechanical Engineering, Politecnico di Milano, Via Previati 1/C, 23826 Lecco, Italy
{pietro.marzaroli,alexpatten.moorhead,marco.tarabini}@polimi.it

[2] E4sport Lab, Politecnico di Milano, Via Golgi 39, 20133 Milan, Italy
manuela.galli@polimi.it

[3] Vibram s.p.a, Via Colombo 5, 21041 Albizzate, Italy
filippo.goi@vibram.com

[4] Sires s.r.l, Via Cavour 2, 22074 Lomazzo, Italy
roberto.caimi@sires.it

**Abstract.** Exposure to mechanical vibration may lead to harmful effects on the human body if it does not occur within a controlled environment. ISO 2631-1 regulates how to measure the vibration exposure and provides safety limits. According to this standard, the acceleration signals should be measured at the interface between the vibrating surface and the human body for a time interval long enough to represent a whole working shift. This is impossible to achieve in the case of foot-transmitted vibration, as standard equipment cannot fit between the foot and the floor. For this reason, a new system of sensors has been developed to be small enough to fit inside a regular foot insole. This system is powered through batteries and transmits the data to a cellphone through the Bluetooth connection, thus enabling a precise and continuous measurement. After production, the system has been validated by comparing the vibration exposure measured with the insoles to the vibration measured by standard piezo-electric accelerometers. The validation process took place both in laboratory controlled conditions and in real, outdoor conditions. The experimental results show a root-mean-squared error in the evaluation of vibration exposure lower than 0.1 m/s$^2$, thus proving the potential of the proposed system.

**Keywords:** Wearable sensors · Mems · Foot-transmitted vibration · Vibration exposure

## 1 Introduction

The harmful effects of occupational exposure to whole-body mechanical vibration are well documented in the scientific literature [1]. These effects may be acute, like discomfort, low back pain [2], nausea, dizziness, temporary loss of sensitivity [3]; or even

P. Perego et al. (Eds.): ICWH 2020, LNICST 376, pp. 188–196, 2021.
https://doi.org/10.1007/978-3-030-76066-3_15

persistent, leading to sciatica [4] or vibration-induced white foot syndrome [5]. Monitoring vibration, therefore, is crucial to the well-being of workers and, in general, of all the people regularly exposed to vibration. ISO 2631-1 [6] was created to regulate how to measure the acceleration and compute the vibration exposure of workers. It imposes that the acceleration must be measured at the interface between the vibrating surface and the part of the human body in contact with it. The regulation distinguishes three main contexts in which the mechanical stimulus can enter in the human body: while sitting, while laying and while standing. Seats and beds are generally thick enough to contain regular accelerometers and data acquisition systems. Measuring acceleration at the interface between the feet and floor, however, is challenging for two main reasons. The first is the small space available, while the second is the need for a wireless system, as wired shoes may prove to be cumbersome to wear and will obstruct natural movement. Given these problems, this paper presents a new measurement system, small enough to be placed inside a regular pair of shoes insoles, able to evaluate the vibration exposure and wirelessly transmit the data acquired to a cell phone.

The acceleration between the feet and the supporting surface as well as the overall environmental conditions of the feet can be directly measured through a two-sensor system placed inside the insoles of the shoes, in dedicated slots; one below the heel and one in correspondence of the forefoot. The sensors used to compose each system are tri-axis MEMS accelerometer ST LIS3DH [7], manufactured by STMicroelectronic (Plan-les-Ouates, Chemin du Champ-des-Filles 39, CH), and the force sensitive resistor 402 FSR, manufactured by Interlink Electronics (31248 Oak Crest, Westlake Village, CA United States). The acceleration range for the accelerometers is to $\pm 4$ g, and the acceleration data are acquired with a frequency of 200 Hz. The pressure data are read with a frequency of 10 Hz. The change of resistance of the FSR is evaluated through a voltage divider configuration, as was done by Spinsante et al. [8]. Given the documented uncertainty of such sensors [8, 9], the pressure data are compared to an arbitrary threshold of 1.5 V; below which it is supposed that the load of a person is being applied. The digital temperature sensor STLM75, produced by STMicroelectronic is also included in the system, as low temperature can be a determining factor in the onset of vibration-induced foot pathologies [10]. The system described is shown in Fig. 1, and has nominal dimensions of $30 \times 30 \times 5$ mm.

The vibration exposure is then automatically computed according to ISO 2631-1 by the acquisition system itself, based on the acceleration signals acquired by all four accelerometers available inside the insoles. Each second, the updated values of vibration exposure, together with the pressure and temperature data are then sent to a smartphone through the Bluetooth® low energy protocol by the module SPBTLE-1S, produced by STMicroelectronic, which also includes the CPU for controlling the system. The data can also be stored on board, through the flash memory MX25R1635FZUIL0, produced by Macronix (Hsinchu, Taiwan, R.O.C.). The whole system is powered by a CR2032 battery, which can be recharged through the wireless recharge coil AWCCA-36R36H08-C51-B, produced by Abracon LLC (Spicewood, TX, USA). Two data acquisition modules are inserted inside one insole, as shown in Fig. 2. This allows the measurement of the vibration transmitted to both fore and rear foot, as these two components may play a different role in the transmission of vibration through to foot to the rest of the body [11].

**Fig. 1.** Photograph showing the sensors system

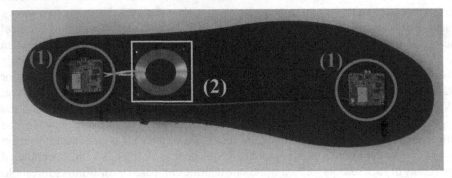

**Fig. 2.** Photograph of the different components of the data acquisition and transmission system inside the insole. (1): Data acquisition and transmission systems (2) Wireless recharge coil and battery

## 2 Method

### 2.1 Participants Information

Experiments were performed with 5, healthy (no injuries or ailments within the previous 6 months), male subjects (age $27 \pm 3$ years, height $178 \pm 5$ cm, mass $73 \pm 14$ kg; mean $\pm$ SD). Three subjects performed the bicycle tests, two subjects performed the ski tests. One of the subjects which participated in both of the outdoor tests also performed the indoor laboratory tests. All subjects were provided and signed informed consents prior to the experiments.

### 2.2 Laboratory Testing

Five pairs of sensorized insoles have been prototyped for the testing and validation phase. Two different tests were performed in laboratory conditions. The first was aimed at evaluating the metrological properties of the system, while the second was aimed at evaluating the effect that the soles of the shoes may have on the measurements. First, the five different prototypes have been placed, one at a time, on a vibrating platform able to move along the three mutually perpendicular spatial axes, with a person standing on them, as shown in Fig. 3. Then, one pair was extracted randomly and placed inside three different shoes: a pair of mountain bike shoes, a pair of working boots with rubber soles and a pair of working boots with polyurethane soles. A person wore the shoes and stood on the same platform used for the tests previously explained. For each prototype and shoe kind, four different signals have been used. For each spatial axis, a white noise signal has been imposed. The nominal RMS amplitude was 0.5 m/s$^2$. The frequency components were between 0.5 Hz and 20 Hz, and the duration was 60 s. Then, a pseudo-random signal was imposed to all three axes simultaneously. The nominal RMS amplitude was 0.5 m/s$^2$, the frequency components were between 0.5 Hz and 50 Hz, and the duration was 120 s. The order of execution of the tests has been randomized. For all tests, the reference acceleration signal was measured through the triaxial accelerometer 356A22 manufactured by PCB Piezotronics (Depew, NY, USA), placed in the middle of the vibrating platform. The data acquisition board National Instruments 9234 (Austin, TX, USA) was used to sample the data with a rate of 2048 Hz. A parallel manipulator specifically made for this purpose actuated the vibrating platform [12].

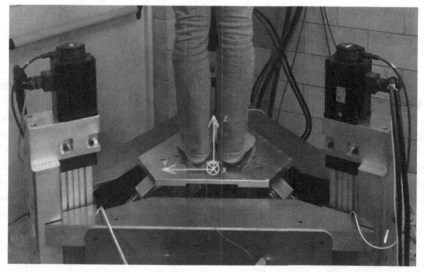

**Fig. 3.** Picture of a person standing on the vibrating platform during the tests of the prototyped insoles.

## 2.3 Outdoor Testing

Two different tests were performed in outdoor conditions and were aimed at evaluating the performances and the reliability of the system in an uncontrolled environment.

Mountain biking was used as the case study for the first test. Three different subjects were asked to repeat a predetermined route inside the university campus five times. The subjects were instructed on the route to follow and to not use the saddle of the bicycle to increase the dose of vibration absorbed through the feet. The same instruments used to acquire the reference signal in the tests executed inside were also used for this tests. In this case, the reference accelerometer was placed on the right pedal of the bike.

Skiing was selected as the second testing condition for the sensors system. Two different subjects took part in this testing activity, and each of them sported a different setup. The instruments used to compose the first setup were the same used for the indoor testing and for the tests on the mountain bike. The triaxial accelerometer was placed close to the right heel, on the ski. The second setup was composed of four single-axis accelerometers 5508 B made by BRÜEL & KJÆR SOUND & VIBRATION MEASUREMENT (Nærum, Denmark). These accelerometers were placed on the skis, close to the heels and to the tips of the feet, to be as close as possible to the sensors placed onside the insoles. Being single-axis, the reference accelerometers were mounted to measure the vertical vibrations, which were found to be the most relevant during the skiing activity [13]. No instructions were given to the subjects about the routes to follow, except that they each had to cover 9 different paths. The test took place on the ski area of Piani di Bobbio (LC, Italy).

### 2.4  Data Analysis

The acceleration signals measured by the reference accelerometers were used to compute the vibration exposure as regulated by ISO 2631-1. The frequency weighting curve "Wk" was applied to the signals measured along the vertical axis, while the frequency weighting curve "Wd" was applied to the signals measured along the two horizontal axes. The vibration exposure was then computed for each direction and measurement point through the running RMS method. Finally, the overall vibration total value was computed as the root-sum-of-squares of the vibration exposures evaluated for each direction and measurement point. The values of vibration exposure measured by both systems were compared by computing their absolute and percentage differences. Since the pressure distribution within the boot or shoe could not be controlled during dynamic tests, the RMS values of all four insole sensors were compared to determine outliers. Tests were eliminated if one of two situations occurred; one, the reference sensor registered a value which was an outlier compared to the other trials of the same subject, or two, the RMS of the four insole sensors resulted in a value which was an outlier compared to the other trials of the same subject.

# 3   Results

## 3.1   Laboratory Testing

Results from the laboratory testing without shoes (Table 1) and with shoes (Table 2) are presented as the mean measurement of the four sensors across all five tests. Results show that the sensorized insoles performed much better being placed inside of shoes than they did being stood upon without shoes. While the percent error is greater than 30% in some instances, particularly without shoes, it should be noted that the absolute difference is still less than 0.1 m/s$^2$ in both cases.

**Table 1.**  Sensorized insole testing without shoes

| Direction of vibration | Mean vibration of 4 insole sensors (m/s$^2$) | Vibration of reference accelerometer (m/s$^2$) | Absolute difference | Percent error |
|---|---|---|---|---|
| X Vibration | 0.241 | 0.176 | 0.065 | 36.669 |
| Y Vibration | 0.223 | 0.170 | 0.053 | 30.825 |
| Z Vibration | 0.352 | 0.376 | 0.024 | 6.416 |
| 3D Vibration | 0.546 | 0.490 | 0.056 | 11.482 |

**Table 2.**  Sensorized insole testing with shoes

| Direction of vibration | Mean vibration of 4 insole sensors (m/s$^2$) | Vibration of reference accelerometer (m/s$^2$) | Absolute difference | Percent error |
|---|---|---|---|---|
| X Vibration | 0.205 | 0.180 | 0.025 | 13.836 |
| Y Vibration | 0.197 | 0.180 | 0.017 | 9.409 |
| Z Vibration | 0.350 | 0.380 | 0.030 | 7.882 |
| 3D Vibration | 0.538 | 0.500 | 0.038 | 7.565 |

## 3.2  Outdoor Testing

Results from the two outdoor tests, riding a bicycle (Table 3) and skiing (Table 4) are presented below, including the tests which were eliminated due to outliers. The means are taken of each column (R Toe, R Heel, L Toe, L Heel) of each subject and the absolute difference as well as the percent error is taken as the difference between the RMS and reference sensor of each row (trial). While the percentage errors among singular trials can occasionally exceed 20% during bicycling, the mean percentage error of all trials for each subject was less than 5% for two of them. The ski tests unfortunately resulted in 7 out of 18 tests being eliminated. Similar to the bicycle tests however, when taking the mean of the valid tests, one of the subjects had a low percent error (just under 6%).

**Table 3.** Outdoor bicycle tests

| Subject.Trial | R Toe | R Heel | L Toe | L Heel | RMS | Ref. | % error |
|---|---|---|---|---|---|---|---|
| S1.T1 | 0.216 | 0.426 | 0.295 | 0.214 | 0.300 | 2.578 | 88.351 |
| S1.T2 | 0.648 | 0.655 | 3.894 | 1.977 | 2.232 | 2.480 | 10.032 |
| S1.T3 | 3.842 | 2.908 | 2.862 | 2.385 | 3.045 | 2.734 | 11.405 |
| S1.T4 | 3.422 | 2.641 | 3.241 | 2.043 | 2.888 | 2.564 | 12.622 |
| S1.T5 | 3.921 | 2.753 | 3.988 | 1.930 | 3.263 | 2.688 | 21.404 |
| RMS S1 | 2.909 | 2.174 | 3.158 | 1.873 | 2.582 | 2.610 | 1.090 |
| S2.T1 | 2.612 | 2.348 | 2.819 | 2.399 | 2.551 | 3.870 | 34.079 |
| S2.T2 | 1.127 | 3.155 | 1.065 | 0.322 | 1.765 | 24.567 | 92.815 |
| S2.T3 | 4.436 | 3.267 | 4.850 | 1.378 | 3.734 | 3.492 | 6.923 |
| S2.T4 | 4.712 | 3.489 | 5.094 | 3.112 | 4.184 | 3.326 | 25.782 |
| S2.T5 | 4.455 | 3.846 | 5.395 | 3.148 | 4.291 | 3.792 | 13.159 |
| RMS S2 | 3.737 | 3.259 | 4.187 | 2.339 | 3.754 | 3.627 | 3.502 |
| S3.T1 | 4.731 | 3.294 | 0.000 | 1.398 | 3.425 | 3.401 | 0.707 |
| S3.T2 | 4.224 | 3.168 | 3.876 | 2.958 | 3.593 | 3.562 | 0.888 |
| S3.T3 | 4.594 | 2.878 | 4.140 | 2.790 | 3.685 | 2.980 | 23.644 |
| S3.T4 | 5.735 | 3.725 | 5.305 | 3.689 | 4.704 | 3.926 | 19.826 |
| S3.T5 | 4.762 | 3.598 | 5.053 | 3.160 | 4.217 | 3.634 | 16.048 |
| RMS S3 | 4.835 | 3.346 | 4.143 | 2.901 | 3.953 | 3.514 | 12.486 |

**Table 4.** Outdoor ski tests

| Subject.Trial | R Toe | R Heel | L Toe | L Heel | Mean | Ref. | % error |
|---|---|---|---|---|---|---|---|
| S1.T1 | 2.657 | 3.473 | 2.744 | 0.948 | 2.624 | 2.643 | 0.699 |
| S1.T2 | 5.234 | 5.560 | 5.836 | 3.080 | 5.046 | 6.716 | 24.866 |
| S1.T3 | 5.632 | 5.173 | 4.173 | 5.952 | 5.275 | 5.688 | 7.254 |
| S1.T4 | 5.003 | 3.720 | 0.874 | 4.155 | 3.771 | 0.928 | 306.343 |
| S1.T5 | 2.014 | 2.603 | 0.102 | 2.345 | 2.021 | 6.317 | 68.006 |
| S1.T6 | 0.108 | 1.702 | 1.459 | 1.772 | 1.430 | 1.780 | 19.655 |
| S1.T7 | 4.156 | 0.640 | 0.000 | 4.337 | 3.488 | 3.529 | 1.186 |
| S1.T8 | 2.323 | 2.833 | 0.000 | 2.766 | 2.650 | 0.698 | 279.460 |
| S1.T9 | 2.364 | 3.038 | 2.284 | 2.794 | 2.638 | 4.169 | 36.716 |
| RMS S1 | 1.810 | 1.787 | 1.393 | 1.769 | 1.793 | 1.899 | 5.584 |
| S2.T1 | 3.305 | 2.934 | 3.324 | 4.450 | 3.549 | 2.896 | 22.526 |
| S2.T2 | - | - | - | - | - | 5.909 | - |
| S2.T3 | - | - | - | - | - | 7.908 | - |
| S2.T4 | - | - | - | - | - | 1.007 | - |
| S2.T5 | - | - | - | - | - | 1.421 | - |
| S2.T6 | 1.971 | 1.483 | 2.092 | 1.466 | 1.776 | 1.876 | 24.969 |
| S2.T7 | 2.662 | 2.143 | 3.056 | 2.306 | 2.566 | 3.950 | 36.783 |
| S2.T8 | 3.370 | 3.097 | 3.674 | 3.160 | 3.333 | 2.676 | 15.625 |
| S2.T9 | 2.243 | 2.099 | 2.460 | 2.401 | 2.305 | 2.643 | 13.860 |
| RMS S2 | 1.646 | 1.533 | 1.709 | 1.660 | 1.645 | 2.016 | 18.420 |

## 4   Discussion and Conclusion

A sensor system has been developed specifically to continuously measure the vibration exposure of subjects exposed to foot-transmitted vibration. The system is fully integrated inside a pair of regular shoe insoles and can transmit the acquired data wirelessly to a smartphone. The system has been validated both in controlled conditions and during realistic use, by comparing the vibration exposure measured by it with the one evaluated by reference piezoelectric accelerometers. The results show that in lab conditions, the insoles function best ($\leq$14% error) while inserted into a pair of shoes as designed rather than outside of the shoes. In outdoor tests, it was found that, while a single test may have an error over- or underestimation of over 30% at times, when averaging the measurements of as few as just 5 tests, the percentage error can drop to as low as nearly 1% during cycling in controlled conditions and 5.6% in uncontrolled skiing tests with just seven trials. The main weakness of the system is related to the wireless data transmission system through the Bluetooth protocol, which is not always reliable, causing a loss of information. This issue may be solved by increasing the time interval after which the new data are sent to the cellphone, thus decreasing the data transmission rate. Another improvement to be made is the implementation of smart algorithm to recognize and neglect corrupted or non-meaningful data set. This algorithm may benefit from the wide variety of measured physical quantities, as it was suggested by the preliminary results obtained from the tests done on the mountain bike (if considering only the sensor with high pressure, i.e. in contact, the error decreases). As the research on foot-transmitted vibration progress, monitoring both forefoot and heel may be a key advantage, in preventing vibration-related diseases and disorders. In particular, a system such as this could be further developed and tested in a greater number of contexts with a larger sample size. With a more in-depth analysis of the system's potential it could offer valuable evaluation of the ergonomics of different types of shoes as well as their comfort and wearability in diverse contexts. Extensive tests, however, are further needed to fully validate the system and prove its potential.

# References

1. Bovenzi, M., Schust, M., Mauro, M.: An overview of low back pain and occupational exposures to whole-body vibration and mechanical shocks. Med. Lav. **108**(6), 419–433 (2017)
2. Bongers, P., et al.: Back pain and exposure to whole body vibration in helicopter pilots. Ergonomics **33**(8), 1007–1026 (1990)
3. Brammer, A.J., Taylor, W., Lundborg, G.: Sensorineural stages of the hand-arm vibration syndrome. Scand. J. Work Environ. Health 279–283 (1987)
4. Burström, L., Nilsson, T., Wahlström, J.: Whole-body vibration and the risk of low back pain and sciatica: a systematic review and meta-analysis. Int. Arch. Occup. Environ. Health **88**(4), 403–418 (2015)
5. Eger, T., et al.: Vibration induced white-feet: overview and field study of vibration exposure and reported symptoms in workers. Work **47**(1), 101–110 (2014)
6. ISO 5349, Mechanical vibration-measurement and evaluation of human exposure to hand transmitted vibration, part 1: general requirements (2001)
7. Tarabini, M., et al.: The potential of micro-electro-mechanical accelerometers in human vibration measurements. J. Sound Vibrat. **331**(2), 487–499 (2012)
8. Spinsante, S., Scalise, L.: Measurement of elderly daily physical activity by unobtrusive instrumented shoes. In: 2018 IEEE International Symposium on Medical Measurements and Applications (MeMeA), pp. 1–5 (2018)
9. Tarabini, M., et al.: Measurement of the force exchanged by orthodontic masks and patients. In: 2018 IEEE International Symposium on Medical Measurements and Applications (MeMeA), pp. 1–6 (2018)
10. Noel, B.: Pathophysiology and classification of the vibration white finger. Journal of the Peripheral Nervous System **5**(4), 242–245 (2000)
11. Chadefaux, D., et al.: Development of a two-dimensional dynamic model of the foot-ankle system exposed to vibration. J. Biomech. 109547 (2019)
12. Marzaroli, P., et al.: Design and testing of a 3-DOF robot for studying the human response to vibration. Machines **7**(4), 67 (2019)
13. Tarabini, M., Saggin, B., Scaccabarozzi, D.: Whole-body vibration exposure in sport: four relevant cases. Ergonomics **58**(7), 1143–1150 (2015)

# ADLs Detection with a Wrist-Worn Accelerometer in Uncontrolled Conditions

Sandro Fioretti, Marica Olivastrelli, Angelica Poli$^{(\boxtimes)}$ ⓘ, Susanna Spinsante ⓘ, and Annachiara Strazza

Dipartimento di Ingegneria dell'Informazione, Università Politecnica delle Marche, 60131 Ancona, Italy
a.poli@staff.univpm.it

**Abstract.** In 2017, the European Commission estimated that 29% of European population will be aged 65 and over, by 2070. The capability of tracking and recognizing people's daily activities may promote and support an active and independent lifestyle. In this regard, Human Activity Recognition allows to obtain meaningful information by monitoring daily activities using wearable devices, that are small, easy to use, and minimally invasive.

In this paper, we discuss the recognition performance of six machine learning classifiers applied to accelerometer data only. Data was collected by 36 individuals, wearing a single wrist-worn sensor to monitor six daily activities pertaining to Hygiene and House Cleaning scenarios. Following a pre-processing phase, both temporal and frequency features were computed to classify and recognize the collected real-world data. The study presents some statistical results obtained from each classifier in order to compare their performance. The findings of experiments are promising for the adoption of the Random Forest classifier in Human Activity Recognition with acceleration data from a single wrist-worn device.

**Keywords:** Human activity recognition · Wearable sensors · Machine learning classifiers

## 1 Introduction

According to the last Ageing Report released by the European Commission [12], the percentage of people aged 65 and over will rise from 19% to 29% of the global European population, while those aged 80 and over will increase from 5%

Authors gratefully acknowledge the support of the *More Years Better Lives JPI* and the Italian Ministero dell'Istruzione, Università e Ricerca (CUP: I36G17000380001), for this research activity carried out within the project PAAL - Privacy-Aware and Acceptable Lifelogging services for older and frail people, (JPI MYBL award number: PAAL_JTC2017). The work was also partly supported by the project "AnzianAbili 3.0 - Percorsi riabilitativi sociosanitari e tecnologici per Anziani vulnerabili" funded by Fondazione Cariverona (Italy).

P. Perego et al. (Eds.): ICWH 2020, LNICST 376, pp. 197–208, 2021.
https://doi.org/10.1007/978-3-030-76066-3_16

to 13%, by 2070. Because of the frailty condition typically associated to older age, developing efficient systems to monitor elderly's life style can help to study their habits, identify misbehaviors, anticipate potential risks and suggest ways to improve their quality of life [2,4]. Recently, the advances in wearable technologies, providing rich sensory information, have led to a wide use of wearable devices as monitoring systems in the broad domain of Activity Recognition (AR) researches [9,17], especially focusing on the automatic classification of indoor Activities of Daily Living (ADLs) [16]. ADLs are defined as *self-care activities important for health maintenance and independent living* [28], and evaluating the capability of subjects to autonomously carry out ADLs gives essential information about their lives, thus allowing to understand needs, difficulties and health conditions [10]. Geriatricians assess ADLs and IADLs as part of assessing an older person's *function*: in fact, problems with ADLs and Instrumented ADLs (IADLs) usually reflect problems with physical and/or cognitive health [29].

In recent years, many researchers have proposed monitoring approaches aimed at HAR and automatic ADLs/IADLs classification, which combine minimally invasive sensing devices to efficient data processing algorithms [30]. An effective example is provided by the use of wrist-worn triaxial accelerometers for unobtrusively collecting ADLs-related signals, joint with effective Machine Learning (ML) algorithms to reach high levels of accuracy in identifying and recognizing different activities [21,22,27]. Wrist-worn triaxial accelerometers are available within smartwatches and smartbands, i.e. consumer electronics devices that are nowadays very common among people of different ages, especially among those interested in monitoring their performances during fitness and sport activities, or in *lifelogging* their daily behaviors. Technologies for *lifelogging* (alternatively known as *quantified self* or *self-tracking*) allow individuals to pervasively capture data about them, their environment, and the people they interact with [13]. The same technologies may enable ADLs detection and classification. Since it is acknowledged that the optimal positioning of a sensor is driven by user acceptance, as well as by the resulting classification accuracy, a meta-analysis of user preferences in the design of wearables indicated that they would like to wear the sensor on the wrist, followed, in descending order, by the trunk, belt, ankle and finally the armpit [3].

In this paper we present the results of a research activity focused on lifelogging for older adults through a non-video based sensing system, namely a wearable accelerometer available on board a smartwatch-like device. An annotated dataset of acceleration signals from the device was collected, from volunteers performing six different ADLs (i.e., Brushing Teeth, Grooming Hair, Washing Hands, Washing Dishes, Ironing Clothes and Dusting) in uncontrolled conditions. The dataset is then exploited to test different automatic classification algorithms, by assessing the impact of activities selected to be performed. In particular, six among the most common supervised ML approaches for classifying human daily activities are applied and compared.

The paper is organized as follows: Sect. 2 shortly reviews the state-of-the-art in the field of HAR and ADLs classification from the wrist-worn accelerometers. Section 3 presents the main steps of the work, aimed at signals collection, pre-processing and features extraction. Section 4 details the classification approaches tested on six different ADLs performed by the volunteers participating in the experiments, and discusses the accuracy attained. Finally, Sect. 5 concludes the paper.

## 2   Background

Typically, the approaches to activity recognition may be classified into vision-based and sensor-based ones. The former solutions exploit different types of cameras (RGB, but also RGBD adding depth information) to capture the agents's activity [7], but they may suffer from physical limitations (occlusions and reduced field of view) and may be perceived as too invasive for the user's privacy. Sensor-based approaches rely on sensors, or installed in the living environment (ambient sensors) or attached to the body of user (wearables), to gather data about the agents' behaviour alongside with the environment where they live. With the development of Micro Electro-Mechanical System (MEMS) technologies, wearable sensors integrated with inertial, acceleration and magnetic sensors are becoming increasingly less expensive, smaller, and lighter. In the framework of lifelogging systems, either ambient and wearable sensors may be used, the latter including smartphones too, that can be seen as smart sensor systems [24].

Gomes et al. [15] present the use of a sensorized wrist device to recognize eating and drinking events, with the aim of triggering automatic reminders to promote independent living of older adults at home. Data measured from accelerometer and gyroscope are used to assess the performance of a single multi-class classification model. Although only two elderly subjects contributed to the data collection process, the results show that it is possible to correctly classify eating and drinking events with acceptable accuracy. In [20], authors propose an approach for personalizing classification rules to a single person. The method improves activity detection from wrist-worn accelerometer data on a four-class recognition problem, where classes are ambulation, cycling, sedentary, and other. The manuscript extends a previously published activity classification method based on support vector machines (SVMs) to estimate the uncertainty of the classification process. Cleland et al. [6] analysed data from ten adults, who were instructed to perform twelve activities with an accelerometer sensor placed on their left wrist. The activities to be classified were divided into stationary - such as standing and sleeping - dynamic - such as walking and running, and transitional activities - such as stand-to-sit and sit-to-stand. The recording sessions lasted five minutes for stationary and dynamic activities, and fifteen seconds for transitional activities repeated fifteen times. Although being useful to monitor the level of physical activity of a monitored subject, the activities considered in this work do not specifically refer to ADLs, differently from those analysed in this paper.

In [19], authors exploit acceleration data from the users' wrist to build up assessment models for quantifying activities, to develop an algorithm for sleep duration detection and to quantitatively assess the regularity of ADLs. A total of ten healthy subjects, by wearing a wrist device, conducted 14 different ADLs, that can be grouped in five main categories: rest/sleep level of activity (i.e., sleeping); sedentary level activities (i.e., sitting and watching TV, sitting and reading newspaper, and sitting and web browsing); light level of activities (i.e., housekeeping, driving, and walking without hand-swing); moderate levels of activities (i.e., walking with hand-swing and up and down stairs, with or without hand-swing); vigorous levels of activity (i.e., jogging with or without hand-swing). Differently from what is presented in this work, the above mentioned paper considered ADLs that were quite different from each other, while in this paper similar ADLs are considered, from the point of view of the type of movements performed by the subject's wrist.

By analyzing the literature, it is possible to see how vastly different wearable recognition systems and accuracies are reported, depending on the activities examined. Additionally, it is important to remember that accelerometers may not be appropriate for some activities, the positioning of sensors also plays an important role, and likely this is a limiting factor for many applications, since sensors positioning is often largely driven by user acceptance rather than optimality of ADLs recognition performance. Finally, in some settings, other sensor modalities may be more appropriate for the activities that are hard to classify using wrist-worn accelerometers.

## 3    Materials and Methods

### 3.1    Data Collection

In this study, a total of 36 recordings (18 from men and 18 from women) were collected from the participants in the data collection phase. The participants, with age around 30 years, were in good health status and no current physical conditions could affect the performed daily-living activities. Activity recordings lasted around 5 min per each activity. Each individual carried out all the scenarios considered, performing each activity three times, in free-living conditions at their own home environment. Two scenarios of activities, namely Hygiene Scenario (i.e., Brushing Teeth, Grooming Hair, Washing Hands) and House Cleaning Scenario (i.e., Washing Dishes, Ironing Clothes, Dusting) were evaluated.

Accelerometer data were recorded by wearing the Empatica E4 wrist-worn device [11] on the dominant wrist, as shown in Fig. 1. According to literature, the wrist is an appropriate place for analysing and recognising some of the activities performed in this work such as grooming hair, brushing teeth and washing hands [5,14,18]. Prior to collecting data, the device was coupled with the Empatica smartphone app, named E4 real-time App, to stream data via Bluetooth, according with manufacturer guidelines. After pressing the button to start the recording, the device takes around 15 s to calibrate the system, thus improving the accuracy of the sensor reading. Accelerometer data from each activity was gathered at a sample rate 32 Hz in a measurable range of ±2g, and then stored in the online cloud platform, called E4 Connect, in the form of .csv files. After this, the recorded files were downloaded and renamed with labels corresponding

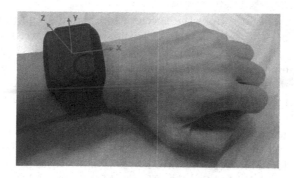

**Fig. 1.** Position of the wrist-worn Empatica E4 with the system of coordinates on the device.

to the scenario and the activity performed. The raw data collection, including acceleration samples used in this study, is available and can be downloaded from the Mendeley platform [26].

### 3.2 Data Pre-processing

The raw acceleration data consists of time instants and acceleration values along the X, Y and Z axes, as represented in Fig. 1. According to the literature, external interferences or loose coupling may generate both high frequency noise and abnormal spikes. In order to clean and validate the collected data, a $4^{th}$ low-pass Butterworth filter with cut-off frequency set 15 Hz, and a $3^{rd}$ order median filter were used to attenuate the signal noise [16, 23]. Additionally, considering the automatic calibration performed by the device, the initial 15 s of signal were discarded from each session acquisition.

Following the filtering step, the accelerometer signal was divided into fixed-size and non-overlapping windows of duration 3 s (corresponding to 96 samples) [1], thus resulting in 92 windows. This short window duration has been previously used because it includes a significant number of samples and it allows to rapidly extract features representative of each activity [16]. Therefore, by choosing the proper window length, the meaningful units about each activity were extracted from each segment, reducing the errors and inaccuracy in the classification phase.

### 3.3 Features Selection and Extraction

Each performed activity can be discriminated by looking for certain motion properties. This way, the corresponding features might be used to classify and distinguish the different activities, by extracting mainly statistical information from the signals. From this idea, a set of 17 common features expressed in time domain were extracted from the collected signals, and computed according to the equations and definitions provided in [8]. As specified in Table 1, some features were computed from the acceleration values along the three X, Y and Z axes, others were obtained from the acceleration Signal Magnitude Vector (i.e. $SMV = \sqrt{a_X^2 + a_Y^2 + a_Z^2}$). In fact, these last features exhibit reduced sensitivity to orientation changes [6]. According to an our previous work [25], the extracted features highly impact the algorithm's performance. Therefore, such distinction in calculating features considered both their corresponding mathematical definitions and their information content, aiming to reduce the potential information redundancy.

Six machine learning algorithms were used for the supervised learning classification tasks, and their performance were assessed. In particular, the Decision Tree (J48), Random Forest (RF), Naïve Bayes (NB), Neural Networks (NNs), k-Nearest Neighbor (kNN) and Support Vector Machines (SVM) were compared. HAR systems can be evaluated using different testing strategies. In this work, we used the 10-fold cross validation, in which all the sessions were divided into training (90% of data) and testing set (10% of data). The overall accuracy, defined as the ratio of correctly-classified activities over the total of activities, was computed as an average over the 10 iterations.

**Table 1.** List of Time-based features.

| Features | Description | Computation |
|---|---|---|
| Mean | Average of values | X, Y, Z axes, SMV |
| Median | Median value | X, Y, Z axes, SMV |
| Standard Deviation | Amount of deviation | X, Y, Z axes, SMV |
| Maximum | Highest value | X, Y, Z axes, SMV |
| Minimum | Lowest value | X, Y, Z axes, SMV |
| Range | Difference between max and min value | X, Y, Z axes, SMV |
| Axis Correlation | Correlation between the three directions | XY, YZ, ZX axes |
| Signal Magnitude Area | The trapezoidal area calculated | SMV |
| Coefficient of Variation | Relationship of the standard deviation to the mean | X, Y, Z axes, SMV |
| Median Absolute Deviation | Variability of the sample | X, Y, Z axes, SMV |
| Skewness | Measurement of symmetry in the distribution of values | X, Y, Z axes, SMV |
| Kurtosis | Sharpness of the feature value distribution | X, Y, Z axes, SMV |
| Zero Crossing | Number of times the signal crosses its median | X, Y, Z axes, SMV |
| Autocorrelation | Comparison between a value at time $t_i$ and the value at $t_{i+1}$ | X, Y, Z axes, SMV |
| Percentiles (20th-50th-80th) | Distribution of values across the sequences | SMV |
| N. of Peaks | Number of peaks | SMV |
| Peak - Peak Amplitude | Distance between two consecutive peaks | SMV |

# 4 Results

## 4.1 Training and Classifiers Evaluation

In supervised learning approaches, the algorithm learns from a set of training examples, which have pre-classified features. For the supervised learning, in fact, labeled classes are provided. In unsupervised learning approaches, instead, the algorithm works without labeled classes: the basic idea is to find patterns in the data using only the input variables. In reinforcement learning approaches, the algorithm learns from feedback after the decision was made, a feedback is sent to the classifier to know which decisions were correct and which instead, were incorrect. Most of the HAR systems work with a supervised learning approach. In general, a supervised approach is the most used thanks to its capability to learn the relationship between the input attributes, the features extracted, the target attributes and the labeled classes. This relationship defines a model, which can be used for predicting the target attribute, knowing only the values of the input data.

The performance of the six machine learning algorithms mentioned in Sect. 3 were assessed by using the WEKA learning tools [31]. The preliminary evaluation of the classification performance provided by the six classifiers is summarized in Table 2, in which the attained accuracy levels are reported.

**Table 2.** Accuracy of tested classifiers.

| J48 | RF | NB | SVM | NNs | kNN |
|---|---|---|---|---|---|
| 99.39% | 98.97% | 52.05% | 83.18% | 96.38% | 89.98% |

Among the six classifiers, J48 and RF algorithms provided the best results with an accuracy higher than 98%, while NB performance was the worst at 52.05%. These three classifiers were considered for further evaluations. In fact, besides the accuracy, the F-measure, sensitivity and precision were computed too, as detailed in Table 3. The F-measure is defined as the harmonic mean of the precision and recall, where precision (positive predictive value) is the fraction of true positive data to total data classified as positive, and recall (sensitivity) is the fraction of true positive data to the total data that should be classified as true.

**Table 3.** Evaluation metrics of J48, RF and NB classifiers.

| Classifiers | J48 | RF | NB |
|---|---|---|---|
| F-measure | 0.993 | 0.989 | 0.502 |
| Sensitivity | 0.993 | 0.984 | 0.521 |
| Precision | 0.986 | 0.989 | 0.561 |

According to such results, the confusion matrix for J48, RF and NB algorithms were reported in Tables 4, 5, and 6, to summarizes how the six activities are classified by each algorithm. The actual classes are in the Y-axis, while the predicted classes are in the X-axis.

**Table 4.** Confusion Matrix for J48.

|  | | Washing Hands | Brushing Teeth | Grooming Hair | Dusting | Ironing Clothes | Washing Dishes |
|---|---|---|---|---|---|---|---|
| | Washing Hands | 546 | 0 | 0 | 0 | 0 | 6 |
| | Brushing Teeth | 1 | 551 | 0 | 0 | 0 | 0 |
| Actual Class | Grooming Hair | 0 | 0 | 547 | 5 | 0 | 0 |
| | Dusting | 0 | 1 | 0 | 550 | 1 | 0 |
| | Ironing Clothes | 0 | 0 | 0 | 0 | 552 | 0 |
| | Washing Dishes | 0 | 1 | 0 | 0 | 0 | 551 |

**Table 5.** Confusion Matrix for RF.

|  | | Washing Hands | Brushing Teeth | Grooming Hair | Dusting | Ironing Clothes | Washing Dishes |
|---|---|---|---|---|---|---|---|
| | Washing Hands | 546 | 0 | 0 | 0 | 0 | 6 |
| | Brushing Teeth | 0 | 535 | 0 | 4 | 13 | 0 |
| Actual Class | Grooming Hair | 0 | 0 | 549 | 3 | 0 | 0 |
| | Dusting | 0 | 1 | 3 | 538 | 7 | 3 |
| | Ironing Clothes | 0 | 1 | 0 | 0 | 547 | 0 |
| | Washing Dishes | 1 | 1 | 0 | 1 | 0 | 549 |

**Table 6.** Confusion Matrix for NB.

Predicted Class

|  | Washing Hands | Brushing Teeth | Grooming Hair | Dusting | Ironing Clothes | Washing Dishes |
|---|---|---|---|---|---|---|
| Washing Hands | 504 | 2 | 1 | 11 | 10 | 24 |
| Brushing Teeth | 5 | 463 | 3 | 22 | 50 | 9 |
| Grooming Hair | 1 | 0 | 141 | 408 | 1 | 1 |
| Dusting | 9 | 120 | 34 | 192 | 167 | 30 |
| Ironing Clothes | 12 | 162 | 1 | 80 | 261 | 36 |
| Washing Dishes | 182 | 64 | 6 | 58 | 79 | 163 |

*(Actual Class, rows)*

# 5  Discussions and Conclusion

In order to support the independent living of older adults, it is crucial to have a robust HAR system. This specific study used a single wrist-worn device for the collection of accelerometer data. The tasks have been examined by testing several well-known classification algorithms in recognizing six daily activities: brushing teeth, grooming hair, washing hands, washing dishes, ironing clothes and dusting. Generally, the performance of classifiers is influenced by the nature of dataset (e.g., the choice of activities to be executed, and the modality of acquisition to be performed). In this case, the non-linearity of dataset along with the acquisitions in uncontrolled conditions affected the NB linear classifier reaching low accuracy. However, the RF and J48 non-linear classifiers provided more than 98% classification accuracy, resulting in good tools for the recognition of the performed activities in uncontrolled conditions.

Also, as it emerges from the confusion matrices presented in the previous Section, the prediction of each classifier in discriminating the activities may depend on the nature of the activities considered. Table 6, for NB algorithm, suggests that some specific misclassifications are more frequent than others: the "Ironing Clothes" class is mostly confused with "Brushing Teeth" class, due to similar patterns for the wrist movements. Also, the "Washing Dishes" class and the "Washing Hands" class, the "Grooming Hair" and the "Dusting" classes are frequently confused, due to the natural randomness in performing these activities exhibited by a subject in free living conditions. Although the number of wrong-predicted activities is low, some observations' errors are evident also in Tables 4 and 5 (i.e., "Washing Dishes"-"Washing Hands" and "Brushing Teeth"-"Ironing Clothes").

Results are promising: the features set used is a suitable set allowing high accuracy results and high interpretability. This work fosters the adoption of wrist-worn devices as unobtrusive and practical tools in healthcare and well-being research. From our findings, a larger population should be involved to improve the reliability of the investigated approaches.

# References

1. Attal, F., Mohammed, S., Dedabrishvili, M., Chamroukhi, F., Oukhellou, L., Amirat, Y.: Physical human activity recognition using wearable sensors. Sensors **15**, 31314–31338 (2015). https://doi.org/10.3390/s151229858
2. Ayse, C., Adem, C.: Testing and analysis of activities of daily living data with machine learning algorithms. Int. J. Adv. Comput. Sci. Appl. **7**, 436–441 (2016). https://doi.org/10.14569/IJACSA.2016.070359
3. Bergmann, J.H.M., McGregor, A.H.: Body-worn sensor design: what do patients and clinicians want? Ann. Biomed. Eng. **39**(9), 2299–2312 (2011). https://doi.org/10.1007/s10439-011-0339-9
4. Chen, Z., Zhu, Q., Soh, Y.C., Zhang, L.: Robust human activity recognition using smartphone sensors via CT-PCA and online SVM. IEEE Trans. Ind. Inf. **13**, 3070–3080 (2017). https://doi.org/10.1109/TII.2017.2712746
5. Chin, Z.H., Ng, H., Yap, T.T.V., Tong, H.L., Ho, C.C., Goh, V.T.: Daily activities classification on human motion primitives detection dataset. In: Chin, Z.H. (ed.) Computational Science and Technology. LNEE, vol. 481, pp. 117–125. Springer, Singapore (2019). https://doi.org/10.1007/978-981-13-2622-6_12
6. Cleland, I., Donnelly, M.P., Nugent, C.D., Hallberg, J., Espinilla, M., Garcia-Constantino, M.: Collection of a diverse, realistic and annotated dataset for wearable activity recognition. In: 2018 IEEE International Conference on Pervasive Computing and Communications Workshops (PerCom Workshops), pp. 555–560, March 2018. https://doi.org/10.1109/PERCOMW.2018.8480322
7. Climent-Pérez, P., Spinsante, S., Mihailidis, A., Florez-Revuelta, F.: A review on video-based active and assisted living technologies for automated lifelogging. Expert Syst. Appl. **139**, (2020). https://doi.org/10.1016/j.eswa.2019.112847
8. Cook, D.J., Krishnan, N.C.: Activity Learning: Discovering, Recognizing, and Predicting Human Behavior from Sensor Data. Wiley, New York (2015). https://doi.org/10.1002/9781119010258.ch3
9. Das Antar, A., Ahmed, M., Ahad, M.A.R.: Challenges in sensor-based human activity recognition and a comparative analysis of benchmark datasets: a review. In: 2019 Joint 8th International Conference on Informatics, Electronics Vision (ICIEV) and 2019 3rd International Conference on Imaging, Vision Pattern Recognition (icIVPR), pp. 134–139. IEEE (2019). https://doi.org/10.1109/ICIEV.2019.8858508
10. Debes, C., Merentitis, A., Sukhanov, S., Niessen, M., Frangiadakis, N., Bauer, A.: Monitoring activities of daily living in smart homes: understanding human behavior. IEEE Signal Process. Mag. **33**, 81–94 (2016). https://doi.org/10.1109/MSP.2015.2503881
11. Empatica Inc.: Empatica E4. Accessed Nov 2019. http://support.empatica.com/hc/en-us/categories/200023126-E4-wristband
12. European Commission: The 2018 ageing report: Underlying assumptions and projection methodologies. Accessed Nov 2019. https://ec.europa.eu/info/sites/info/files/economy-finance/ip065en.pdf

13. Florez-Revuelta, F., Mihailidis, A., Ziefle, M., Colonna, L., Spinsante, S.: Privacy-aware and acceptable lifelogging services for older and frail people: the PAAL project. In: IEEE 8th International Conference on Consumer Electronics - Berlin (ICCE-Berlin), pp. 1–4, September 2018. https://doi.org/10.1109/ICCE-Berlin.2018.8576191

14. Galluzzi, V., Herman, T., Polgreen, P.: Hand hygiene duration and technique recognition using wrist-worn sensors. In: Proceedings of the 14th International Conference on Information Processing in Sensor Networks, pp. 106–117. ACM (2015). https://doi.org/10.1145/2737095.2737106

15. Gomes, D., Mendes-Moreira, J., Sousa, I., Silva, J.: Eating and drinking recognition in free-living conditions for triggering smart reminders. Sensors (Switzerland) **19**(12) (2019). https://doi.org/10.3390/s19122803

16. Hassan, M.M., Huda, M.S., Uddin, M.Z., Almogren, A., AlRubaian, M.A.: Human activity recognition from body sensor data using deep learning. J. Med. Syst. **42**, 1–8 (2018). https://doi.org/10.1007/s10916-018-0948-z

17. Hossain, T., Islam, M., Ahad, M., Inoue, S.: Human activity recognition using earable device. In: 2019 ACM International Joint Conference on Pervasive and Ubiquitous Computing and the 2019 ACM International Symposium, pp. 81–84 (2019). https://doi.org/10.1145/3341162.3343822

18. Huang, H., Lin, S.: Toothbrushing monitoring using wrist watch. In: Proceedings of the 14th ACM Conference on Embedded Network Sensor Systems CD-ROM, pp. 202–215. ACM (2016). https://doi.org/10.1145/2994551.2994563

19. Lin, W.Y., Verma, V.K., Lee, M.Y., Lai, C.S.: Activity monitoring with a wrist-worn, accelerometer-based device. Micromachines **9**(9) (2018). https://doi.org/10.3390/mi9090450

20. Mannini, A., Intille, S.: Classifier personalization for activity recognition using wrist accelerometers. IEEE J. Biomed. Health Inf. **23**(4), 1585–1594 (2019). https://doi.org/10.1109/JBHI.2018.2869779

21. Mauceri, S., Smith, L., Sweeney, J., McDermott, J.: Subject recognition using wrist-worn triaxial accelerometer data. In: Nicosia, G., Pardalos, P., Giuffrida, G., Umeton, R. (eds.) MOD 2017. LNCS, vol. 10710, pp. 574–585. Springer, Cham (2018). https://doi.org/10.1007/978-3-319-72926-8_48

22. Nguyen, M., Fan, L., Shahabi, C.: Activity recognition using wrist-worn sensors for human performance evaluation. In: 2015 IEEE International Conference on Data Mining Workshop (ICDMW), pp. 164–169. IEEE (2015). https://doi.org/10.1109/ICDMW.2015.199

23. Ni, Q., Cleland, I., Nugent, C., Hernando, A.B.G., de la Cruz, I.P.: Design and assessment of the data analysis process for a wrist-worn smart object to detect atomic activities in the smart home. Pervasive Mob. Comput. **56**, 57–70 (2019). https://doi.org/10.1016/j.pmcj.2019.03.006

24. Pires, I.M., et al.: Recognition of activities of daily living and environments using acoustic sensors embedded on mobile devices. Electronics **8**(12) (2019). https://doi.org/10.3390/electronics8121499

25. Poli, A., Cosoli, G., Scalise, L., Spinsante, S.: Impact of wearable measurement properties and data quality on ADLs classification accuracy. IEEE Sensors J. 1 (2020). https://doi.org/10.1109/JSEN.2020.3009368

26. Poli, A., Spinsante, S.: Activities of Daily Living by 3-Axis Accelerometer - Mendeley Data, V1. https://data.mendeley.com/datasets/b9py72hwxs/1. Accessed 19 Oct 2020

27. Poli, A., Spinsante, S., Nugent, C., Cleland, I.: Improving the collection and under-standing the quality of datasets for the aim of human activity recognition. In: Chen, F., García-Betances, R.I., Chen, L., Cabrera-Umpiérrez, M.F., Nugent, C. (eds.) Smart Assisted Living. CCN, pp. 147–165. Springer, Cham (2020). https://doi.org/10.1007/978-3-030-25590-9_7

28. Troyer, A.K.: Activities of Daily Living (ADL), pp. 28–30. Springer, New York (2011). https://doi.org/10.1007/978-0-387-79948-3_1077

29. Wales, K., Clemson, L., Lannin, N., Cameron, I.: Functional assessments used by occupational therapists with older adults at risk of activity and participation limitations: a systematic review. Plos One 11(2), 1–20 (2016). https://doi.org/10.1371/journal.pone.0147980

30. Wang, Y., Cang, S., Yu, H.: A survey on wearable sensor modality centred human activity recognition in health care. Expert Syst. Appl. 137, 167–190 (2019). https://doi.org/10.1016/j.eswa.2019.04.057

31. Witten, I.H., Frank, E., Hall, M.A., Pal, C.J.: Data Mining. Morgan Kaufmann, 4th edn. (2017). https://www.cs.waikato.ac.nz/ml/weka

# Author Index

Printed in the United States
by Baker & Taylor Publisher Services